A Text Book Of

INFORMATION TECHNOLOGY IN BUSINESS OPERATIONS

For

**BBM (IB) Semester - II (Course Code: 206)
As Per Revised Syllabus
Effective from June 2013**

Gautam Bapat
M.C.A., P.G.D.B.M. (Marketing)
Asst. Professor, Computer Science & Applications
Mitsom College
Pune

N2946

Information Technology in Business Operations ISBN 978-93-83525-98-0

Third Edition : January 2016
© : Author

The text of this publication, or any part thereof, should not be reproduced or transmitted in any form or stored in any computer storage system or device for distribution including photocopy, recording, taping or information retrieval system or reproduced on any disc, tape, perforated media or other information storage device etc., without the written permission of Author with whom the rights are reserved. Breach of this condition is liable for legal action.

Every effort has been made to avoid errors or omissions in this publication. In spite of this, errors may have crept in. Any mistake, error or discrepancy so noted and shall be brought to our notice shall be taken care of in the next edition. It is notified that neither the publisher nor the author or seller shall be responsible for any damage or loss of action to any one, of any kind, in any manner, therefrom.

Published By :
NIRALI PRAKASHAN
Abhyudaya Pragati, 1312, Shivaji Nagar
Off J.M. Road, PUNE – 411005
Tel - (020) 25512336/37/39, Fax - (020) 25511379
Email : niralipune@pragationline.com

Printed By :
Repro Knowledgecast Limited,
Thane

☞ DISTRIBUTION CENTRES

PUNE
Nirali Prakashan : 119, Budhwar Peth, Jogeshwari Mandir Lane, Pune 411002, Maharashtra
Tel : (020) 2445 2044, 66022708, Fax : (020) 2445 1538
Email : bookorder@pragationline.com, niralilocal@pragationline.com

Nirali Prakashan : S. No. 28/27, Dhyari, Near Pari Company, Pune 411041
Tel : (020) 24690204 Fax : (020) 24690316
Email : dhyari@pragationline.com, bookorder@pragationline.com

MUMBAI
Nirali Prakashan : 385, S.V.P. Road, Rasdhara Co-op. Hsg. Society Ltd.,
Girgaum, Mumbai 400004, Maharashtra
Tel : (022) 2385 6339 / 2386 9976, Fax : (022) 2386 9976
Email : niralimumbai@pragationline.com

☞ DISTRIBUTION BRANCHES

JALGAON
Nirali Prakashan : 34, V. V. Golani Market, Navi Peth, Jalgaon 425001,
Maharashtra, Tel : (0257) 222 0395, Mob : 94234 91860

KOLHAPUR
Nirali Prakashan : New Mahadvar Road, Kedar Plaza, 1st Floor Opp. IDBI Bank
Kolhapur 416 012, Maharashtra. Mob : 9850046155

NAGPUR
Pratibha Book Distributors : Above Maratha Mandir, Shop No. 3, First Floor,
Rani Jhanshi Square, Sitabuldi, Nagpur 440012, Maharashtra
Tel : (0712) 254 7129

DELHI
Nirali Prakashan : 4593/21, Basement, Aggarwal Lane 15, Ansari Road, Daryaganj
Near Times of India Building, New Delhi 110002
Mob : 08505972553

BENGALURU
Pragati Book House : House No. 1, Sanjeevappa Lane, Avenue Road Cross,
Opp. Rice Church, Bengaluru – 560002.
Tel : (080) 64513344, 64513355,Mob : 9880582331, 9845021552
Email:bharatsavla@yahoo.com

CHENNAI
Pragati Books : 9/1, Montieth Road, Behind Taas Mahal, Egmore,
Chennai 600008 Tamil Nadu, Tel : (044) 6518 3535,
Mob : 94440 01782 / 98450 21552 / 98805 82331,
Email : bharatsavla@yahoo.com

niralipune@pragationline.com | www.pragationline.com
Also find us on www.facebook.com/niralibooks

Preface ...

I take this opportunity to present this book entitled as **"Information Technology in Business Operations"** to the students of Second Semester (BBM [IB]). The object of this book is to present the subject matter in a most concise and simple manner. The book is written strictly according to the Revised Syllabus.

The book has its own unique features. It brings out the subject in a very simple and lucid manner for easy and comprehensive understanding of the basic concepts, its intricacies, procedures and practices. This book will help the readers to have a broader view on Information Technology in Business Operations. The language used in this book is easy and will help students to improve their vocabulary of Technical terms and understand the matter in a better and happier way.

I sincerely, thank Shri. Dineshbhai Furia and Shri. Jignesh Furia of Nirali Prakashan, for the confidence reposed in me and giving me this opportunity to reach out to the students of management studies.

I thank Mr. Amar Salunkhe for his important inputs time to time and Mr. Akbar Shaikh who painstakingly attended to all the details to make this book appear good.

I also thank Ms. Chaitali Takale, Mr. Ravindra Walodare, Mr. Mahesh Swami, Mr. Vijay Shete, Mr. Sachin Shinde, Nikunj Joshi, Nilesh Deshmukh, Ashok Bodke, Moshin Sayyed and Nitin Thorat.

I have given my best inputs for this book. Any suggestions towards the improvement of this book and sincere comments are most welcome on niralipune@pragationline.com.

AUTHOR

Syllabus ...

Unit 1: Computers [10 Lectures]
  1.1 Introduction
  1.2 Characteristics of Computers
  1.3 Block Diagram Of Elements of digital computer-their functions-memory-CPU
  1.4 Data Organization
    1.4.1 Drives
    1.4.2 Files
    1.4.3 Directories
  1.5 Types of Memory (Primary And Secondary)
    1.5.1 RAM
    1.5.2 ROM
    1.5.3 PROM
    1.5.4 EPROM
    1.5.5 Secondary Storage Devices (DVD, CD, HD, magnetic tape, Pen drive)
  1.6 I/O Devices
    1.6.1 Scanners
    1.6.2 Digitizers
    1.6.3 Plotters
    1.6.4 Printer
    1.6.5 LCD
    1.6.6 Plasma Display
  1.7 Hardware and Software
    1.7.1 Types of computers and features
    1.7.2 Mini Computers
    1.7.3 Micro Computers
    1.7.4 Mainframe Computers
    1.7.5 Super Computers
    1.7.6 Laptop

Unit 2: System Concept [6 Lectures]
  2.1 Introduction to system Analysis and design
  2.2 Types of system
  2.3 Characteristic of system
  2.4 System Development Life Cycle
  2.5 Prototyping

Unit 3: Operating System and Services in O.S. [6 Lectures]
- 3.1 Dos - History
- 3.2 Files and Directories
- 3.3 Internal and External Commands
- 3.4 Batch Files
- 3.5 Types of O.S

Unit 4: Introduction To R.D.B.M.S with Practical of Oracle8i basic Commands [6 Lectures]
- 4.1 Advantages and Limitations
- 4.2 Normalization
- 4.3 Entity Relationships
- 4.4 Use Of simple SQL Commands involving both single table and simple joins.

Unit 5: Management Information System (MIS) [10 Lectures]
- 5.1 Cryptography - Encryption, Decryption
- 5.2 Digital Signature
- 5.3 IT Act
- 5.4 Security Threats to information
    - 5.4.1 Virus
    - 5.4.2 Hacking
    - 5.4.3 Natural Calamities
    - 5.4.4 Failure of system
- 5.5 Preventive measures and data recovery
    - 5.5.1 Antivirus
    - 5.5.2 Firewall
    - 5.5.3 Data Recovery methods

Unit 6: MS-Office with Practical [10 Lectures]
- 6.1 MS Word
- 6.2 MS Excel
- 6.3 MS Powerpoint

•••

Contents ...

1. Computers — 1.1 – 1.88

2. System Concept — 2.1 – 2.16

3. Operating System and Services in Operating System — 3.1 – 3.42

4. Introduction to R.D.B.M.S. — 4.1 – 4.60

5. Management Information System (MIS) — 5.1 – 5.32

6. MS-Office — 6.1 – 6.57

Question Papers - October 2014, April 2015, October 2015 — P.1 – P.3

Chapter 1...

Computers

Contents ...

1.1 Introduction
    1.1.1 What is a Computer? / Meaning of Computer
    1.1.2 Definition
    1.1.3 Generations of Computers
    1.1.4 Advantages of Computers
    1.1.5 Disadvantages of Computers
    1.1.6 Computer Applications
1.2 Characteristics of Computers
1.3 Block Diagram of Computer
1.4 Data Organisation
    1.4.1 Drives
    1.4.2 Files
        1.4.2.1 Definition of File
        1.4.2.2 File Organisation
    1.4.3 Directories
1.5 Types of Memory (Primary and Secondary)
    1.5.1 Primary Memory
        1.5.1.1 RAM
        1.5.1.2 ROM (PROM and EPROM)
    1.5.2 Secondary Memory
    1.5.3 Secondary Storage Devices
        1.5.3.1 Magnetic Tape
        1.5.3.2 Magnetic Disks
        1.5.3.3 Optical Disks (CD and DVD)
        1.5.3.4 Pen Drive
1.6 I/O (Input/Output) Devices
    1.6.1 Input Devices
        1.6.1.1 Keyboard
        1.6.1.2 Mouse
        1.6.1.3 Scanner
        1.6.1.4 MICR

    1.6.1.5 OMR
    1.6.1.6 Digital Camera
    1.6.1.7 Digitizer
    1.6.1.8 Joystick
    1.6.1.9 Light Pen
    1.6.1.10 Trackball
    1.6.1.11 OCR
    1.6.1.12 Bar Code Readers
  1.6.2 Output Devices
    1.6.2.1 Monitor (CRT and LCD)
    1.6.2.2 Plasma Display
    1.6.2.3 Printers
    1.6.2.4 Plotters
1.7 Hardware and Software
  1.7.1 Computer Hardware
  1.7.2 Computer Software
1.8 Types of Computers
  1.8.1 Super Computers
  1.8.2 Mainframe Computers
  1.8.3 Mini Computers
  1.8.4 Micro Computers
  1.8.5 Laptop
- Questions

1.1 Introduction

- Now-a-days, computer are an integral part of our lives. They are used for the reservation of tickets for airplanes and railways, payment of telephone and electricity bills, deposit and withdrawal of money from banks, processing of business data, forecasting of weather conditions, diagnosis of diseases, searching for information on the internet, etc.
- Computer are also used extensively in schools, universities, organisations, music industry, movie industry, scientific research, law firms, fashion industry, etc.
- The term computer is derived from the Latin word 'compute'. The word 'compute' means to calculate.
- A computer is an electronic machine that accepts data from the user, processes the data by performing calculations and operations on it, and generates the desired output results.
- Computer performs both simple and complex operations, with speed and accuracy.
- A computer is a general purpose device that can be programmed to carry out a finite set of arithmetic or logical operations.

- A computer is an electronic device that manipulates information or data. It has the ability to store, retrieve, and process data.
- A computer is a programmable machine. The two **principal characteristics of a computer** are:
  1. Computer responds to a specific set of instructions in a well-defined manner, and
  2. Computer can execute a pre-recorded list of instructions (a program).

1.1.1 What is a Computer? / Meaning of Computer

- A computer is an advanced electronic device that takes raw data as input from the user and processes these data under the control of set of instructions (called program) and gives the result (output) and saves output for the future use.
- A computer can process both numerical and non-numerical (arithmetic and logical) calculations.
- A computer has following functions:
  1. **Input (Data):** Input is the raw information entered into a computer from the input devices. It is the collection of letters, numbers, images etc.
  2. **Process:** Process is the operation of data as per given instruction. It is totally internal process of the computer system.
  3. **Output and Storage:** Output is the processed data given by computer after data processing. Output is also called as Result. We can save these results in the storage devices for the future use.

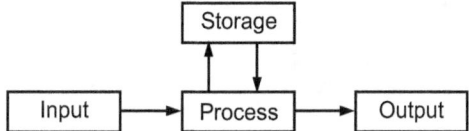

Fig. 1.1: Functions of a computer

1.1.2 Definition

- A computer is a programmable machine that can store, retrieve, and process data.

OR

- A computer is an extremely fast and accurate electronic data processing machine that receives data as input, performs arithmetic and logical operations on them according to a program stored in the memory and produces the desired output.

OR

- Computer is an electronic machine made up of various electronic devices (parts) to process the data to produce useful information.

OR

- A computer is an electronic device which is capable of receiving information (data) in a particular form and of performing a sequence of operations in accordance with a predetermined but variable set of procedural instructions (program) to produce a result in the form of information or signals.

1.1.3 Generations of Computers

- Generation in computer terminology is a change in technology a computer is/was being used.
- A generation in computer talk is a step in technology. Computer developed after ENIAC have been classified into five generations depending upon the technology used, processing techniques, computer languages, memory systems.

1. First Generation Computer (1942-1955):

- The first generation computer were using Vacuum Tubes and machine languages were used for giving instructions. The computer of this generation were very large in size and their programming was a difficult task.
- The first commercial electronic digital computer capable of using stored programs was called "Universal Automatic Calculator" (UNIVAC) built by Macuchy and Eckert in 1951. Punched cards were used for feeding and retrieving of information.
- The major first generation computer were UNIVAC-1, IBM-701, IBM-650, ENIAC, EDVAC, EDSAC, etc.

(a) 1st generation computer (b) Vacuum tube

Fig. 1.2

- First generation computer were the fastest calculating devices of their time. They could perform computations in milliseconds. Vacuum tube technology made possible the advent of electronic digital computers.

Advantages:
  (i) First generation computer were fastest calculating devices of their time.
  (ii) Support parallel processing.

Disadvantages:
  (i) Air conditioning is required.
  (ii) Bulky in size (required large rooms) for assembly on installation.
  (iii) Vacuum tube required very high power consumption.
  (iv) Commercial production of these computer was difficult and costly.
  (v) Time consuming for assembling and installation.
  (vi) These computer required very high constant maintenance.
  (vii) Difficult to use and programming.

Application:
- They were used for scientific applications as they were the fastest computing device of their time.

2. Second Generation Computer (1955-1964):
- Computer are entered into second generation by the introduction of Transistors.
- Vacuum tubes were replaced by tiny solid-state components called transistors.
- Transistors were highly reliable, requires less power and faster than vacuum tubes. High Level Languages such as FORTRAN, COBOL, BASIC etc. were introduced.
- The practice of writing programs in Machine languages were replaced by High Level Languages.
- Punched cards were used for input-output operations.
- Major second generation computer were IBM-1400 series, 7000 series, Honeywell 200, CDC 3600, UNIVAC 1108 etc.

(a) 2nd generation computer   (b) Transistor

Fig. 1.3

Advantages:
(i) They used transistor technology as transistor are faster than vacuum tube.
(ii) More reliable.
(iii) Cheaper.
(iv) Smaller in size.
(v) Less power consumption.
(vi) Support parallel processing.

Disadvantages:
(i) Time consuming for assembly and installation.
(ii) Air-conditioning required.
(iii) Difficult for commercial production.
(iv) Costly for commercial production.
(v) Maintenance is high.

3. Third Generation Computer (1964-1975):
- The third generation computer used the new technology, Transistor Integrated Circuits (IC) intended by Jack and Noyce in 1958.

- All electronic components like transistors, resistor and capacitor were fabricated on silicon chips. Computer were designed by making use of ICs.
- IC has higher speed, larger storage capacity and smaller size. Operating systems were introduced for use in computers.
- Significant advances in hardware technology made the introduction of keyboards and monitor for data input and output. More high level languages like Pascal, RPG were also introduced.
- Major third generation computer were IBM -360 series, ICL -1900 series, CDC's CYBER - 175, TDC-316, IBM 370/168 etc.

(a) 3rd generation computer   (b) ICs

Fig. 1.4

Advantages:
(i) Required small space (portable).
(ii) More reliable.
(iii) Faster in speed.
(iv) Support high level languages.
(v) Commercial production is raised.
(vi) Installation is required in less time.
(vii) Low maintenance.

Disadvantages:
(i) Air-conditioning required.
(ii) Cost is more than fourth generation computers.
(iii) Highly sophisticated technology required for the manufacturing chips.

Application:
- Computer became accessible to mass audience. Computer were produced commercially and were smaller and cheaper than their predecessors.

4. Fourth Generation Computer (1975-1989):
- The ICs used in third generation computer had about 10 to 100 transistor per unit.
- This technology was called Small-Scale Integration (SSI). Later, with the advancement of technology for manufacturing ICs, it is possible to integrate 10,000 transistor in an IC.
- This technology is called Large-Scale Integration (LSI). Very Large Scale Integration (VLSI) can pack a million or more transistor on a single chip. LSI and VLSI technologies led to the introduction of Microprocessors.

- Computer which are designed using Microprocessor become the fourth generation computers. Magnetic disks become the primary means for external storage.
- Intel introduced the first microprocessor 4004 using LSI. The languages C, LISP, Prolog become popular. Present day computer are fourth generation computers.
- Major fourth generation computer are IBM System 370, CRAY–MPC, WIPRO 860, IBM AS/400/B60, IBM ps/2 MODEL 80, HCL Magnum, etc.

(a) 4th generation computer   (b) Microprocessor

Fig. 1.5

Advantages:
- (i) Portable in size.
- (ii) Cheaper.
- (iii) More reliable.
- (iv) Easy for installation.
- (v) Support high level language.
- (vi) Support networking.
- (vii) Support GUI (Graphical User Interface).
- (viii) Less time required for manual assembly.

Disadvantages:
- (i) Air-conditioning is required.
- (ii) Expensive.
- (iii) Single user oriented.

Application:
- They became widely available for commercial purposes. Personal computer became available to the home user.

5. Fifth Generation Computer (1989 onwards):
- Fifth generation computer are capable of parallel processing, high speed computing and artificial intelligence.
- They have an architecture which allows more neural problem solving ability. These machines uses the principle of Artificial Intelligence.
- They have the ability to understand natural languages like English, Malayalam, etc. it can converse with human beings.
- Computer languages such as LISP, PROLOG, C, C++, etc., are available to program such computers.

- The goal of fifth generation computing is to develop computer that are capable of learning and self-organisation. The fifth generation computer use Super Large Scale Integrated (SLSI) chips that are able to store millions of components on a single chip. These computer have large memory requirements.

Fig. 1.6: 5th generation computer

Advantages:

(i) More smaller and handy than computer of fourth generation, allowing user to use the computing facility even while travelling.

(ii) Very less power required.

(iii) No air-conditioning required.

(iv) Use for large scale organisations.

(v) Support standard HLL (High Level Language).

(vi) User friendly interface.

(vii) Faster in speed.

(viii) More reliable.

(ix) Easy for installation.

(x) Very short time required for manual assembly.

(xi) Support very high powerful applications (multimedia).

1.1.4 Advantages of Computers

- Following list demonstrates the advantages of computer in today's arena:

  1. **High Speed:** Computer is a very fast device. It can perform millions of calculations in few seconds as compared to man who can spend many months for doing the same task.

  2. **Accuracy:** Computer are very accurate. The computer can perform calculations 100% error free.

  3. **Storage Capability:** Computer can store large amount of data using memory. Computer can store any type of data such as images, videos, text, audio and any other type.

  4. **Versatility:** A computer is a very versatile machine. Computer machine can be used to solve the problems relating to various different fields.

  5. **Automation:** Automation means ability to perform the task automatically. Computer is a automatic machine. Once, a program (instruction) is given to computer i.e. stored in computer memory, the program and instruction can control the program execution without human interaction.

6. **Diligence:** Unlike human beings, a computer is free from monotony, tiredness and lack of concentration. Computer can work continuously without creating any error and boredom and it can do repeated work with same speed and accuracy.
7. **Reliability:** A computer is a reliable machine and modern electronic components have failure free long lives. Computer are designed to make maintenance easy and simple.
8. **Reduction in Cost:** Though the initial investment for installing a computer is high but it substantially reduces the cost of each of its transaction.
9. **Reduction in Paper Work:** The use of computer for data processing in an organisation leads to reduction in paper work and speeds up the process.

1.1.5 Disadvantages of Computers

- Various disadvantage of computers are listed below:
    1. **No intelligence:** A computer is a machine and has no intelligence of its own to perform any task. Each and every instruction has to be given to computer. A computer can not take any decision on its own.
    2. **Environment:** The operating environment of computer should be dust free and suitable to it.
    3. **No feeling:** Computer has no feeling or emotions.
    4. **Dependency:** Computer can perform function as instructed by user, so it is fully dependent on human being. Computer cannot make Judgment based on feeling, taste, experience and knowledge unlike a human being.
    5. **Violation of Privacy:** It is crucial that personal and confidential records stored in computers be protected properly.
    6. **Health Risks:** Prolonged or improper computer use can lead to disorders. Computer user can protect themselves from health risks through proper workplace design, good posture while at the computer and appropriately spaced work breaks.
    7. **Impact on the Environment:** Computer manufacturing processes and computer waste are depleting natural resources and polluting the environment.

1.1.6 Computer Applications

- Various application of computer in various fields are listed below:

1. **Banking:**
- Today Banking is almost totally dependent on computer.
- Banks provide following facilities:
    (i) Banks, on-line accounting facility, which include current balances, deposits, overdrafts, interest charges, shares and trustee records.
    (ii) ATM machines are making it even easier for customer to deal with banks.

2. **Business:**
- Computer used in business organisation for payroll calculations, budgeting, sales analysis, financial forecasting, managing employees database and maintenance of stocks etc.

3. **Education:**
   - The computer has provided a lot of facilities in the education system.
   - The uses of computer provide a tool in the Education system is known as CBE (Computer Based Education).

4. **Marketing:**
   - In Marketing uses of computer are following:

     (i) **Home Shopping:** Home shopping has been made possible through use of computerised catalogs that provide access to product information and permit direct entry of order to be filled by the customers.

     (ii) **Advertising:** With computers, advertising professionals create art and graphics, write and revise copy, and print and disseminate ads with the goal of selling more products.

5. **Insurance:**
   - Insurance companies are keeping all records up to date with the help of computer.
   - The insurance companies, finance houses and stock broking firms are widely using computer for their concerns.
   - Insurance companies are maintaining a database of all clients with information showing how to continue with policies, starting date of the policies, next due installment of a policy, maturity date, interests due, survival benefits bonus and so on.

6. **Communication:**
   - Communication means to convey a message, an idea, a picture or speech that is received and understood clearly and correctly by the person for whom it is meant.
   - Some main areas in this category are: E-mail, Chatting, Usenet, FTP, Telnet, Video-conferencing and so on.

7. **Health Care:**
   - The computer are being used in hospitals to keep the record of patients and medicines. It is also used in scanning and diagnosing different diseases.
   - ECG, EEG, Ultrasounds and CT Scans etc. are also done by computerised machines. Some of major fields of health care in which computer are used:

     (i) **Pharma Information System:** Computer checks Drug-Labels, expiry dates, harmful drug side effects etc.

     (ii) **Diagnostic System:** Computer are used to collect data and identify cause of illness.

     (iii) **Patient Monitoring System:** These are used to check patient's signs for abnormality such as in cardiac arrest, ECG etc.

     (iv) Now-a-days, computer are also used in **performing surgery**.

     (v) **Lab-diagnostic System:** All tests can be done and reports are prepared by computer.

8. Military:
- Computer are largely used in defence. Modern tanks, missiles, weapons etc. employ computerized control systems.
- Some military areas where a computer has been used are: missile control, military communication, military operation and planning, smart weapons and so on.

9. Government Applications:
- Computer play an important role in government applications.
- Some major fields in this category are: budgets, sales tax department, income tax department, male/female ratio, computerization of voter lists, computerization of driving licensing system, computerization of pan card, weather forecasting and so on.

10. Engineering Design:
- Computer are widely used in Engineering purposes. Some fields are:
    (i) **Industrial Engineering:** Computer deals with design, implementation and improvement of integrated systems of people, materials and equipments.
    (ii) **Architectural Engineering:** Computer help in planning towns, designing buildings, determining a range of buildings on a site using both 2D and 3D drawings.
    (iii) **Structural Engineering:** Requires stress and strain analysis required for design of ships, buildings, budgets, airplanes etc.

1.2 Characteristics of Computers

- The main characteristics (capabilities) of computer, which makes them powerful and useful are:
    1. **Automation:** Computer has automation power that means computer can perform the task automatically by using programs.
    2. **Speed:** Computer are of high speed in its operation. The speed is measured in terms of Instructions Per Second (IPS). All modern computer can process information at a speed of a couple of Million Instructions Per Second (MIPS).
    3. **Accuracy:** Computer are highly accurate in its operations. They either give correct answer or do not answer at all. Error can occur in computer but these are mainly due to human rather than technological weakness.
    4. **Reliability:** It is the ability of a computer to perform the same job exactly in the same way in any number of times.
    5. **Versatility:** A computer is capable of performing almost any task provided that the task can be reduced to a series of logical steps.
    6. **Integrity:** It is the ability of a computer to carry out a sequence of instructions.
    7. **No feelings:** Computer are devoid of emotions. They have no feeling because they are machines.
    8. **Diligence continuity:** A computer is free from monotony, tiredness, lack of concentration, etc. It can work for hour without creating any error.
    9. **Power of remembering:** Computer can store and recall any amount of information because of its storage capability.

1.3 Block Diagram of Computer

- Fig. 1.7 shows block diagram of a computer.

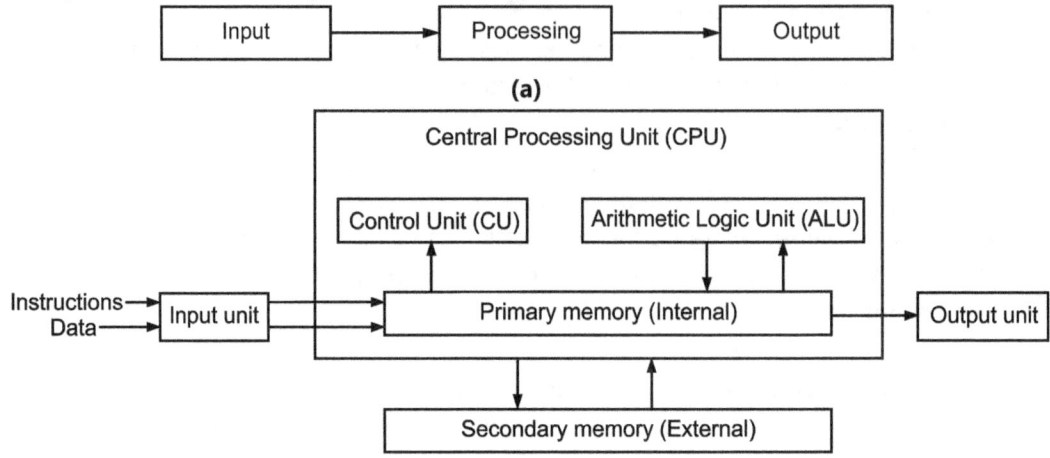

(b) Block diagram of a computer

Fig. 1.7

- Various parts of computer are described below:

1. Input Unit:

- Input unit contains devices with the help of which we enter data into computer. This unit makes link between user and computer.
- The input devices translate the human readable information into the form understanddable by computer.
- Some important input devices which are used in computer systems are: keyboard, mouse, joystick, light pen, track ball, scanner, graphic tablet, microphone, Magnetic Ink Card Reader (MICR), Optical Character Reader (OCR), bar code reader, optical mark reader (OMR).
- An input device performs the following functions:
   (i) It accepts (i.e. reads) the list of instruction and data from the user.
   (ii) It converts these instructions and data in binary form which is understood by the computer.
   (iii) It supplies the converted instructions and data to the computer for further processing.

2. CPU:

- The task of performing operations like arithmetic and logical operations is called processing.
- The Central Processing Unit (CPU) takes data and instructions from the storage unit and makes all sorts of calculations based on the instructions given and the type of data provided. It is then sent back to the storage unit.

- Central Processing Unit (CPU) is the heart of every computer system that performs the user instructions.
- The CPU is like brain performs the following functions:
  (i) It performs all calculations.
  (ii) It takes all decisions.
  (iii) It controls all units of the computer.
- CPU itself has following three components:

1. **Arithmetic Logical Unit (ALU):**
   After we enter data through the input device it is stored in the primary storage unit. The actual processing of the data and instruction are performed by Arithmetic Logical Unit (ALU). The major operations performed by the ALU is addition, subtraction, multiplication, division, logic and comparison. Data is transferred to ALU from storage unit when required. After processing the output is returned back to storage unit for further processing or getting stored. This unit consists of two subsection namely:

   (a) Arithmetic section: Function of arithmetic section is to perform arithmetic operations like addition, subtraction, multiplication and division. All complex operations are done by making repetitive use of above operations.

   (b) Logic Section: Function of logic section is to perform logic operations such as comparing, selecting, matching and merging of data.

   Functions of ALU:
   (i) All calculations are performed in the Arithmetic Logic Unit (ALU) of the computer. The ALU can perform basic operations such as addition, subtraction, multiplication, division, etc and does logic operations viz, $>$, $<$, $=$, 'etc.
   (ii) It also supplies or gives out the information and results for computation to the outside world.

2. **Control Unit (CU):**
   It controls all other units in the computer. The control unit instructs the input unit, where to store the data after receiving it from the user. It controls the flow of data and instructions from the storage unit to ALU. It also controls the flow of results from the ALU to the storage unit. The control unit is generally referred as the central nervous system of the computer that control and synchronizes its working.

   The main function of control unit is to control all operations like input, processing, output etc. Control Unit (CU) acts as the supervisor seeing that things are done in proper fashion. Control Unit is responsible for coordinating various operations using time signal. The control unit determines the sequence in which computer programs and instructions are executed. Things like processing of programs stored in the main memory, interpretation of the instructions and issuing of signals for other units of the computer to execute them. It also acts as a switch board operator when several user access the computer simultaneously. Thereby it coordinates the activities of computer's peripheral equipments as they perform the input and output.

   Control unit controls the operations of all parts of computer. It does not carry out any actual data processing operations.

Functions of control unit are:
  (i) It is responsible for controlling the transfer of data and instructions among other units of a computer.
  (ii) It manages and coordinates all the units of the computer.
  (iii) It does not process or store data.
  (iv) It obtains the instructions from the memory, interprets them and directs the operation of the computer.
  (v) It communicates with Input/Output (I/O) devices for transfer of data or results from storage.

3. **Memory or Storage Unit:**
- Memory unit can store instruction, data and intermediate results. This unit supplies information to the other units of the computer when needed.
- It is also known as internal storage unit or main memory or primary storage or Random Access Memory (RAM).
- Its size affects speed, power and capability. There are two types of memories in the computer namely primary memory and secondary memory.
- **Function of memory unit** are:
  (i) It stores all the data to be processed and the instructions required for processing.
  (ii) It stores intermediate results of processing.
  (iii) It stores final results of processing before these results are released to an output device.
  (iv) All inputs and outputs are transmitted through main memory.

4. **Secondary Memory (Storage):**
- To supplement the limited storage capacity of the primary storage section, most computer have secondary storage capabilities.
- These devices are connected directly to the processor which accept data/program instructions for the processor, retain them, and then write them back to the processor as needed to complete the processing tasks.
- Magnetic tape, disks are the examples of secondary storage.

5. **Output Unit:**
- Output is the process of producing results from the data for getting useful information. Similarly the output produced by the computer after processing must also be kept somewhere inside the computer before being given to you in human readable form. Again the output is also stored inside the computer for further processing. The result of computer processing is called as output. This result is communicated to user through a device called output devices.
- Output unit consists of devices with the help of which we get the information from computer. This unit is a link between computer and users.
- Output devices translate the computer's output into the human readable form.

- Few of the important output devices which are used in computer systems are: Monitors, Graphic plotter, Printer etc.
- The following **functions are performed by an output** unit:
  (i) It accepts results produced by the computer which are in binary coded form and hence cannot be understood by user.
  (ii) It converts these coded results to human readable form.
  (iii) It supplies the converted form to the user.

1.4 Data Organization

- A group of symbol used to express a value of characteristic of an object is called data.
- Data can be defined as "a representation of facts, concepts or instruction in a formalized manner which should be suitable for communication, interpretation or processing by human or electronic machine".
- Data is represented with the help of character like alphabets (A-Z,a-z), digits (0-9) or special characters(+,-,/,*,<,>,= etc).
- A data which has been processed and organized so that it can be used to draw meaningful conclusion is called information.
- Information is organised or classified data so that it has some meaningful values to the receiver.
- Example: 2225860 is a number data. When we say that it is a telephone number, then we get information from the data.

Difference between Data and Information:

Data	Information
1. It is the information which processing is done.	1. An organized fact is called information.
2. A data has neither fixed nor define meaning.	2. An information has not only fixed but also define meaning.
3. Data is similar to raw material.	3. Information is similar to finish goods.

Data Processing:

- Data processing is the re-structuring or re-ordering of data by people or machine to increase their usefulness and add values for particular purpose.
- Data processing is "a sequence of operations performed on data, especially by a computer, in order to extract information, reorder files, etc."
- Data processing may involve various processes, including:
  1. **Data validation:** Ensuring that supplied data is "clean, correct and useful."
  2. **Sorting:** "Arranging items in some sequence and/or in different sets."
  3. **Data aggregation:** Combining multiple pieces of data.
  4. **Statistical analysis:** The "collection, organization, analysis, interpretation and presentation of data.".
  5. **Reporting:** List detail or summary data or computed information.

1.4.1 Drives

- A disk driver is a device driver that allows a specific disk drive to communicate with the remainder of the computer.
- It is a machine that reads data from and writes data onto a disk. A disk drive rotates the disk very fast and has one or more heads that read and write data.
- There are different types of disk drives for different types of disks.

1. Hard Disk Drive (HDD):

- The mechanism that reads and writes data on a hard disk. Hard disk drives (HDDs) for PCs generally have seek times of about 12 milliseconds or less. Many disk drives improve their performance through a technique called caching.
- There are several interface standards for passing data between a hard disk and a computer. The most common are IDE and SCSI.
- Hard disk drives are sometimes called Winchester drives, Winchester being the name of one of the first popular hard disk drive technologies developed by IBM in 1973.

2. Floppy Disk Drive (FDDs):

- A Floppy Disk Drive, or FDD or FD for short, is a computer disk drive that enables a user to save data to removable diskettes.
- Although 8" disk drives were first made available in 1971, the first real disk drives used were the $5^{1/4}$" floppy disk drives, which were later replaced with $3^{1/2}$" floppy disk drives.
- Today, because of the limited capacity and reliability of floppy diskettes many computer no longer come equipped with floppy disk drives and are being replaced with CD-R, other writable discs, and flash drives.

1.4.2 Files

- A file is a collection of related records. In other words, a file is a collection of data or information usually stored on disk.
- A record is a collection of data items arranged for processing by a program.
- The files can be viewed as logical files and physical files.
- Logical file is a very viewed in terms of what data items, its record contain and what processing operations may be performed upon the file. The user of the file will normally adopt such a view.
- Physical file is a file viewed in terms of how the data is stored on a storage device and how the processing operations are made possible.

1.4.2.1 Definition of File

- File is a structured collection of data i.e. a collection of related records.

OR

- We can define file as "a set of logically related records".

1.4.2.2 File Organisation

- File organisation refer to the way records are physically arranged on a storage device.

- The term "file organisation" refer to the way in which data is stored in a file and consequently the methods by which it can be accessed.
- File organisation refer to the relationship of the key of the record to the physical location of that record in the computer file.

Definition of File Organisation:
- File organisation refer to the way records are physically arranged on a storage device. File organisation refer to the arrangement of records within a database.

OR

- "File organisation" refer to the logical relationships among the various records that constitute the file, particularly with respect to the means of identification and access to any specific record. "File structure" refer to the format of the label and data blocks and of any logical record control information.
- File organisation may be either **physical file** or a **logical file**.
- A physical file is a physical unit, such as magnetic tape or a disk.
- A logical file on the other hand is a complete set of records for a specific application or purpose.
- A logical file may occupy a part of physical file or may extend over more than one physical files.
- **The objectives of computer based file organisation are:**
    1. Ease of file creation and maintenance
    2. Efficient means of storing and retrieving information.
- The organisation of a given file may be sequential, relative, or indexed.

1. Sequential File Organisation:
- In sequential file organisation, records are arranged sequentially.
- A sequential file is a file whose records can be accessed on the order of their appearance in the file.
- The order in which the records are stored is determined by the order in which they are written when the file was prepared. This order does not change. Records may be added at the end of file only.
- The records may be accessed in the order on which they were originally written into a file.
- A magnetic tape file, such as printer, can only have a sequential organisation.
- A sequentially organized file may be stored on either a serial–access or direct access storage medium.
- The task of file handling is the responsibility of the system software known as Input-Output Control System (IOCS). Block is used to group a number of consecutive records. IOCS takes care of blocking. IOCS reserves a memory space equal to the size of a block of the file.

- Sequential files may be recorded in variable-length of fixed-length record form. If a file consists of variable-length records, each logical record is preceded by control information that indicates the size of the logical record.
- If a file consists of fixed-length records, the record size is established at the time the file is opened and is the same for every logical record on the file. Therefore, there is no need to record any control information with the logical record.
- Sequential files are normally created and stored on magnetic tape using batch processing method.

Advantages:
   (i)   Simple to understand and implement.
   (ii) Easy to maintain and organize.
   (iii) Loading a record requires only the record key.
   (iv) Relatively inexpensive I/O media and devices can be used.
   (v)   Easy to reconstruct the files.
   (vi) The proportion of file records to be processed is high.

Disadvantages:
   (i)   Entire file must be processed, to get specific information.
   (ii) Very low activity rate stored.
   (iii) Transactions must be stored and placed in sequence prior to processing.
   (iv) Data redundancy is high, as same data can be stored at different places with different keys.
   (v)   Impossible to handle random enquiries.

Area of Use:
- Sequential files are most frequently used in commercial batch oriented data processing applications where there is the concept of a master file to which details are added periodically. Example: Payroll applications.

2. Index Sequential File Organisation:
- When there is need to access records sequentially by some key value and also to access records directly by the same key value, the collection of records may be organized in an effective manner called index sequential file organisation.
- In index sequential file organisation, the records are stored in the key sequence order usually in ascending order. Some index tables are also created and maintained with the file.
- Index table provide to identify the groups of records in the file. When an indexed file is accessed randomly, the programmer control the sequence on which the records are accessed by specifying the value of a data item called record key.
- When the new records are inserted in the data file, the sequence of records needs to be preserved and also the index is accordingly updated.

Advantages:
(i) In indexed sequential file organisation, the item in the table can be examined sequentially if all the records in the file must be accessed.
(ii) Indexed sequential file organisation is very useful when a random access or records by specifying the key is required.
(iii) Updating is easily accommodated.
(iv) Random access is possible.

Area of Use:
- Index sequential file organisation support applications that selectively access individual records rather than searching through the entire collection in sequence.
- Example: Train Enquiry System, Reservation Enquiry System and so on.

3. Direct/Random/Relative File Organisation:
- In direct access file organisation, records are placed randomly throughout the file.
- Records need not be in sequence because they are updated directly and rewritten back in the same location.
- New records are added at the end of the file or inserted in specific locations based on software commands.
- Records are accessed by addresses that specify their disk locations. An address is required for locating a record, for linking records, or for establishing relationships.
- Addresses are of two types:
    1. **An absolute address** represents the physical location of the record. It is usually stated in the format of sector/track/record number. One problem with absolute address is that they become invalid when the file that contains the records is relocated on the disk.
    2. **A relative address** gives a record location relative to the beginning of the file. There must be fixed length records for reference. Another way of locating a record is by the number of bytes it is from the beginning of the file. When the file is moved, pointer need not be updated because the relative location remains the same.

Advantages:
(i) Records can be immediately accessed for updation.
(ii) Several files can be simultaneously updated during transaction processing.
(iii) Transaction need not be sorted.
(iv) Existing records can be amended or modified.
(v) Very easy to handle random enquiries.
(vi) Most suitable for interactive online applications.

Disadvantages:
(i) Data may be accidentally erased or over written unless special precautions are taken.
(ii) Risk of loss of accuracy and breach of security. Special backup and reconstruction procedures must be established.
(iii) Less efficient use of storage space.

(iv) Expensive hardware and software are required.
(v) High complexity in programming.
(vi) File updation is more difficult when compared to that of sequential method.

Area of Use:
- Relative (Random/Direct) file organisation is used where the records of a file are updated for a number of times during a working day. Price list can be a file, which is to be constantly interrogated during a billing run.

4. **Indexed Files:**
- An indexed file, which must be allocated in the execution activity to two or more random mass storage files (one for the index, and one or more for the data) is organized such that each record is uniquely identified by the value of key within the record.
- An index is a data structure that organizes data records on disk to optimize certain file operations. An index allows us to efficiently search or retrieve all records. Using an index, we can achieve a fast search of data records.
- In order to create and maintain index files a computer create a data file and an index file. The data file contains the actual contents (data) of the record and index file contains the index entries. The one field in a file is the primary key, which identifies a record uniquely.
- Files are organized in the following ways:
    (i) The data file is stored in the order of the primary key values.
    (ii) The index file contains two fields: the key value and the pointer to the data record.
    (iii) One record in the index file thus, consists of a key value and a pointer to the corresponding data record. The pointer points to the first entry within the range of data records.
- **Example:**

Index File

Key 1 ptr 1		Key 2 ptr 2		Key 3 ptr 3		- - - - -
10	1	20	11	30	21	

Record 1	Record 2	Record 3	- - - -	Record 10

Record 11	Record 12	- - - - - - - - - - - - -	Record 20

Record 21	Record 22	- - - - - - - - - - - -	Record 30

Fig. 1.8: Index file organisation

- Generally, the key value is the largest primary key value in a given range of records.
- In the Fig. 1.8, the first index entry is 10, which is highest primary key value in the first data block of 1 to 10. The pointer from this index entry points to the start of this range i.e. 1.

- There are several types of ordered indexes:
    1. **Primary Index:** A primary index is an index specified on the ordering key field of an ordered records. Every record has unique value for that field.
    2. **Clustering Index:** If the ordering field is not a key field i.e. if several records in the file can have the same value for the ordering field then a clustering index can be used. Notice that, a file can have atmost one physical ordering field, so it can have at most one primary index or one clustering index, but not both.
    3. **Secondary Index:** The third type of index, called a secondary index, can be specified on any non-ordering field of a file. A file can have several secondary indexes in addition to its primary access method.

1.4.3 Directories

- Files contain text or data. Directories contain files. Directories should be organized in hierarchical manner.
- A directory is a named group of related files that are separated by the naming convention from other groups of files.
- A directory is file system cataloging structure in which references to other computer files, and possibly other directories, are kept.
- Consequently we can identify:
    1. Parent directories, and
    2. Child directories.
- Top most directory is the root directory. The directory you are in is you current directory.
- When you log in the OS places you in your home directory (usually a child of the directory users).

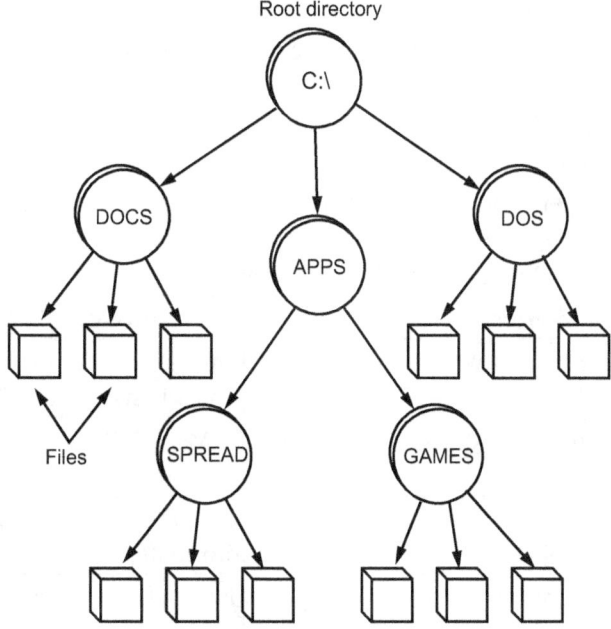

Fig. 1.9: Directory structure

- Directories contain bookkeeping information about files that are, figuratively speaking, beneath them in the hierarchy. You can think of a directory as a file cabinet that contains folder that contain files. Many graphical user interfaces use the term folder instead of directory.
- Computer manuals often describe directories and file structures in terms of an inverted tree. The files and directories at any level are contained in the directory above them. To access a file, you may need to specify the names of all the directories above it. You do this by specifying a path.
- The topmost directory in any file is called the root directory. A directory that is below another directory is called a subdirectory. A directory above a subdirectory is called the parent directory. Under DOS and Windows, the root directory is a back slash (\).
- To read information from, or write information into, a directory, you must use an operating system command. You cannot directly edit directory files.
- For example, the DIR command in DOS reads a directory file and displays its contents:

1.5 Types of Memory (Primary and Secondary)

- Computer memory is any physical device capable of storing information temporarily or permanently.
- Computer data storage, often called storage or memory, is a technology consisting of computer components and recording media used to retain digital data.
- Memory refer to the physical devices used to store programs (sequences of instructions) or data (e.g. program state information) on a temporary or permanent basis for use in a computer or other digital electronic device.
- The main function of memory is to store the information or data.
- There are two types of memories:
  1. **Volatile memory** is a type of memory (storage) whose contents are erased when the system's power is turned off or interrupted.
  2. **Non-volatile memory** is any memory or storage that will be saved regardless if the power to the computer is on or off.

Comparison between Volatile and Non-volatile memories:

Volatile Memories	Non-volatile Memories
1. Information stored is lost when power is switched OFF.	1. Information stored is retained even after power is switched OFF.
2. All RAMs are volatile memories.	2. ROMs, EPROMS are non-volatile memories.
3. Stored information is retained as long as power is ON.	3. No effect of power, on stored information.
4. Used for temporary storage of information.	4. Used for permanent storage of information.

- Fig. 1.10 shows classification of memories.

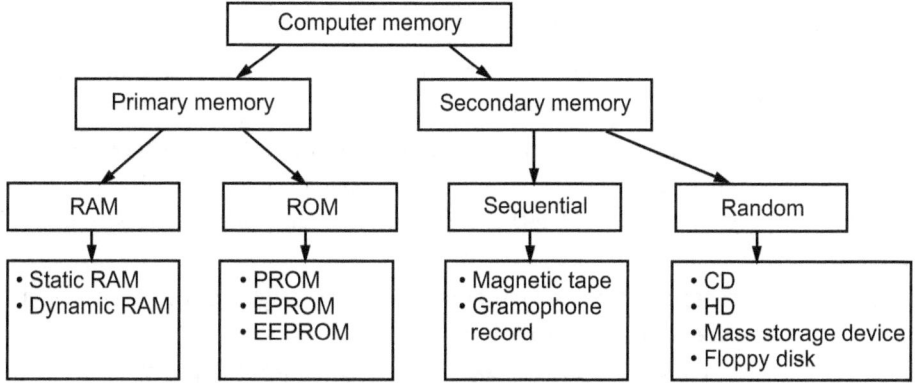

Fig. 1.10: Classification of computer memories

1.5.1 Primary Memory

- Primary memory (primary storage or main memory or internal memory), often referred to simply as memory, is the only one, directly accessible to the CPU.
- The CPU continuously reads instructions stored there and executes them as required.
- Any data actively operated on is also stored there in uniform manner.
- Primary memory holds only those data and instructions on which computer is currently working. It has limited capacity and data get lost when power is switched off.
- It is generally made up of semiconductor device. These memories are not as fast as registers. The data and instruction required to be processed earlier reside in main memory.
- Primary memory is divided into two subcategories RAM and ROM.

Characteristic of main (Primary) memory:
1. Primary memories are semiconductor memories.
2. Usually volatile memory.
3. Data is lost in case power is switched off.
4. It is working memory of the computer.
5. Faster than secondary memories.
6. A computer cannot run without primary memory.

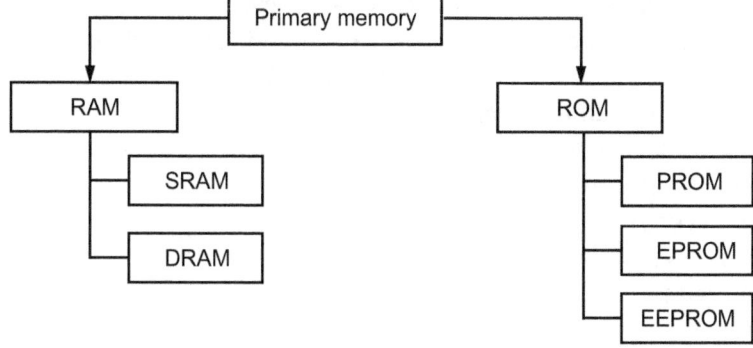

Fig. 1.11

1.5.1.1 RAM

- RAM stands for Random Access Memory.
- A RAM constitutes the internal memory of the CPU for storing data, program and program result. It is read/write memory.
- RAM is volatile, i.e. data stored in it is lost when we switch off the computer or if there is a power failure. Hence, a backup Uninterruptible Power System (UPS) is often used with computers. RAM is small, both in terms of its physical size and in the amount of data it can hold.
- This memory is accessible from any memory location anytime. one can switch to one place to another place in memory randomly.
- RAM is of two types i.e. Static RAM (SRAM) and Dynamic RAM (DRAM).

1. SRAM:

- SRAM (Static Random Access Memory) is a type of semiconductor memory where the word static indicates that, it does not need to be periodically refreshed, as SRAM uses bistable latching circuitry to store each bit.
- SRAM is volatile in the conventional sense that data is eventually lost when the memory is not powered.
- Static RAM is used as cache memory needs to be very fast and small.

Characteristic of the Static RAM:

(i) It has long data lifetime.
(ii) There is no need to refresh.
(iii) Faster.
(iv) Used as cache memory.
(v) Large size.
(vi) Expensive.
(vii) High power consumption.

2. DRAM:

- DRAM (Dynamic Random Access Memory) is a type of random access memory that stores each bit of data in a separate capacitor within an integrated circuit.
- Since, real capacitor leak charge, the information eventually fades unless the capacitor charge is refreshed periodically. Because of this refresh requirement, it is a dynamic memory as opposed to SRAM and other static memory.

Characteristic of the Dynamic RAM:

(i) It has short data lifetime.
(ii) Need to refresh continuously.
(iii) Slower as compared to SRAM.
(iv) Used as RAM.
(v) Lesser in size.
(vi) Less expensive.
(vii) Less power consumption.

Comparison between Static RAM and Dynamic RAM:

Static RAM (SRAM)	Dynamic RAM (DRAM)
1. Each static RAM cell is a flip-flop.	1. A dynamic RAM cell consists of a MOSFET and a capacitor.
2. Less number of memory cells/unit area.	2. More number of memory cells/unit area.
3. More number of components per cell.	3. Only two components per cell.
4. Does not require refreshing.	4. Require refreshing.
5. Faster memories.	5. Slower memories.
6. Power consumption is less.	6. More power consumption.

1.5.1.2 ROM (PROM and EPROM)

- ROM stands for Read Only Memory.
- The memory from which we can only read but cannot write on it.
- This type of memory is non-volatile. The information is stored permanently in such memories during manufacture.
- Read only memory, also known as firmware, is an integrated circuit programmed with specific data when it is manufactured. ROM chips are used not only in computers, but in most other electronic items as well like washing machine and microwave oven.
- A ROM, stores such instruction as are required to start computer when electricity is first turned on, this operation is referred to as bootstrap.

Advantages of ROM:
1. Non-volatile in nature.
2. These can not be accidentally changed.
3. Cheaper than RAMs.
4. Easy to test.
5. More Reliable than RAMs.
6. These are static and do not require refreshing.
7. Its contents are always known and can be verified.

Types of ROMs:
1. **MROM**
   - MROM stands for Masked ROM.
   - The very first ROMs were hard-wired devices that contained a pre-programmed set of data or instructions.
   - These kind of ROMs are known as masked ROMs.
   - MROM is inexpensive ROM.
2. **PROM**
   - PROM stands for Programmable Read Only Memory.
   - PROM is read-only memory that can be modified only once by a user. The user buys a blank PROM and enter the desired contents using a PROM programmer.

- Inside the PROM chip there are small fuses which are burnt open during programming. It can be programmed only once and is not erasable.
- A Programmable Read-Only Memory or Field Programmable Read-Only Memory (FPROM) is a form of digital memory where the setting of each bit is locked by a fuse or antifuse.

3. **EPROM**
   - EPROM stands for Erasable and Programmable Read Only Memory.
   - An EPROM is a type of memory chip that retains its data when its power supply is switched off. The EPROM can be erased by exposing it to ultra-violet light for a duration of up to 40 minutes. Usually, a EPROM eraser achieves this function.
   - During programming an electrical charge is trapped in an insulated gate region. The charge is retained for more than ten year because the charge has no leakage path.
   - For erasing this charge, ultra-violet light is passed through a quartz crystal window (lid). This exposure to ultra-violet light dissipates the charge. During normal use the quartz lid is sealed with a sticker.

4. **EEPROM**
   - EEPROM stands for Electrically Erasable and Programmable Read Only Memory. EEPROM also written as E^2PROM.
   - EEPROM is a type of non-volatile memory used in computer and other electronic devices to store small amounts of data that must be saved when power is removed,
   - The EEPROM is programmed and erased electrically. It can be erased and reprogrammed about ten thousand times. Both erasing and programming take about 4 to 10 ms (milli second).
   - In EEPROM, any location can be selectively erased and programmed. EEPROMs can be erased one byte at a time, rather than erasing the entire chip. Hence, the process of re-programming is flexible but slow.

Comparison between E^2PROM and EPROM:

E^2PROM	EPROM
1. E^2PROM stands for Electrically Erasable Programmable Read Only Memory.	1. EPROM stands for Erasable Programmable Read Only Memory.
2. Can be programmed and erased electrically.	2. Cannot be erased electrically and require UV rays to erase the EPROM.
3. Can be erased in a small time of 10 ms.	3. Requires 20 to 30 min. for erasing the contents.
4. Not required to remove the chip from the circuit for erasing and reprogramming.	4. Chip has to be removed from the circuit for erasing and reprogram-ming.
5. Low density	5. High density
6. Expensive than EPROM.	6. Cheaper than E^2PROM.

Difference between RAM and ROM:

RAM	ROM
1. RAM stands for Random Access Memory.	1. ROM stands for Read Only Memory.
2. It is temporary memory.	2. It is permanent memory.
3. RAM is volatile memory.	3. ROM is non-volatile memory.
4. Information stored by user.	4. Information stored by manufacturer.
5. Read/write operations can be performed.	5. Only read can be performed.
6. Every location can be accessed directly or randomly.	6. Longer access time.
7. RAM stores data, program instructions during program execution.	7. ROM stores system software are programs for basic operations.

Cache Memory:
- Cache memory is a very high speed memory placed in between RAM and CPU. Cache memory increases the speed of processing.
- Cache memory is a storage buffer that stores the data that is used more often, temporarily, and makes them available to CPU at a fast rate.
- During processing, CPU first checks cache for the required data. If data is not found in cache, then it looks in the RAM for data.
- To access the cache memory, CPU does not have to use the motherboard's system bus for data transfer.
- Cache memory is built into the processor, and may also be located next to it on a separate chip between the CPU and RAM.
- Cache built into the CPU is faster than separate cache, running at the speed of the microprocessor itself. However, separate cache is roughly twice as fast as RAM.

Flash Memory:
- It is an extension of EEPROMs.
- It uses floating gate principle.
- It is designed such that large blocks of memory can be erased all at once rather than just one word at a time.

Applications of Flash Memory:
1. To store photograph in a digital camera.
2. To store voice in compressed form in a voice recorder.
3. To store message in mobile phone.

1.5.2 Secondary Memory
- Secondary storage (also known as external memory or auxiliary storage or secondary storage), differ from primary storage in that it is not directly accessible by the CPU.

- The computer usually uses its input/output channels to access secondary storage and transfer the desired data using intermediate area in primary storage.
- Secondary storage does not lose the data when the device is powered down—it is non-volatile. Per unit, it is typically also two order of magnitude less expensive than primary storage.
- Consequently, modern computer systems typically have two order of magnitude more secondary storage than primary storage and data are kept for a longer time there.
- Secondary memory is slower than main memory.
- CPU directly does not access these memories instead they are accessed via input-output routines.
- Contents of secondary memories are first transferred to main memory, and then CPU can access it. For example: disk, CD-ROM, DVD etc.

Characteristic of secondary memory:

1. These are magnetic and optical memories.
2. It is known as backup memory.
3. It is non-volatile memory.
4. Data is permanently stored even if power is switched off.
5. It is used for storage of the data in the computer.
6. Computer may run without secondary memory.
7. Slower than primary memories.

Comparison between Primary and Secondary Memories:

Primary Memory	Secondary Memory
1. It is a part of CPU.	1. It is not a part of CPU.
2. It is the internal or main memory.	2. It is the external memory and resides on disk.
3. The access time is less a few nanoseconds.	3. The access time is more a few milliseconds.
4. It is a medium capacity memory.	4. It is a high capacity memory.
5. It is further classified as RAM and ROM.	5. There are different types of secondary storage devices such as hard disk, floppy disk, CD-ROM etc.
6. Most Primary Storage is temporary.	6. All secondary storage is permanent.
7. Primary storage is expensive and smaller.	7. Secondary storage is usually cheaper and large.
8. Primary storage is usually faster therefore more expensive.	8. Secondary storage connects to the CPU via cables and therefore is slower.

1.5.3 Secondary Storage Devices
1.5.3.1 Magnetic Tape
- Magnetic tape is now principally used only as a backup medium. It is also used to archive records of past transactions for long-term storage, as it is cheap, robust and easily used to store large quantities of data.
- Magnetic tape is a recording medium consisting of a thin tape with a coating of a fine magnetic material, used for recording analog or digital data.
- A device that stores computer data on magnetic tape is a tape drive.

Fig. 1.12 (a): Magnetic tape

- The magnetic tape drive is similar to the audio tape recorders. Before the data on magnetic tape can be processed, the tape must be placed in a machine called tape drive or tape transport.
- We can read/write data from the tape. Writing data on the tape destroys the previous tape contents.
- When the tape is accelerated to its full speed no recording can be done. The distance traversed by the tape during this time is called as Inter Block Gap (IBG). The beginning of the tape is indicated by a metal foil called a marker.
- When a write command is given, the block of data is written on the tape and after the IBG the next block of data is written. A metal foil is used again to indicate the end of tape. The data which is stored on the tape has to be accessed sequentially.

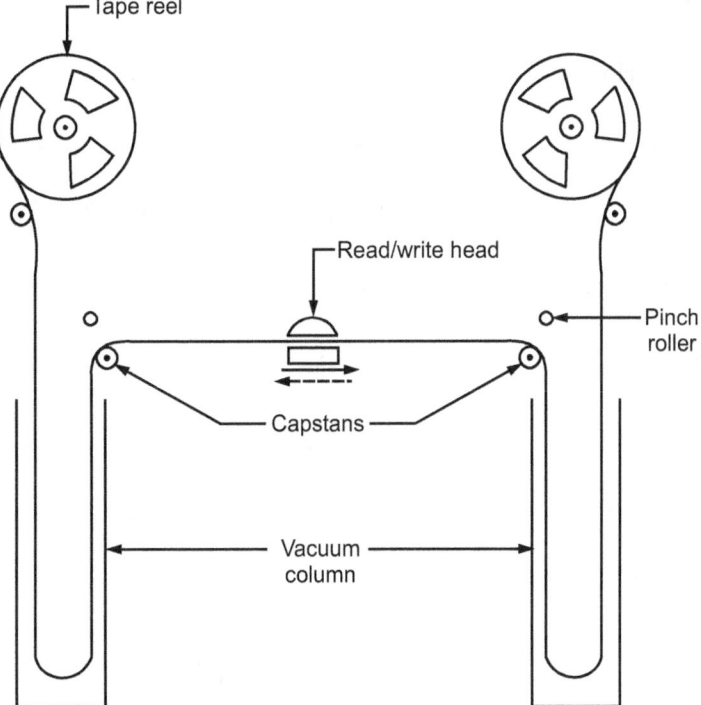

Fig. 1.12 (b): Magnetic tape drive

- Advantages of magnetic tape include the fact that it's generally the cheapest option for memory storage and it holds plenty of data (often 1 terabyte per tape). The disadvantages include that readers are becoming more obsolete over time, processing is slow, and searching within the data is cumbersome.

1.5.3.2 Magnetic Disks

1. Floppy Disk:
- The floppy disk is made up of thin flexible plastic (Mylar) material of circular shape. As the thickness of the Mylar is few thousands of an inch it is called floppy.
- The information can be stored on single side or both sides of the disk. Depending on the recording technique used, they are classified as single density and double density diskettes.
- The different sizes available are:
    1. 8" disk which is used in order computer which is presently obsolete.
    2. $5^{1/4}$" disk having capacity 1.2 MB called mini floppy.
    3. $3^{1/2}$" disk having capacity 1.44 MB called micro floppy.

Fig. 1.13 (a): A floppy

Characteristics of a Floppy Disk:
1. A "track" is a narrow recording band that forms a full circle on the surface of the disk.
2. The disk's storage locations are then divided into pie-shaped sections, which break the tracks into small arcs called sectors (can hold 512 bytes of data).
3. Floppy Disks store data on both sides. Each side consists of 80 tracks with 18 sectors per track.
4. To read from and write on the disk, sectors are grouped into clusters (consist of 2 to 8 sectors).
5. A cluster is the smallest unit of space used to store data.

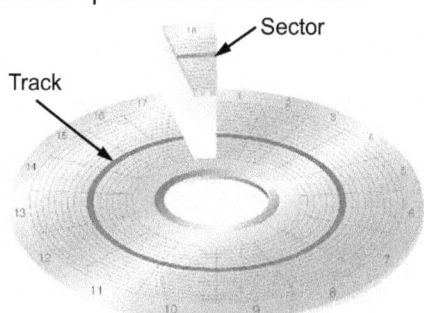

Fig. 1.13 (b)

- **Construction of floppy disk:** The floppy disk is coated with magnetic material and enclosed in a protective jacket. There is a large slot on jacket through which head reads and writes data on the disk.

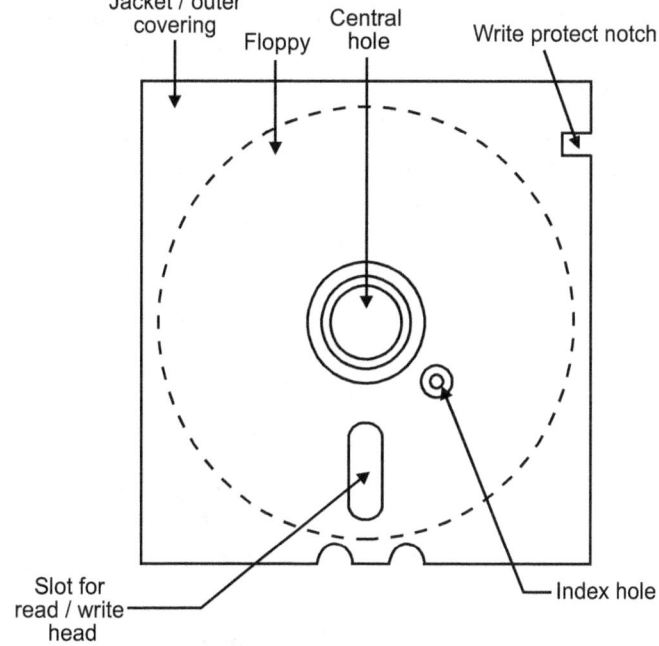

Fig. 1.14: Parts of a floppy

- A hole is provided at the centre called hub for clamping the floppy so that it can rotate easily without slipping. Near the centre a small hole is punched on the diskette called index hole.
- This hole indicates the beginning of a track. Writing is done on the floppy disk only after sensing the index hole.
- A write protect notch is provided. If this notch is open, writing on diskette is permitted. If this notch is covered by a paper or sticker then writing is not permitted.
- **Principle of working:** Floppy is made of number of tracks and each track is divided into a number of sectors. Data is stored on the track bit by bit using electromagnetic techniques, the data is read (or stored) from (on) the disk.
- There are two heads, one for writing on the top side of the disk and the other on the bottom side of the disk. In a write operation the write data line contains both clock pulses and data pulses.
- Current is passed through read/write head and flux transition is created for each clock or data pulse. In read operation e.m.f. is induced into the read head because of rotation of floppy disk which causes flux transitions. The induced e.m.f. is amplified and shaped by the amplifier circuit in FDD.
- In a write operation the data pulses as well as the clock pulses are stored on the disk or else it becomes difficult to differentiate between no data and zero data.

(i) Micro Floppy:

- It is of the size $3^{1/2}$ inch and its capacity is 1.44 MB. The 3.5" is so designed that one end is truncated which prevents improper insertion of the diskette.
- There is a round plastic sheet (mylar), coated with magnetic material and is enclosed in a hard plastic jacket. It uses a more finely grained medium with buffer magnetic properties so its capacity is more.
- A hole with slider is provided along the side of the plastic jacket. One can read/write if the hole is blocked by the slider. One can only read the data if the hole is visible.

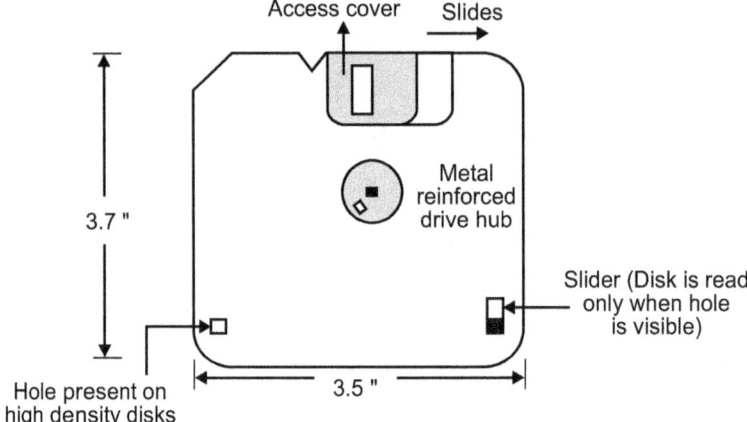

Fig. 1.15: Micro floppy

- It uses a metal hub so the disk can be centered very easily. If one more hole is provided it indicates the diskette has double density.

(ii) Mini Floppy:

- A mini floppy is of size of $5^{1/4}$ inch floppy disk. A floppy diskette is an ultra thin plastic piece in circular shape.

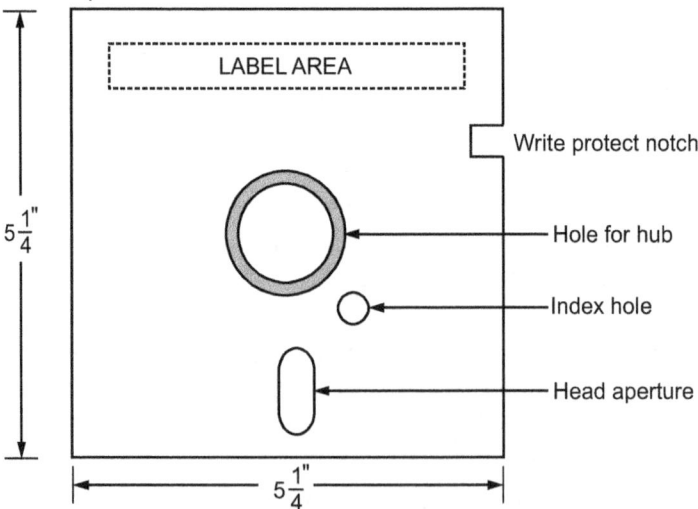

Fig. 1.16: Mini floppy

- It is coated with a magnetic material and enclosed in a protective jacket. An oval access hole is made on the jacket so as to provide contact between the read/write head and the diskette.
- On floppy there is write protect notch. If this notch is kept uncovered then you can write to the floppy, but if it is covered by a sticker then floppy becomes read only and you cannot write on to it.
- When index hole of upper cover and mini floppy matches each other then there is first block/sector on read/write head slot. It is widely used in present day computer including PCs, PC-XTs, PC-ATs, etc.

Advantages of Floppy Disk:
  (i) Information can be directly encoded onto the disk.
  (ii) Bulky media is not used, so ease in handling and transportation.
  (iii) Used for storage, input and output.
  (iv) It is cheap.
  (v) Density is high.
  (vi) It can be reused many times.

Disadvantages of Floppy Disk:
  (i) It should be handled carefully.
  (ii) It is sensitive to environment conditions such as heat, dust etc.

2. **Hard Disk:**
- The hard disk is the most widely used mass storage device for PCs. On the hard disk all the programs and data are stored which can be accessed instantly thus making the system faster.
- The hard disk drive or hard disk is the main, and usually largest data storage device in a computer.
- It is a non-volatile, random access digital magnetic data storage device.
- A hard drive is made up of platter which stored the data, and read/write heads to transfer data.
- A hard drive is generally the fastest of the secondary storage devices, and has the largest data storage capacity, approximately the same as magnetic tapes. Hard drives however, are not very portable and are primarily used internally in a computer system.

Construction of Hard Disk:
- Hard disks use a circular hard platter to store data on. They are in pristine condition with a mirror like finish to them. These platter are locked away inside a steel casing as unclean air can easily ruin a hard disk.
- This is why we should never remove the casing from the hard disk as it is very unlikely that we will be able to put it back together as a working component.

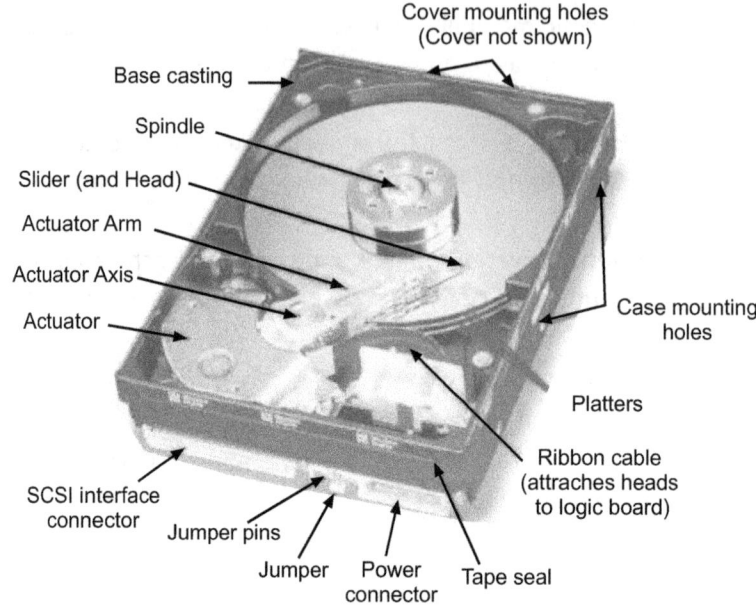

Fig. 1.17: Parts of hard disk

- Fig. 1.17 shows a labelled diagram of a hard disk.
- The model is a SCSI (Small Computer Scientific Interface) shows the hard platter on top of each other with a set of arms which hold the read/write head.
- The speed of the arm is truly amazing as well as the accuracy of the head which can read and write to perfection on a platter which is rotating around 7200 rpm.
- The hard disk looks a very simple idea and probably is, however a lot goes on before the simple writing to the disk itsself.
- Hard disk should have two parts i.e. physical part like platter read/write head, and
- Logical parts like track, sector, pie, shape and cylinder.
- A hard disk is divided into tracks and sectors, data on this hard disk is positioned into these tracks and sector so they can be easily read by the heads and also to help reduce fragmentation on the hard disk.
- Fig. 1.18 depicts how a hard disk is divided into tracks and sectors.

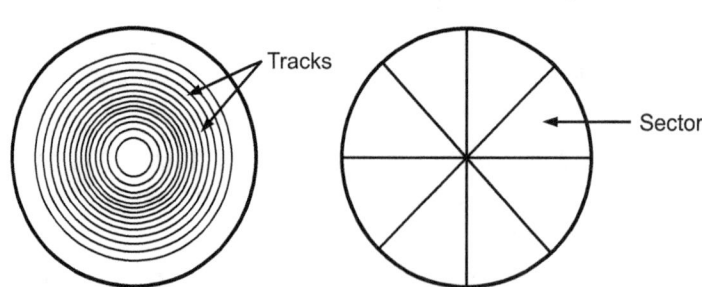

Fig. 1.18: Track and sector in harddisk

- Data on a hard drive are accessed by two methods:
    1. **Fixed Head:** Hard disks with fixed heads have a read/write head for each track on the hard disk, since there is no moving of heads to access data, the data access time is generally faster for fixed head hard drives.
    2. **Moving Head:** A moving head hard disk is one in which one or more read-write heads are attached to a movable arm which allows each head to cover many tracks of information.
- Each access to the hard drive to read or write data causes the read/write heads to burst into a furious flurry of movement – which must be performed with microscopic precision. The tolerances in a disk drive are equivalent to a jumbo jet flying at an altitude of less than a centimetre.
- Data is stored in a very orderly pattern on each platter. Bits of data are arranged in concentric, circular paths called tracks. Each track is broken up into smaller areas called sectors. Part of the hard drive stores a map of sector that have already been used up and other that are still free.
- When the computer wants to store new information, it takes a look at the map to find some free sectors
- Typically, data up to 100 GB's can be stored on single platter.
- With so much information stored in such a tiny amount of space, a hard drive is a remarkable piece of engineering.

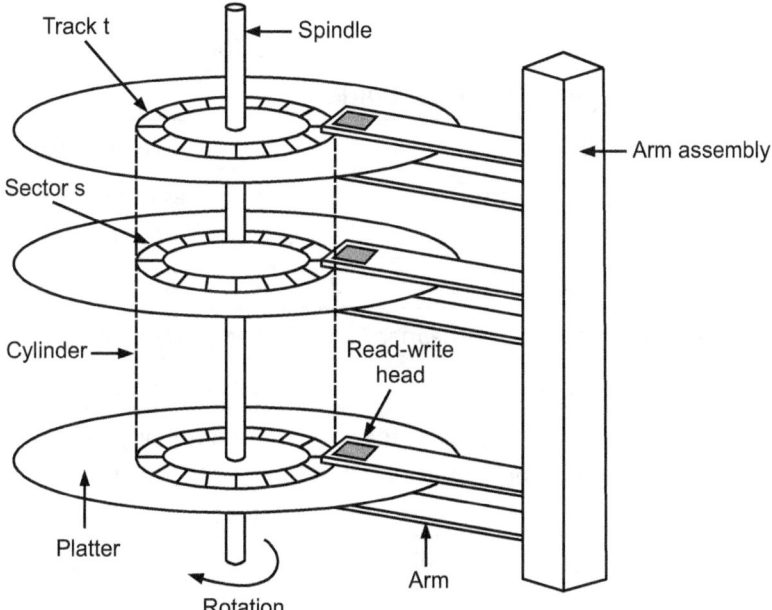

Fig. 1.19: Hard disk cylinder, R/W head spindle assembly

Comparison between Tape drive and Hard disk/Floppy disk:

Tape drive	Hard disk/Floppy disk
1. Data cannot be accessed directly, it has to be accessed sequentially.	1. Data can be accessed directly or sequentially
2. The data cannot be accessed and immediately updated.	2. The data can be accessed and updated in a few milliseconds.
3. It is cheaper than magnetic disks.	3. It is nearly 20 times more expensive than tape drive.
4. Easy to maintain security of tape files than files stored on a disk.	4. Security of files is less compared to tape drive.

Difference between Floppy disk and CD-ROM:

Floppy disk	CD-ROM
1. It has lower storage capacity 1.44 MB.	1. It has higher storage capacity upto 700 MB.
2. It uses magnetic technology.	2. It uses laser technology.
3. Data is recorded on both sides.	3. Data is recorded on one side.
4. It is affected by dust, moisture.	4. It is not affected by dust, mositure.
5. It is read/write medium.	5. It is read only medium.
6. Used to store low volumes of data.	6. Used to store high volumes of data such as encyclopaedia, telephone, directory etc.

Difference between Floppy disk and Hard disk:

Floppy disk	Hard disk
1. It is a removable, low storage capacity secondary storage medium.	1. It is not easily removable, high capacity secondary storage medium.
2. It provides off-line storage of data.	2. It can provide on-line storage of data.
3. It has more access time, but it is cheaper.	3. The access time is less but it is costly.
4. It has a write-protect notch.	4. It does not have a notch.
5. There are two read/write heads in the drive, one for each side of the floppy.	5. There are many read/write heads in the drive because the disk contains many plotters.
6. The read/write head touches the surface of floppy.	6. The read/write head never touches the surface.

1.5.3.3 Optical Disks (CD and DVD)

- Optical disk is an electronic data storage medium from which data is read and written to by using a low-powered laser beam.
- It is flat, circular, plastic or glass disk on which data is stored in the form of light and dark pits.
- There are three basic types of optical disks: Read-Only Optical Disks, Write Once Read Many Optical Disks and Rewritable Optical Disks.
- Two main types of optical disks are CD and DVD.

1. CD:
- CD stands for Compact Disk.

Fig. 1.20: A CD

- CD is an abbreviation of Compact Disk, and is a form of data storage that can transfer data up to the speed of 7800 KB/s.
- A standard 120 mm CD holds up to 700 MB of data, or about 70 minutes of audio. There are two types of CD: CD-ROM and CD-RW.
- CD-ROM are stands for CD-Read Only Memory and they function the same way Read Only Memory does.

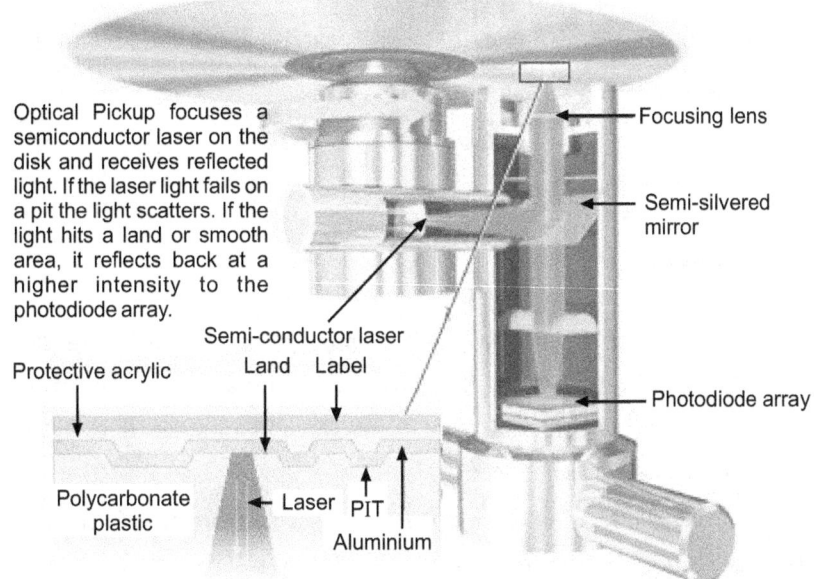

Fig. 1.21: Working of CD

- CD-RW stands for CD-Rewritable, these disks can be erased and rewritten at any time.
- The Compact Disk (CD) is storage media that hold content in digital form and that are written and read by a laser; these media include all the CD and DVD variations, as well as optical jukeboxes and autochangers.
- Optical media have a number of advantages over magnetic media such as the floppy disk. Optical disk capacity ranges up to 6 gigabytes; that's 6 billion bytes compared to 1.44 megabytes (MB) – 1,440,000 bytes – of the floppy.
- One optical disk holds about the equivalent of 500 floppies worth of data. Durability is another feature of optical media; they last up to seven times as long as traditional storage media.

2. **DVD:**
- DVD is an abbreviation of Digital Versatile Disc, and is an optical disc storage media format that can be used for data storage.
- The DVD supports disks with capacities of 4.7 GB to 17 GB and access rates of 600 Kbps to 1.3 mbps.
- A standard DVD disc store up to 4.7 GB of data. There are two types of DVD's: DVD-ROM and DVD-RW.
- DVD-ROM are stands for DVD-Read Only Memory and they function the same way Read Only Memory does.
- DVD-RW stands for DVD-Rewritable, these disks can be erased and rewritten at any time.

Fig. 1.22: DVDs

- A DVD is composed of several layer of plastic, polycarbonate base, totaling about 1.2 millimeter thick. Writing data to the DVD is done by a red laser beam modulated by the serial data stream. When the beam turns on and hits the dye layer, a distortion (known as a pit) on the surface is made.
- Dual layer recording allows DVD-R and DVD+R discs to store significantly more data, up to 8.54 GB's per side, per disc, compared with 4.7 GB's for single-layer discs. While you will need as much as 300 DVD's to be able to store that data.

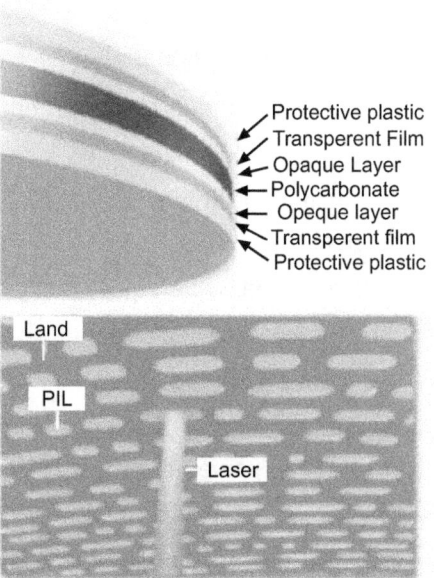

Fig. 1.23: Working of DVD

Comparison of CD and DVD:

Terms	CD	DVD
Stands for	Compact Disc	Digital Versatile Disc
Purpose	CDs are made with the purpose of holding audio files as well as program files.	DVDs are made with the purpose of holding video files, movies, substantial amount of programs, etc.
Media type	Optical disc	Optical disc
Encoding	Various	Various
Capacity	Typically up to 700 MiB (up to 80 minutes audio)	DVD can range from 4.7 GB to 17.08 GB.
Read mechanism	780 nm wavelength (infrared and red edge) semiconductor laser, 1200 Kib/s (1×)	650 nm laser, 10.5 Mbit/s (1×)
Write mechanism	1200 Kib/s (1×)	10.5 Mbit/s (1×)
Types	CD-R, CD-RW, CD-Text, CD + Graphics, CD + Extended Graphics, Super Audio CD, CD-MIDI, CD-ROM, Video CD, Super Video CD, Photo CD, CD-I, Enhanced CD, VinylDisc and Bootable CD.	DVD-RW, DVD+RW, DVD-RAM and Blu-Ray.
Developed by:	Philips, Sony	Philips, Sony, Toshiba, and Panasonic

1.5.3.4 Pen Drive

- Pen drive is type of Universal Serial Cable (USB) flash drive.
- It is a kind of memory card that can be plugged into a computer's USB port.
- It is termed "Pen drive" with reference to its size.
- It is a small and compact thus naming it fit into the palm of our hand. It is often flat and rectangular like a highlighter pen.
- A pen drive is used to store data and has a storage capacity of 64 MB to 32 GB.
- It is removable and rewritable. It is mostly used as a backup for CD-ROMs or floppy disks.

Technical Mechanism:

- Pen drive consists of a small printed circuit board. This circuit board provides a strong base for the pen drive's form and also serves as a means to collection information.
- The circuit board consists of a small microchip within it. This microchip enables the pen drive to extract or feed in data. This process requires relatively low electrical power compared to CD-R's or Floppy. It based on EEP-ROMS technology that allows writing and ensure process in a computer system.
- The data that is to be transferred is connected through a computer programme. It is then read, transmitted or rewritten from a pen drive to a computer or vice versa. Thus the required data gets copied to any selected derive on the computer for further use.
- When a pen drive is connected to a USB port, it is activated. The USB parts gives the pen drive access to the information on a specific computer drive. Most of the open drives are designed in such a way that they are compatible with any USB port of a computer.
- The data that is to be transferred is connected through a computer programme. It is then read, transmitted or rewritten from a pen drive to a computer or vice versa. Thus the required data gets copied to any selected drive on the computer for further use.
- Internal parts of a typical USB flash drive are, (See Fig. 1.24).
    1. US connector.
    2. USB mass storage controller device.
    3. Test points.
    4. Flash memory chip.
    5. Crystal oscillator.
    6. LED.
    7. Write-protect switch (Optional)
    8. Space for second flash memory chip.

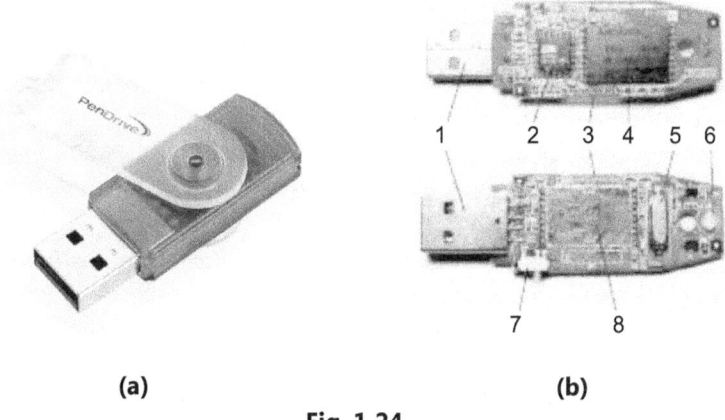

(a)   (b)

Fig. 1.24

Advantages:
1. Reliable than make external storage devices like CD, floppy etc.
2. Cost effective.
3. Easily Transportable in case of CD we need a pouch.
4. Can be used as a bootable device.
5. No prior software needed to write or read data, in case of CD writing we need software like Nero etc.

Disadvantages:
1. It does have a cyclic life span.
2. If items like dust goes inside then it will not work properly.
3. While the pen drive is portable and convenient, it also has the risk of being easily lost, as well as the fact that it has a limited number of write and erase cycles.

1.6 I/O (Input/Output) Devices

- The terms input and output are used both as verbs to describe the process of entering or displaying the data, and as nouns referring to the data itself entered into or displayed by the computer.
- Input devices allow us to enter raw data into a computer. The computer processes the data and then produces outputs that we can understand using an output device.

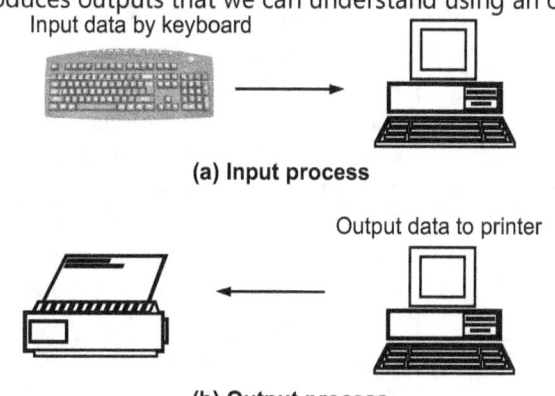

(a) Input process

(b) Output process

Fig. 1.25: I/O (Input/Output) process

- Any information or data that is entered or sent to the computer to be processed is considered input and anything that is displayed from the computer is output.
- Therefore, an input device such as a computer keyboard is capable of having information sent to the computer, but does not display (output) any information.
- An output device such as a computer printer can print information from the computer but does not send any information (input) to the computer.

1.6.1 Input Devices

- The devices which are used to input the data and the programs in the computer are known as Input Devices.
- Input device can read data and convert them to a form that a computer can understand and use.
- An input device is equipment used to capture information and commands.

1.6.1.1 Keyboard

- Keyboard is most common input device is used today. Keyboard are used for inputting data to computer.
- The data and instructions are input by typing on the keyboard. The message typed on the keyboard reaches the memory unit of a computer. It is connected to a computer via a cable. Apart from alphabet and numeral keys, it has other function keys for performing different functions.
- The layout of the keyboard is like that of traditional typewriter, although there are some additional keys provided for performing some additional functions.
- Keyboard are of two sizes 84 keys or 101/102 keys, but now 104 keys or 108 keys keyboard is also available for Windows and Internet.
- The keys are following:

Sr. No.	Keys	Description
1.	Typing Keys	These keys include the letter keys (A-Z) and digits keys (0-9) which are generally arranged in same layout as that of typewriters.
2.	Numeric Keypad	It is used to enter numeric data or cursor movement. Generally, it consists of a set of 17 keys that are laid out in the same configuration used by most adding machine and calculators.
3.	Function Keys	The twelve functions keys are present on the keyboard. These are arranged in a row along the top of the keyboard. Each function key has unique meaning and is used for some specific purpose.
4.	Control keys	These keys provides cursor and screen control. It includes four directional arrow key. Control keys also include Home, End,Insert, Delete, Page Up, Page Down, Control (Ctrl), Alternate (Alt), Escape(Esc).
5.	Special Purpose Keys	Keyboard also contains some special purpose keys such as Enter, Shift, Caps Lock, Num Lock, Space bar, Tab, and Print Screen.

- Fig. 1.26 shows a keyboard with its keys.

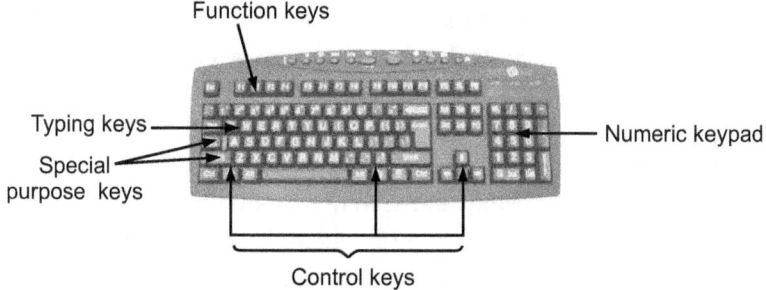

Fig. 1.26: Computer keyboard with different types of keys

1.6.1.2 Mouse

- Mouse is most popular pointing device.
- Mouse is a very famous cursor-control device.
- Mouse is a small palm size box with a round ball at its base which senses the movement of mouse and sends corresponding signals to CPU on pressing the buttons.
- Generally it has two buttons called left and right button and scroll bar is present at the mid wheel, (See Fig. 1.27).
- Mouse can be used to control the position of cursor on screen, but it cannot be used to enter text into the computer.

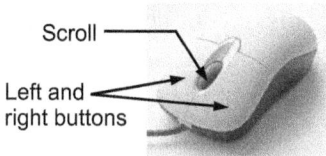

Fig. 1.27: Mouse

Advantages:
1. Easy to use.
2. Not very expensive.
3. Moves the cursor faster than the arrow keys of keyboard.

1.6.1.3 Scanner

- Scanner is an input device which works more like a photocopy (Xerox) machine.
- Scanner are used to enter information directly into the computer's memory.
- The scanner converts any type of printed or written information including photographs into digital pulses, which can be manipulated by the computer.
- Scanner is used when some information is available on a paper and it is to be transferred to the hard disc of the computer for further manipulation.
- Scanner captures images from the source which are then converted into the digital form that can be stored on the disc. These images can be edited before they are printed.

- There are several types of scanners, all of which serve a variety of functions:
    1. **Flatbed scanner:** This versatile scanner is usually found on a desktop. You lay the document on a glass panel, and a scan head moves beneath it. These scanners are great for scanning the occasional newspaper article, book chapter, or photograph; or for those who may need to scan or bulky items such as the cover of a DVD.
    2. **Sheet-fed scanner:** With this scanner, you place documents into a feeder, and they move through the scanner while the scan head remains still.
    3. **Handheld scanner:** In this case, the scan head is passed over the documents. These scanners don't usually produce high-quality images.
    4. **Drum scanner:** This kind of scanner uses a photomultiplier tube to reproduce very detailed images. Drum scanners are often used in the publishing industry.

Fig. 1.28: Scanner

Advantages:
1. A scanner is not having to go to the printers or library to make a copy of documents when you are in need of a copy.
2. It also makes keeping records of your finances and important documents a great deal less time consuming because you can make a digital copy of them.
3. Using scanner fast and convenient to have a copy done.

Disadvantages:
1. One of the biggest disadvantages of having a scanner is that they are relatively slow.
2. A good scanner is a little on the expensive side.
3. Quality of scan not the same as original.
4. In scanner we only can scan on the surface but not above it.

1.6.1.4 MICR

- MICR is an input device.
- MICR is a very fast and reliable as a means of entering data into a computer.
- Magnetic Ink Card Reader (MICR) input device is generally used in banks because of a large number of cheques to be processed every day.
- The bank's code number and cheque number are printed on the cheques with a special type of ink that contains particles of magnetic material that are machine readable.
- This reading process is called Magnetic Ink Character Recognition (MICR). The main advantage of MICR is that it is fast and less error prone.
- MICR is a character recognition system that uses special ink and characters.

Fig. 1.29: MICR

Advantages:
1. The use of iron oxide-based ink ensures MICR characters are readable even if a document is obscured by miscellaneous marks or overprinted.
2. MICR systems provide a high level of security since MICR characters are required to follow a stringent format and use precise iron oxide ink, which makes the documents difficult to forge.
3. The error rate for reading MICR characters is small as compared to other character recognition systems.

Disadvantages:
1. MICR readers are expensive and capable of recognizing only MICR fonts written in a specific format.
2. The printing of MICR is demanding, setting precise but difficult-to-achieve standards, which is a distinct disadvantage in terms of time consumption.

1.6.1.5 OMR

- Optical Mark Reader (OMR) is the process of gathering data with an optical scanner by measuring the reflectivity of light at predetermined positions on a surface.
- OMR is a special type of optical scanner used to recognize the type of mark made by pen or pencil.
- OMR is used where one out of a few alternatives is to be selected and marked.
- OMR is specially used for checking the answer sheets of examinations having multiple choice questions.

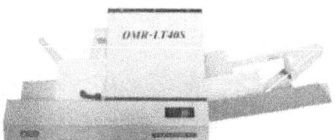

Fig. 1.30

Advantages:
1. A fast method of inputting large amount of data.
2. OMR is much accurate than data being keyed in by a user.
3. There is a large number of document to justify designing and printing them.
4. The user can only make marks and cannot write any information.

Disadvantages:
1. Document for mark reader are complicated to design.
2. Input of the data to computer is slow.
3. It is difficult for a computer to check marked data.
4. The person putting the marks on the document has to follow the instruction.

1.6.1.6 Digital Camera

- Digital camera is an input device.
- Digital cameras are becoming increasingly popular as they become cheaper and photo sharing websites become common.
- Digital camera is a device that captures digital photographs. Most digital cameras do not directly input data into a computer - they store photographs on memory cards.
- The photographs can later be transferred to a computer. A modern digital camera can capture 10 Megapixels or more per photograph - that's 10,000,000 colored dots (pixels) in every photo.

Fig. 1.31: Digital camera

1.6.1.7 Digitizer

- Digitizer is an input device which converts analog information into a digital form.
- Digitizer can convert a signal from the television camera into a series of number that could be stored in a computer.
- Digitizer can be used by the computer to create a picture of whatever the camera had been pointed at.
- Digitizer is also known as Tablet or Graphics Tablet because it converts graphics and pictorial data into binary inputs.
- A graphic tablet as digitizer is used for doing fine works of drawing and image manipulation applications.

Fig. 1.32: Digitizer

1.6.1.8 Joystick

- Joystick is also a pointing device which is used to move cursor position on a monitor screen.

- Joystick is a stick having a spherical ball at its both lower and upper ends. The lower spherical ball moves in a socket. The Joystick can be moved in all four directions.
- The function of joystick is similar to that of a mouse.
- Joystick is mainly used in Computer Aided Designing (CAD) and playing computer games.

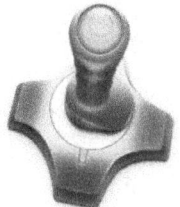

Fig. 1.33: Joystick

Advantages:
1. A joystick is that it is very easy to learn to use and they have a very simple design so they can be inexpensive.
2. The advantage of joystick is that it gives the player a real-time or virtual experience of the game.

Disadvantage:
1. A joystick is that some player finds it more difficult to control than using a mouse.
2. Joysticks are only limited to forward, backward, left and right.

1.6.1.9 Light Pen

- Light pen is an input device which is used to draw lines or figures on a computer screen.
- Light pen is a pointing device which is similar to a pen. It is used to select a displayed menu item or draw pictures on the monitor screen.
- Light pen consists of a photocell and an optical system placed in a small tube.
- When light pen's tip is moved over the monitor screen and pen button is pressed, its photocell sensing element detects the screen location and sends the corresponding signal to the CPU.

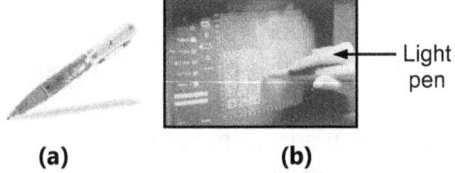

(a)   (b)

Fig. 1.34: Light pen

Advantages
(i) Light pens are easy to use.
(ii) They have extremely good positional accuracy on a computer screen, much more than is possible with a mouse or a touch screen.
(iii) They are ergonomically designed for ease of hand movement and are excellent for all drawing and pointing tasks.

(iv) They don't require extra desk space and are easily modified for use by people with disabilities.
(v) When used for bar code reading, they are lightweight, able to come in direct contact with the bar codes and have no moving parts.

Disadvantages
(i) Light pens are easily damaged.
(ii) They can only be used on some computer screens; they do not work with LCD screens.
(iii) They usually lack high resolution capability.
(iv) They can be fatiguing to the hand if overused.
(v) They can impair viewing of the computer screen on which they're being used. When used as bar code readers, they have a high error rate.

1.6.1.10 Track Ball

- Track ball is an input device that is mostly used in notebook or laptop computer, instead of a mouse.
- This is a ball which is half inserted and by moving finger on ball, pointer can be moved.
- Since, the whole device is not moved, a track ball requires less space than a mouse. A track ball comes in various shapes like a ball, a button and a square.
- Track ball is similar to the upside- down design of the mouse.
- The user moves the ball directly, while the device itself remains stationary. The user spins the ball in various directions to effect the screen movements.

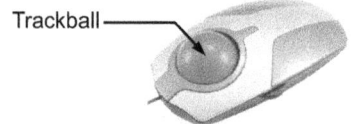

Fig. 1.35: Track ball

1.6.1.11 OCR

- OCR stands for Optical Character Reader.
- OCR is a device which detects alpha numeric character printed or written on a paper.
- The text which is to be scanned is illuminated by a low frequency light source.
- The light is absorbed by the dark areas but reflected from the bright areas. The reflected light is received by the photocells.
- OCR is an input device used to read a printed text.
- OCR scans text optically character by character, converts them into a machine readable code and stores the text on the system memory.

Fig. 1.36: OCR

1.6.1.12 Bar Code Readers

- A bar code reader reads bar codes and coverts them into electric pulses to be processed by a computer. A bar code is nothing but data coded in form of light and dark bars.
- Bar coded data is generally used in labelling goods, numbering the books etc. It may be a hand held scanner or may be embedded in a stationary scanner.
- Bar code reader scans a bar code image, converts it into an alphanumeric value which is then fed to the computer to which bar code reader is connected.

Fig. 1.37: Barcode reader

Advantages:
  (i) Much smaller in size.
  (ii) Less expensive i.e. barcodes are directly printed onto plastic or paper materials, therefore the only cost involved is the ink; a tiny overall cost.
  (iii) Barcodes work with the same accuracy on various materials in which they are placed.
  (iv) Barcode readers are helpful in stores in order to maintain accurate and updated inventory monitoring.

Disadvantages:
  (i) Barcode scanners need a direct line of sight to the barcode to be able to read.
  (ii) They are very labour intensive; as they must be scanned individually.
  (iii) Barcodes are more easily damaged; as the line of sight is needed to scan, the printed bar code has to be exposed on the outside of the product.
  (iv) Scratched or crumpled barcodes may cause problems.
  (v) Data must be coded in the barcode.
  (vi) In laser scanning, durability and cost are the two disadvantages.

1.6.2 Output Devices

- Output device can produce the final product of machine processing into a form usable by users. It provides machine to man communication.
- The output devices accept the results after processed by the CPU, converts it into human acceptable form and supplies it to the user.
- An output device is equipment used to see, hear, or otherwise accept the results of information processing requests.

1.6.2.1 Monitor (CRT and LCD)

- Monitor commonly called as Visual Display Unit (VDU) is the main output device of a computer.
- Monitor forms images from tiny dots, called pixels, that are arranged in a rectangular form. The sharpness of the image depends upon the no. of the pixels.

- The monitor displays the video and graphics information generated by the computer through the video card.
- Monitors are very similar to televisions but usually display information at a much higher resolution.
- The monitor is also known as screen, display, video display or video screen.
- Monitors come in two major types i.e. LCD and CRT.

1. CRT (Cathode Ray Tube):
- CRT monitor look much like old-fashioned televisions and are very deep in size. A monitor contains a Cathode Ray Tube (CRT), hardware to control an electronics beam and a power supply.
- A CRT is used to display numbers, letter and graphics.
- In the CRT display is made up of small picture elements called pixels for short. The smaller the pixels, the better the image clarity, or resolution. It takes more than one illuminated pixel to form whole character, such as the letter e in the word help.
- A finite number of character can be displayed on a screen at once. The screen can be divided into a series of character boxes - fixed location on the screen where a standard character can be placed.
- The most screens are capable of displaying 80 character of data horizontally and 25 lines vertically.

Fig. 1.38: CRT monitor

How CRT Monitor works?
- CRT monitor looks like TV screen. This kind of screen uses the Cathode Ray Tube (CRT) technology.
- CRT is a partially evacuated glass tube which is filled with an inert gas at very low pressure.
- Images are formed in this CRT by an electron gun shooting a stream of electrons at the surface of phosphorescent. Deflection coils are used to divert electron beam and strike on the exact position of phosphorescent surface.
- The CRT screen can be classified into two types in terms of color capability:
    - **(i) Monochrome Monitor:** Monochrome monitor actually displays only two colors, one for the background and other for the foreground.
    - **(ii) Color Monitor:** Color Monitor display color but the number of color they can display depends on the video adaptor capabilities as well as the monitors. Color monitor can display from 1 to 16 million different colors. Color monitor are sometime called RGB monitor because they accept three separate signal RED, GREEN and BLUE.

- Fig. 1.39 shows structure of CRT.

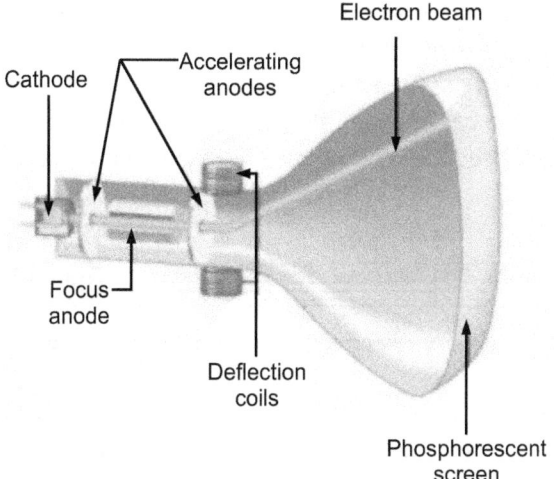

Fig. 1.39: Structure of CRT (internal)

- There are some disadvantage of CRT:
  (i) Large in size, and
  (ii) High power consumption.

2. **LCD (Liquid Crystal Display):**
- LCD monitor are much thinner, use less energy, and provide a greater graphics quality.
- LCD monitor have completely obsoleted CRT monitor due to their higher quality, smaller footprint on the desk, and decreasing price.
- The flat-panel display refer to a class of video devices that have reduced volume, weight and power requirement compared to the CRT.
- We can hang them on walls or wear them on your wrists. Current uses for flat-panel displays include calculators, videogames, monitors, laptop computer, graphics display.

Fig. 1.40 (a): LCD monitor

- The flat-panel display are divided into two categories:
  (i) Emissive Displays: The emissive displays are devices that convert electrical energy into light. Example are plasma panel and LED (Light-Emitting Diodes).
  (ii) Non-Emissive Displays: The Non-emissive displays use optical effects to convert sunlight or light from some other source into graphics patterns. Example is LCD (Liquid-Crystal Device).

How LCD Monitor Works?

- In LCD or liquid crystalline material is sandwich between two glass or plates as shown in Fig. 1.41 (LCD monitor). The front plate is transparent and the back plate is reflective.
- The less expensive LCD's are called passive matrix LCD's. The expensive LCD's are called active matrix LCD's (also called thinfil transistor - TFT) used transistor to control the color of each screen pixel. Speed and color quality is improved on passive matrix LCD's.

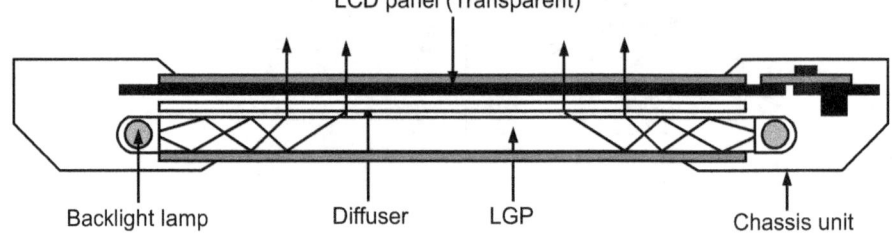

Fig. 1.41: Working of LCD monitor

Advantages:
(i) Power consumption is low.
(ii) Cost is less.

Disadvantages:
(i) Turn-on and Turn-off is large hence they are slow devices.
(ii) Their life span is less when used on DC.
(iii) They occupy large area.
(iv) Most monitor are in a widescreen format and range in size from 17" to 24" or more. This size is a diagonal measurement from one corner of the screen to the other.

1.6.2.2 Plasma Display

- A plasma display is a computer video display in which each pixel on the screen is illuminated by a tiny bit of plasma or charged gas, somewhat like a tiny neon light. Plasma displays are thinner than Cathode Ray Tube (CRT) displays and brighter than Liquid Crystal Displays (LCD).
- Plasma displays are sometimes marketed as "thin-panel" displays and can be used to display either analog video signals or display modes digital computer input.

Fig. 1.42: Plasma display

How Plasma Displays Work?

- The xenon and neon gas in a plasma television is contained in hundreds of thousands of tiny cells positioned between two plates of glass. Long electrodes are also sandwiched between the glass plates, on both sides of the cells.
- The address electrodes sit behind the cells, along the rear glass plate. The transparent display electrodes, which are surrounded by an insulating dielectric material and covered by a magnesium oxide protective layer, are mounted above the cell, along the front glass plate.

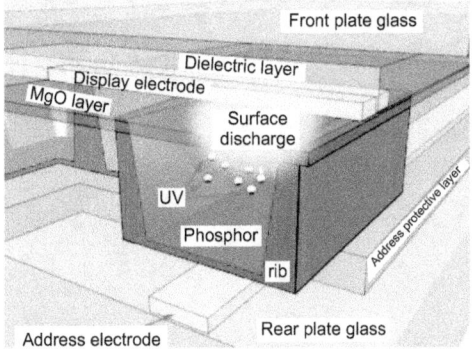

Fig. 1.43

- To ionize the gas in a particular cell, the plasma display's computer charges the electrodes that intersect at that cell. It does this thousands of times in a small fraction of a second, charging each cell in turn.

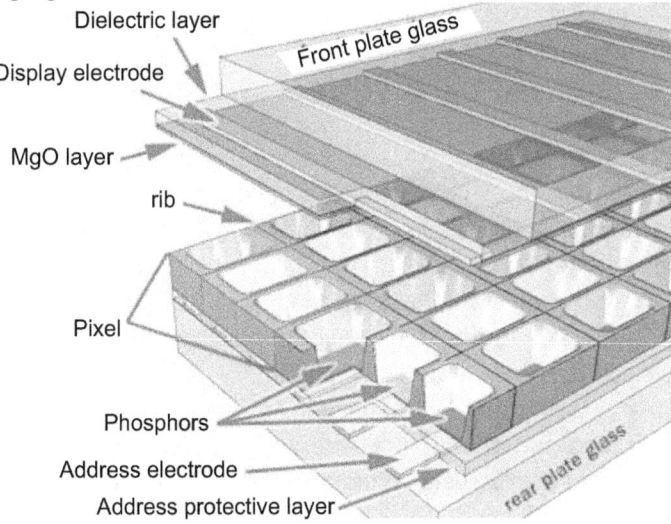

Fig. 1.44

- When the intersecting electrodes are charged (with a voltage difference between them), an electric current flows through the gas in the cell. As we saw in the last section, the current creates a rapid flow of charged particles, which stimulates the gas atoms to release ultraviolet photons.

- The released ultraviolet photons interact with phosphor material coated on the inside wall of the cell. Phosphors are substances that give off light when they are exposed to other light.
- When an ultraviolet photon hits a phosphor atom in the cell, one of the phosphor's electrons jumps to a higher energy level and the atom heats up. When the electron falls back to its normal level, it releases energy in the form of a visible light photon.

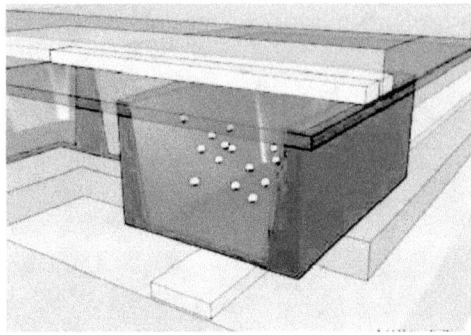

Fig. 1.45

Advantages:
1. Best picture quality.
2. Capable of producing deeper blacks allowing for superior contrast ratio.
3. Wider viewing angles than those of LCD; images do not suffer from degradation at high angles like LCD's.
4. Less visible motion blur, thanks in large part to very high refresh rates and a faster response time, contributing to superior performance when displaying content with significant amounts of rapid motion.

Disadvantages:
1. Earlier generation displays were more susceptible to screen burn-in and image retention, although most recent models have a pixel orbiter that moves the entire picture slower than is noticeable to the human eye, which reduces the effect of burn-in but does not prevent it.
2. Generally do not come in smaller sizes than 37 inches.
3. Heavier than LCD due to the requirement of a glass screen to hold the gases.
4. Use more electricity, on average, than an LCD TV.
5. Do not work as well at high altitudes due to pressure differential between the gases inside the screen and the air pressure at altitude. It may cause a buzzing noise. Manufacturer rate their screens to indicate the altitude parameters.

1.6.2.3 Printers
- Printer is a peripheral which produces a hard copy (permanent readable text and/or graphics) of documents stored in electronic form, usually on physical print media such as paper or transparencies.
- Printer is the most important output device, which is used to print information on paper.

- The quality of printer depends on following factors:
    1. **Speed:** The impact printer is slower than non-impact printer. The speed of dot matrix printer depends on number of pins. The expensive printer is faster than non-expensive printers. Generally, color printer is also slow.
    2. **Resolution:** The sharpness of text and image per inch is called resolution of computer. The quality of output depends on resolution. The high-resolution computer is expensive than low-resolution computers.
    3. **Memory:** The costly input/output device has own local memory to hold data at the time of processing. The printer is slower than the processor so, if it has its own memory to hold processed data, the speed can be increased. So, high memory printer is preferred for quality and fast printings.
    4. **Color:** The color is a part of information. The colorful text and graphics are more attractive than plain text and graphics. So, color printer is also a part of quality printings.
- Fig. 1.46 shows types of printers.

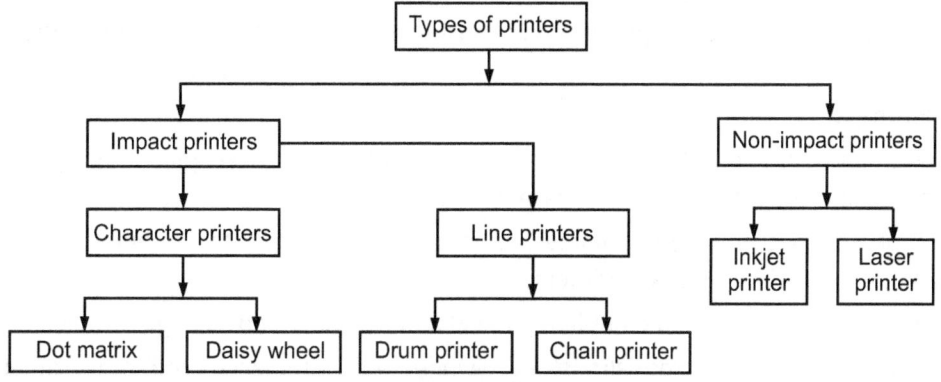

Fig. 1.46: Types of computer printer

1. Impact Printers:
- The printer that print the character by striking against the ribbon and onto the paper, are called impact printers.
- An impact printer is like a typewriter and the character are formed by physically striking the type devices against an inked ribbon.
- Impact printer can produce a page, a line, or a character at a time. Print quality is low, but these printer are mainly used for printing backup copies of large amounts of data.
- Some of the examples of impact printer are: Dot matrix printer, Daisy wheel printers, Drum printer and Chain printers.

Characteristics of Impact Printers:
   (i) Very low consumable costs.
   (ii) Impact printer are very noisy.
   (iii) Useful for bulk printing due to low cost.
   (iv) There is physical contact with the paper to produce an image.

- Impact printer are of two types:
    (i) Character printers: Character printer are printer which print one character at a time. These are of further two types Dot Matrix Printer (DMP) and Daisy wheel printer.
    (ii) Line printers: A line printer is a high-speed printing device that is able to store and print a complete line of information at a time. Line printer are printer which print one line at a time. Large computer system typically use line printer. Line printer are of further two types Drum printer and Chain printer.

Advantages of Impact Printers:
   (i) Design and functioning of this kind of printer is easier than that of non-impact printer.
   (ii) Since, the image is produced as a result of impact, multiple copies can be produced by the use of carbon paper.

Disadvantages of Impact Printer:
   (i) They are noisy in operation.
   (ii) The wear and tear of printer head causes the periodical replacement of the printer head.

2. Non-impact Printers:
- Non-impact printer generally, use specially coated or sensitized paper that respond to thermal or electrostatic stimuli to form an image.
- The printer that print the character without striking against the ribbon and onto the paper, are called non-impact printers.
- Non-impact printer print a complete page at a time, also called as page printers.
- Non-impact printers, used almost everywhere now, are faster and more quiet than impact printer because they have fewer moving parts.
- Non-impact printer are of two types Laser printer and Inkjet printers.

Characteristics of Non-impact printers:
   (i) Faster than impact printers.
   (ii) They are not noisy.
   (iii) High quality.
   (iv) Support many fonts and different character size.

Advantages of non-impact printer:
   (i) Soundless operation.
   (ii) High quality output.

Disadvantages of non-impact printer:
   (i) Multiple copies cannot be produced in a single pass.
   (ii) They are costly.

Comparison between Impact and Non-impact printers:

Impact printer	Non-impact printer
1. Impact printer are usually cheap.	1. Non-impact printer are usually more expensive that impact printer.
2. Impact printer is not quiet.	2. Non-impact printer is quitter.
3. Produce poor quality print.	3. Produce better quality print.
4. Its prints non-electrically.	4. Its prints electrically.
5. **Example:** Dot-matrix, daisy wheel etc.	5. **Example:** Inkjet, thermal, Laser etc.

(i) Character Printer:
- These printers prints one character at a time. Dot matrix printer and Daisy wheel printers are the character printers.

1. Dot Matrix Printer:
- In the general sense many printer rely on a matrix of pixels, or dots, that together form the larger image. However, the term dot matrix printer is specifically used for impact printer that use a matrix of small pins to create precise dots.
- A dot matrix printer or impact matrix printer refer to a type of computer printer with a print head that runs back and forth on the page and prints by impact, striking an ink-soaked cloth ribbon against the paper, much like a typewriter.
- Dot matrix technology uses a series or matrix of pins to create printed dots arranged to form character on a piece of paper. Because the printing involves mechanical pressure, these printer can create carbon copies and carbonless copies.
- The print head mechanism pushes each pin into the ribbon, which then strikes the paper. Many offices and government agencies use them because they can make multiple copies at lowest cost.

Fig. 1.47: Dot matrix printer

Working of Dot Matrix Printer:
- Fig. 1.48 shows working of dot matrix printer.
- Dot matrix refer to the way the printer creates character or images on paper.
- This is done by several tiny pins, aligned in a column, striking an ink ribbon positioned between the pins and the paper, creating dots on the paper.
- Character are composed of patterns of these dots by moving the printhead laterally across the page in very small increments.

- The pins, contained in the printhead, are about one inch long and are driven by several hammer which force each pin into contact with the ink ribbon (and paper) at a certain time.
- The force on these hammer comes from the magnetic pull of small wire coils (solenoids) which are energized at a particular time, depending on the character to be printed.
- Timing of the signals sent to the solenoids is programmed into the printer for each character, and translated from information sent by the computer about which character to print.

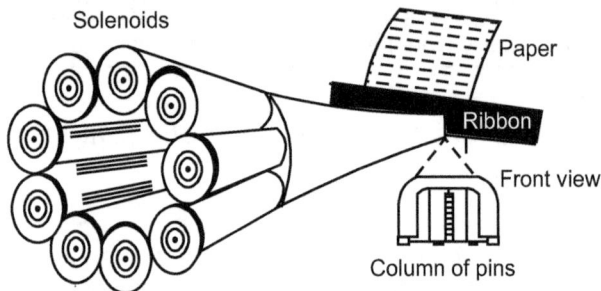

Fig. 1.48: Working of dot matrix printer

Advantages:
   (i) They can print on multi-part stationary or make carbon copies.
   (ii) Low printing cost.
   (iii) They can bear environmental conditions.
   (iv) Long life.

Disadvantages:
   (i) These printer are noisy.
   (ii) Low resolution.
   (iii) Very limited color performance.
   (iv) Low speed.
   (v) Servicing cost of this printer is more than buying a new one.

2. **Daisy Wheel Printer:**
- A daisy wheel printer is an electronic device that can be connected to a word processor or computer to allow documents to be printed from that machine.
- The basic functionality of these devices is similar to other printers, such as dot matrix or inkjet printers, though the way in which a document is printed is quite different.
- A daisy wheel printer uses a printing mechanism known as a "daisy wheel," which consists of numerous raised letter and number arrayed in a circle.
- Head is lying on a wheel and Pins corresponding to character are like petals of Daisy (flower name) that is why it is called Daisy Wheel Printer.
- These printer are generally used for word-processing in offices which require a few letter to be send here and there with very nice quality representation.

Fig. 1.49: Daisy wheel

Working of Daisy wheel printer:
- Daisy wheel printer operate in much the same fashion as a typewriter. A hammer strikes a wheel with petals (the daisy wheel), each petal containing a letter form at its tip.
- The letter form strikes a ribbon of ink, depositing the ink on the page and thus printing a character.
- By rotating the daisy wheel, different character are selected for printing.
- These printer were also referred to as letter-quality printer because, during their heyday, they could produce text which was as clear and crisp as a typewriter (though they were nowhere near the quality of printing presses).
- The fastest letter-quality printer printed 30 character per second.

Advantages:
1. More reliable than dot matrix printers.
2. Better quality.
3. The fonts of character can be easily changed.

Disadvantages:
1. Slower than dot matrix printers.
2. Noisy in operation.
3. More expensive than dot matrix printers.

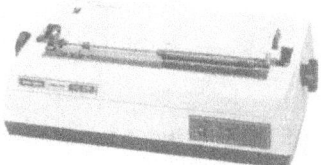

Fig. 1.50: Daisy wheel printer

(ii) Line Printers:
- Line printer are print one line at a time.

1. Drum Printer:
- Drum printer is like a drum in shape so it called drum printer.
- Drum Printer consists of a drum which consists of a number of characters; those are printed on the drum. And the number of character or number of tracks are divided, after examining the width of the paper.
- The surface of drum is divided into number of tracks. Total tracks are equal to size of paper i.e. for a paper width of 132 characters, drum will have 132 tracks.

- A character set is embossed on track. The different character sets are available in market 48 character set, 64 and 96 character set. One rotation of drum prints one line.
- Drum printer are fast in speed and speed is in between 300 to 2000 lines per minute.

Working of Drum Printer:
- In a typical drum printer design, a fixed font character set is engraved onto the periphery of a number of print wheels, the number equals the number of columns (letter in a line) the printer could print.
- The wheels, joined to form a large drum (cylinder), spin at high speed and paper and an inked ribbon are stepped (moved) past the print position.
- As the desired character for each column passes the print position, a hammer strikes the paper from the rear and presses the paper against the ribbon and the drum, causing the desired character to be recorded on the continuous paper.
- Because the drum carrying the letterforms (characters) remains in constant motion, the strike-and-retreat action of the hammer had to be very fast.

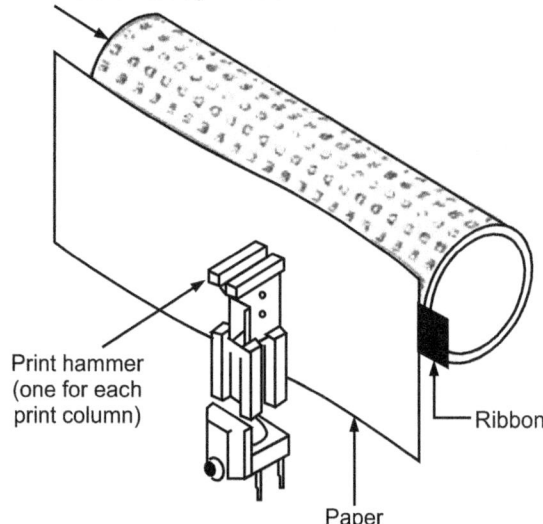

Fig. 1.51: Working of drum printer

Advantages:
(i) Very high speed.

Disadvantages
(i) Very expensive.
(ii) Character fonts can not be changed.

2. Chain Printer:
- In this printer chain of character sets are used so it is called chain printers.
- A standard character set may have 48, 64, 96 characters.
- These are also line printers, which print one line at a time. All the character are printed on the chain and the set of character are placed on the chain.

- There are 48 and 64 and 96 character set printer are available. There are also some hammers, those are placed in front of the chain, and paper is placed between the hammer and the inked ribbon.
- The total number of hammer will be equal to the total number of print positions.

Working of Chain Printer:
- Chain printer (also known as train printers) placed the type on moving bar (a horizontally-moving chain).
- As with the drum printer, as the correct character passed by each column, a hammer was fired from behind the paper. Compared to drum printers, chain printer had the advantage that the type chain could usually be changed by the operator.
- By selecting chains that had a smaller character set (for example, just number and a few punctuation marks), the printer could print much faster than if the chain contained the entire upper - and lower - case alphabets, numbers, and all special symbols.

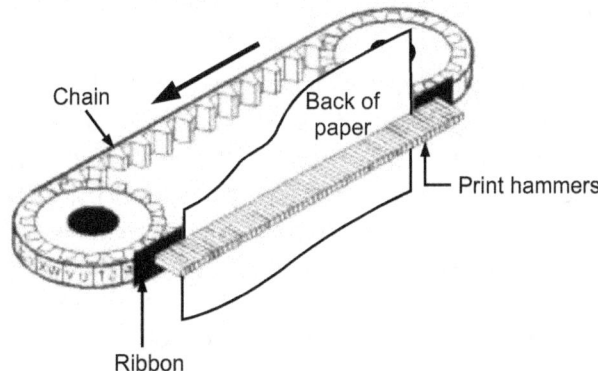

Fig. 1.52: Working of chain printer

Advantages:
  (i) Character fonts can easily be changed.
  (ii) Different languages can be used with the same printer.

Disadvantages:
  (i) Noisy in operation.
  (ii) Do not have the ability to print any shape of characters.

4. **Inkjet Printers:**
- Inkjet printer are non impact character printer based on a relatively new technology.
- Inkjet printer print character by spraying small drops of ink onto paper.
- Inkjet printer produce high quality output with presentable features.
- Inkjet printer make less noise because no hammering is done and these have many styles of printing modes available.
- Using inkjet printer, colour printing is also possible. Some models of Inkjet printer can produce multiple copies of printing also.

Fig. 1.53: Inkjet printer

- An inkjet printer is a type of computer printer that creates a digital image by propelling droplets of ink onto paper.
- Inkjet printer are the most commonly used type of printer and range from small inexpensive consumer models to very large professional machines that can cost up to thousands of dollars. Its consumable is called inkjet cartridge.

Working of Inkjet Printers:
- Inkjet printer operate by propelling variably-sized droplets of ink onto almost any sized page. They are the most common type of computer printer for the general consumer due to their low cost, high quality of output, capability of printing in different colors.
- A typical inkjet receives control info from your printer driver/PC, or may process the printout in its onboard electronics. Either way, roller advance a page from your paper tray (1) under a sliding printhead/cartridge assembly (2). Then, the printhead stepper motor (3), kicks in, drawing the assembly on a sliding rod (4), to its starting position, usually via a belt (5).
- The printhead (6) proper is an incredible piece of miniaturization, in some cases fabricated via an etching process similar to semiconductor manufacture. On some printers, the head and ink cartridge (7) are one unit.
- The head's microscopic nozzles (8) anywhere from dozens to literally thousands-are outlets for incredibly tiny ink chamber (9), which are fed by the cartridge's reservoirs. Microscopic droplets (10), measured in millionths of a millionth of a liter, fire through the nozzles.

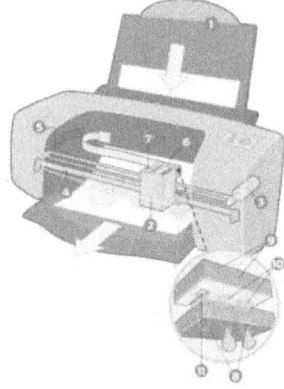

Fig. 1.54: Working of inkjet printer

Advantages:
   (i) High quality printing.
   (ii) More reliable.
   (iii) Low printer cost.
   (iv) Compact size.
   (v) Low noise.

Disadvantages:
   (i) Expensive as cost per page is high.
   (ii) Slow as compare to laser printer.
   (iii) The ink is often very expensive.
   (iv) Lifetime of inkjet prints produced by inkjet printer is limited. They will eventually fade and the color balance may change.
   (v) Easily get blur if get water drop.
   (vi) Easy to get clogging on inkjet nozzles.

5. **Laser Printer:**
- Laser printers are non impact printers.
- Laser printer use laser lights to produces the dots needed to form the character to be printed on a page.

Fig. 1.55: Laser printer

- Laser printing is the most advance technology.
- In laser printing, a computer sends data to the printer. Printer translates this data into printable image data. This kind of printer use xerographic principle.
- A laser beam discharges photo sensitive drum.
- A latent image is created on drum, during development process toner is attracted to the drum surface and then transferred to the paper. Its consumable called toner cartridge or laser toner.

Working of Laser Printer:
- Static electricity is the principle behind laser printers.
- A revolving drum or cylinder builds up an electrical charge.

- A tiny laser beam pointed at the drum discharges the surface in the pattern of the letter and images to be printed creating a surface with positive and negative areas.
- The surface is then coated with toner, a fine powder that is positively-charged so it clings only to the negatively-charged areas, and is then passed onto the paper to form the positive image.
- The paper then passes through heated roller fusing the toner to the paper. Color laser make multiple passes, in order to mix the different color toners.

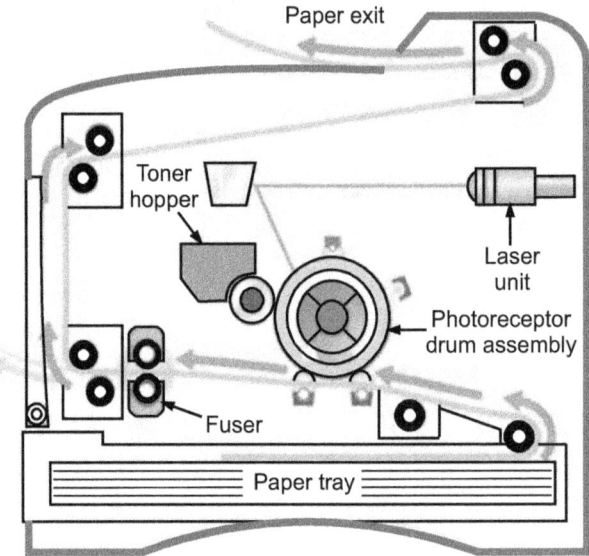

Fig. 1.56: Working of laser printer

Advantages:

(i) Very high speed.

(ii) Very high quality output.

(iii) Low noise in printing operation.

(iv) Support many fonts and different character size.

(v) Low cost per page as compare to inkjet printer.

(vi) Give good and high graphics quality.

Disadvantages:

(i) Laser printer are more expensive, but getting more affordable these days.

(ii) Cannot be used to produce multiple copies of a document in a single printing.

(iii) Their size is generally larger.

Comparison between Laser, Inkjet and Dot Matrix Printers:

Terms	Laser Printers	Inkjet Printers	Dot Matrix Printers
Invented	1969 by Gary Starkweather.	Developed in the early 1950s.	Introduced by Digital Equipment Corporation in 1970.
How it works	Laser printer use fine ink powder and heat the powder on the paper.	Inkjet printer spray liquid ink on paper through microscopic nozzles.	Dot Matrix works having pins pushed against an ink soaked ribbon to paper.
Types	Personal and Office printers. Black and White or color printers.	Continuous (CIJ) and drop-on demand (DOD).	Serial Dot Matrix printer and Line Dot Matrix.
Price per page	USD 0.6 for black and white page. Much higher for a color page.	USD 0.20 color page; USD 0.4-0.5 black and white page.	Copies are quite cheap.
Cost for basic printer	Approximately USD 60-1000, depending on the size and use of the printer.	Approximately USD 100-150	Basic cost of printer is quite expensive. Compared to an inkjet, dot matrix can cost between two to ten times more.
Printing speed	20 pages a minute	6 pages a minute	30-550 character per second.
Quality	Printing quality is adequate. Best for black and white.	Printing quality is good, specially for smaller fonts.	Printing quality is bad if printing images. In terms of text, printing is fine.
Color Printing	Basic models only offer black and white, with higher models providing color printing.	Yes provides color printing.	Limited color printing.
Black and White Quality	Black and white quality is adequate, best for bulk printing.	Black and white quality is excellent, specially with small fonts.	Can print adequate quality images.

contd. ...

Color Quality	Color quality is a bit poor, with banding.	Color printing is sharp and excellent.	Only works best with low-res images.
Size	Smaller is available but is more common in larger sizes.	Smaller and more compact.	Size ranges depending on usage. New compact ones are also available.
Features	Offer scanner and faxing machines built in. Has bigger input trays, direct connecting facilities (wireless)	Can be used for wider range of paper (photo paper, vinyl, self-adhesive papers), accurate photographic images, ink is not waterproof.	Used for a variety of purposes. Can print on various types of papers.
Usage	Most commonly used for commercial purposes and places that require black and white printing.	More commonly used for homes as the unit is smaller and ink is cheaper.	Used to be used for office uses, but now only used by select places such as banks.
Maintenance	Expensive	Cheaper	Expensive, parts are hard to come by.
Advantages	Prints faster, bigger input trays.	Quieter in operation, high print quality, no warm up time, low cost per page	Cheaper to print as ribbon is cheap.
Disadvantages	More susceptible to paper jams. Toner is very expensive, print quality for color is adequate, device itself is expensive, has health hazards if not properly maintained.	Ink is expensive, issues with 'intelligent' ink cartridges, lifetime of inkjet prints produced by aqueous inks is shorter, ink is not waterproof, and nozzle is prone to clogging.	Initial purchase is expensive, maintenance is expensive, prints is not fast, makes noise.

1.6.2.4 Plotters

- A plotter is a device that draws images on paper after receiving a command from a computer.
- A plotter is a special output device used to produce hardcopies of graphs and designs on the paper.
- A plotter is typically used to print large-format graphs or maps such as construction maps, engineering drawings and big posters.
- Plotter are divided into two types drum plotter and flatbed plotter.

1. **Drum Plotter:**
   - A drum plotter is also known as roller plotter.
   - Drum plotter consists of a drum or roller on which a paper is placed and the drum rotates back and forth to produce the graph on the paper.
   - Drum plotter also consists of mechanical device known as Robotic Drawing Arm that holds a set of colored ink pens or pencils.
   - The robotic drawing arm moves side to side as the paper are rolled back and forth through the roller. In this way, a perfect graph or map is created on the paper. This work is done under the control of computer.
   - Drum plotter are used to produce continuous output, such as plotting earthquake activity.

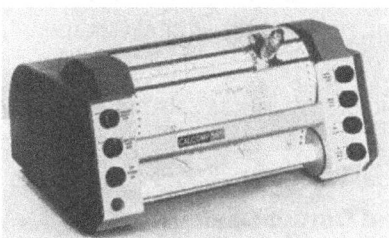

Fig. 1.57: Drum plotter

2. **Flatbed Plotter:**
   - A flatbed plotter is also known as table plotter.
   - Flatbed plotter plots on paper that is spread and fixed over a rectangular flatbed table.
   - The flatbed plotter uses two robotic drawing arms, each of which holds a set of colored ink pens or pencils. The drawing arms move over the stationary paper and draw the graph on the paper. Typically, the plot size is equal to the area of a bed.
   - The plot size may be 20 by 50 feet. It is used in the design of cars, ships, aircrafts, buildings, highways etc. Flatbed plotter is very slow in drawing or printing graphs. The large and complicated drawing can take several hour to print.
   - The main reason of the slow printing is due to the movement mechanical devices.

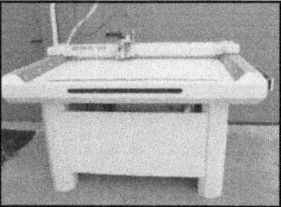

Fig. 1.58: Flatbed plotter

   - Today, mechanical plotter have been replaced by thermal, electrostatic and inkjet plotters. These systems are faster and cheaper. They also produce large size drawings.

Advantages:

(i) Plotters are faster than other types of printing machines, including the desktop printer.

(ii) The versatility of plotter is another major advantage. A plotter can be hooked up to any computer. There are a number of plotter configuration options as well, depending on the model and series we buy.

(iii) Plotter allows us to print and manipulate the plotter in a number of ways, and it also allows it to be connected to any type of machine. Plotter also have their own interfaces in some cases, which allow the user to operate and control them without resetting the paper or having to maintain the plotter during operation.

(iv) The precision of the plotter is the main advantage for engineering drawings. Plotter have advanced technology that allows them to print more precise lines. When printing a set of drawings for a bridge or skyscraper, it is imperative that each line be precise.

(v) Color accuracy and picture quality are also improved with the overall precision of the plotter. This is an advantage for a business looking for an inexpensive and efficient way to print promotional materials, banner and more.

Difference between Input and Output Devices:

Input devices	Output devices
1. An input device for a computer is anything that sends information to the CPU to perform a specific function.	1. Output is processed data or information.
2. A computer has the ability to use many different types of input devices to provide a unique experience to each user.	2. Output is data that has been processed into useful form, called information.
3. Computer input devices include many types of hardware such as a keyboard, mouse, webcam, scanner as well as a microphone.	3. The most common types of output are text, graphics, audio and video.
4. Input device are usually smaller.	4. Output device are large in size.
5. Cheaper in cost.	5. Costly in price.
6. Example: Keyboard, Microphone, Mouse etc.	6. Example: Speaker, Monitor, Printers etc.

1.7 Hardware and Software

- A computer system consists of hardware and software.
- The computer hardware cannot perform any task on its own. It needs to be instructed about the tasks to be performed.

- Software is a set of programs that instructs the computer about the tasks to be performed. Software tells the computer how the tasks are to be performed; hardware carries out these tasks.
- The physical parts, which you can see and touch, are collectively called hardware, on the other hand software, refer to the instructions, or programs, that tell the hardware what to do.

1. **Relationship between Computer Hardware and Software:**
- Hardware and Software have a symbiotic relationship, this means that without software hardware is very limited; and without hardware, software would not be able to run at all. They need each other to fulfill their potential.
- Computer hardware and software must work together. Nothing useful can be done with the computer hardware on its own, and computer software cannot be utilized without supporting hardware.
- The following important points show the relationships between computer hardware and software:
    (i) Both i.e. computer hardware and software are complementary to each other.
    (ii) Except for upgrades hardware is normally a one-time expense, whereas software is a continuing expense.
    (iii) Computer hardware and software are necessary for a computer to do useful job or task.
    (iv) The same hardware can be loaded with different software to make a computer system perform different types of jobs or tasks.

2. **Logical System Architecture:**
- The logical architecture of a computer system is shown in Fig. 1.59. The architecture of computer system basically depicts the relationship among the hardware, system software, application software and user of computer system.
- As shown in Fig. 1.59, at the center of any computer system is the hardware, which comprises of the physical devices/ components of the computer system.
- Surrounding the hardware is the system software layer, which constitutes the operating and programming environment of the computer system.
- Surrounding the system software is the application software layer, which consists of a wide range of softwares, which are designed to do a specific task, or solve a specific problem.
- The final layer is the layer of user who normally interact with the computer system via the user interface provided by the application software.

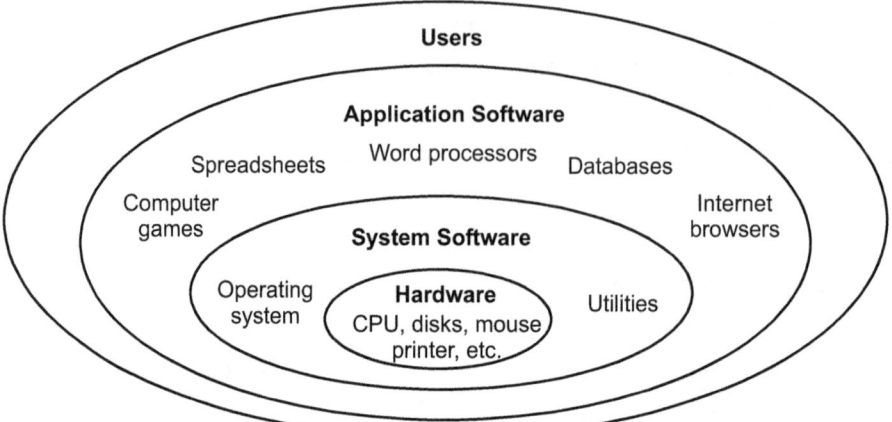

Fig. 1.59: Relationship between computer hardware, system software, application software and users

1.7.1 Computer Hardware

- Hardware, in the computer world, refer to the physical components that make up a computer system.
- Computer hardware is a term used for physical devices that you are able to touch and see. For example, the monitor on which you are viewing this page is a computer hardware. Similarly, the keyboard and mouse you use are also hardware. These devices you are actually able to see and touch.
- The actual physical components that constitute a computer are known as Computer Hardware.
- Hardware consists of the mechanical parts that make up the computer as a machine.
- In other words, anything in the computer that you can touch and see is the hardware. For example, CPU, monitor, keyboard, ICs, resistors, etc.
- Hardware represents the physical and tangible components of the computer i.e. the components that can be seen and touched.

Components of Computer Hardware:

1. **Input/Output (I/O) Unit:** The I/O unit consists of the input unit and the output unit. CPU performs calculations and processing on the input data, to generate the output. The memory unit is used to store the data, the instructions and the output information. The user interacts with the computer via the I/O unit. The Input unit accepts data from the user and the Output unit provides the processed data i.e. the information to the user. The input unit converts the data that it accepts from the user, into a form that is understandable by the computer. Similarly, the output unit provides the output in a form that is understandable by the user.

2. **Central Processing Unit (CPU):** Central Processing Unit (CPU) controls, coordinates and supervises the operations of the computer. It is responsible for processing of the input data. CPU consists of Arithmetic Logic Unit (ALU) and Control Unit (CU).
   (i) ALU performs all the arithmetic and logical operations on the input data.
   (ii) CU controls the overall operations of the computer i.e. it checks the sequence of execution of instructions and controls and coordinates the overall functioning of the units of computer.

3. **Memory Unit:** Memory unit stores the data, instructions, intermediate results and output, temporarily, during the processing of data. This memory is also called the main memory or primary memory of the computer. The input data that is to be processed is brought into the main memory before processing. The instructions required for processing of data and any intermediate results are also stored in the main memory. The output is stored in memory before being transferred to the output device. CPU can work with the information stored in the main memory. Another kind of storage unit also referred to as the secondary memory of the computer. The data, the programs and the output are stored permanently in the storage unit of the computer. Magnetic disks, optical disks and magnetic tapes are examples of secondary memory.

- Examples of Hardware:
  - **Input devices:** Keyboard, mouse etc.
  - **Output devices:** Printer, monitor etc.
  - **Secondary storage devices:** Hard disk, CD, DVD etc.
  - **Internal components:** CPU, motherboard, RAM etc.
- Fig. 1.60 various hardware parts of a computer system.

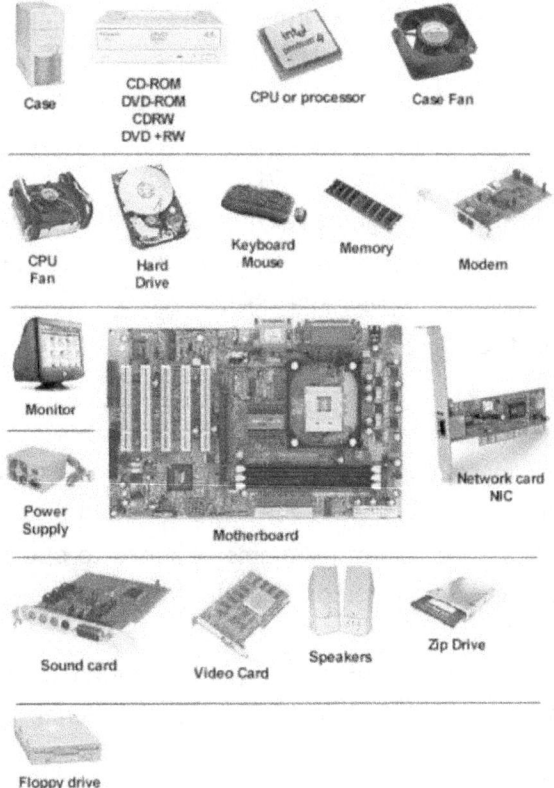

Fig. 1.60: Various hardware parts of a computer

1.7.2 Computer Software

- A set of programs and documents are collectively called software. The hardware of the computer system cannot perform any task on its own.
- Computer software is a term used for a set of code and instructions that tell a computer (including hardware) as to how to perform a task.
- In other words, software is a collection of computer programs, procedures and documentation that perform some task on a computer system.
- Unlike hardware, you cannot usually touch and see the computer software. However, you may be able to read the set of instructions.
- Thus, we can say that CD or Pen Drive are hardware, whereas the programme which is loaded in the CD/Pen Drive is a software. You can touch CD and Pen Drive but cannot touch the programme which is loaded in the CD/Pen Drive.
- Software is a set of instructions that tells the computer about the tasks to be performed and how these tasks are to be performed.
- Program is a set of instructions, written in a language understood by the computer, to perform a specific task.
- The hardware needs to be instructed about the task to be performed. Software instructs the computer about the task to be performed.

Definition of Software:

- The instructions or programs that are required to operate the hardware are known as software.

OR

- Software is a set of instructions that are required to operate the computer hardware.
- Software is not the physical part rather they are the logical parts of a computer. For example, operating system, compiler, assemblers, etc.
- There are two types of softwares:

1. System Software:

- System software provides basic functionality to the computer. System software is required for the working of computer itself. The user of computer does not need to be aware about the functioning of system software, while using the computer.
- The system software is collection of programs designed to operate, control and extend the processing capabilities of the computer itself. System software are generally prepared by computer manufactures.
- System software controls how the various technology tools work together along with the application software. System software includes both operating system software and utility software.
- Examples of system software are Operating systems, Language translator like Compiler, Assembler, etc.

2. Application Software:

- The software that a user uses for accomplishing a specific task is the application software. Application software may be a single program or a set of programs.
- A set of programs that are written for a specific purpose and provide the required functionality is called as a software package.
- Application software is written for different kinds of applications—graphics, word processors, media players, database applications, telecommunication, accounting purposes etc.
- Application software are the software that are designed to satisfy a particular need of a particular environment. All softwares prepared by programmer in the computer lab can come under the category of Application software.
- Application software is used for specific information processing needs, including payroll, customer relationship management, project management, training, and many others. Application software is used to solve specific problems or perform specific tasks.
- Example of application software are Excel, Tally for Accounting, MS-Word for word processing etc.

Comparison of Computer Hardware and Software:

Terms	Hardware	Software
Definition	Physical devices used to store and execute various softwares.	Set of instructions that enables a user to interact with the computer. It enables the computer to perform a specific task.
Types	Input Devices, Output Devices, Storage Devices, Processing Devices, Control Devices.	System software, Programming software and Application software.
Function	Hardware acts as the delivery system for software solutions. Once installed, hardware is not required to be changed on day to day basis.	Software is used to perform the specific task. Although software is generally not needed to be amended on day to day basis, but data is regularly fed for certain software. New versions are released for software from time to time.
Reliability	Hardware are reliable and no buys are usually noticed in its life time.	Software needs constant testing and any deficiencies/bugs noticed are to be fixed from time to time.
Chances of failure	Hardware failure is random. As the hardware becomes older, the chance of failure increases.	Software failure is systematic. With the passage of time and fixing of bugs, software have lesser chances of failure.
Lifetime	Hardware wears out over time.	Software does not wear out over time.
Nature	It is physical in nature.	It is logical in nature.
Examples	Monitor, CPU, Keyboard, Mouse, CD-ROM, Pen Drives, Printer, Scanners, Modern etc.	Microsoft Word, Microsoft Excel, Acrobat Readers, Window XP.

1.8 Types of Computers

- Computer can be classified based on their principles of operation or on their configuration.
- By configuration, we mean the size, speed of doing computation and storage capacity of a computer.
- Types of computer according to the principles of operation and configuration are shown in Fig. 1.61.

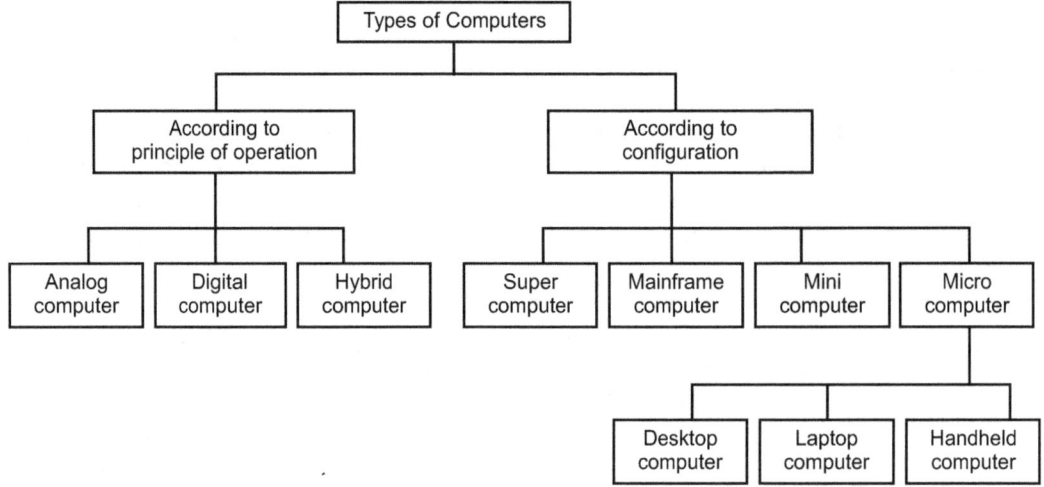

Fig. 1.61: Types of computers

1. Analog Computers:

- The earliest computer were analog computers. Analog computer is a computing device that works on continuous range of values. The results given by the analog computer will only be approximate since they deal with quantities that vary continuously.
- Analog computer generally deals with physical variables such as voltage, pressure, temperature, speed, etc.
- Analog computer are used for measuring parameter that vary continuously in real time, such as temperature, pressure and voltage.
- Analog computer may be more flexible but generally less precise than digital computers.
- Slide rule, Antikythera mechanism, astrolabe, differential analyzer, Deltar, Kerrison Predictor are the example of an analog computers.

Definition:

- An analog computer (spelled analogue) is a form of computer that uses electrical, mechanical or hydraulic phenomena to model the problem being solved.

OR

- Analog computer is a mechanical, electrical, or electronic computer that performs arithmetical operations by using some variable physical quantity, such as mechanical movement or voltage, to represent numbers.

Advantages:
  (i) Continuous representation of all data within the range of the machine.
  (ii) Fast and inexpensive when implemented with same technology as digital computer.
  (iii) Parallel and real-time operation many signal values can be computed simultaneously.
  (iv) Computation can be done for some applications without the requirement for transducer to convert the inputs/outputs to/from digital electronic form.

Disadvantages:
  (i) Computation elements have a limited useful dynamic range, usually not much more than 120 dB, about 6 significant digits of accuracy.
  (ii) Useful solution of problems of any size can take an inordinate amount of setup time.
  (iii) For a given size (mass) and power consumption, digital computer can solve larger problems.
  (iv) Solutions appear in real (or scaled) time, and may be difficult to record for later use or analysis.
  (v) The range of useful time constants is limited. Problems that have components operating on vastly different time scales are difficult to deal with accuracy.

2. Digital Computers:

- A digital computer uses distinct values to represent the data internally. All information are represented using the digits 0s and 1s.
- The computer that we use at our homes and offices are digital computers.
- The digital computer is designed using digital circuits in which there are two levels for an input or output signal. These two levels are known as logic 0 and logic 1. Digital computer can give more accurate and faster results.
- Digital computer is well suited for solving complex problems in engineering and technology. Hence digital computer have an increasing use in the field of design, research and data processing.
- UNIVAC, IBM-360 and other mainframe computer are examples of digital computers.

Definition:
- A computer that performs calculations and logical operations with quantities represented as digits, usually in the binary number system.

OR

- Digital computer is an electronic computer in which the input is discrete rather than continuous, consisting of combinations of numbers, letters, and other character written in an appropriate programming language and represented internally in binary notation.

Advantages:
  (i) Greater flexibility and precision.
  (ii) It can store large amount of facts, instructions, and information.

Disadvantage:
  (i) Its higher cost and complexity.

Difference between Digital and Analog Computers:

	Terms	Digital computers	Analog computers
1.	Definition	A computer that performs calculations and logical operations with quantities represented as digits, usually in the binary number system (0's and 1's).	Analog computer is a mechanical, electrical, or electronic computer that performs arithmetical operations by using some variable physical quantity, such as mechanical movement or voltage, to represent numbers.
2.	Computing power	Digital computers, however, are not limited specific types of applications, but have a more general purpose in terms of usage.	Analog computer are limited to performing restrictive and specialized mathematical calculations such as the measurement and analysis of electrical voltages.
3.	Output	Digital computer produce number as output. The computer uses display screens, printers, disc drives and other peripherals to capture this output.	Analog computer output voltage signals, and has sets of analog meter and oscilloscopes to display the voltages.
4.	Electronic circuits	Digital computer use a variety of on-off switching circuits, such as microprocessors, clock pulse generator and logic gates.	Analog computer circuits use op-amps, signal generator and networks of resistor and capacitors. These circuits process continuous voltage signals.
5.	Discrete versus Continuous signals	Digital signals have two discrete states, on or off. The off state is usually zero volts, and the on state is typically five volts.	Analog signals are continuous. They may have any value between two extremes, such as -15 and +15 volts. An analog signal's voltage may be constant or vary with time.
6.	Size	Digital computer range from tiny microchips a few millimeter square to room-sized server installations.	Analog computer vary in size from small desktop systems the size of a large book to tall racks laden with equipment.
7.	Data storage	The numeric, discrete nature of digital computer makes data storage simple. A memory circuit copies and retains the discrete states of another circuit.	For analog computers, storing data is more difficult, as they use continuous signals. A circuit that stores an analog signal is prone to drift over time.
8.	Speed and Accuracy	Digital computer can give more accurate and faster results.	Analogue computer can give less accurate and slow results.
9.	Cost	Cost is high.	Cost is low.

3. **Hybrid Computers:**
- A hybrid computer combines the desirable features of analog and digital computers.
- Hybrid computer is mostly used for automatic operations of complicated physical processes and machines.
- Now-a-days analog-to-digital and digital-to-analog converter are used for transforming the data into suitable form for either type of computation.

Definition:
- Hybrid computer is a computer that combines the characteristics of a digital computer and an analog computer by its capacity to accept input and provide output in either digital or analog form and to process information digitally.

OR

- Hybrid computer as the name suggests are a hybrid of analog and digital computers. The analog part of the hybrid computer computes higher mathematical calculations such as differential equations while the digital part takes care of the logical computation and also controls the overall process.

Advantages:
  (i) Hybrid computer have tremendous computing speed enabled by the all-parallel configuration provided by the analog subsystem.
  (ii) The results provided by hybrid computer are precise, accurate, more detailed and much more useful when compared to their earlier counterparts.

Uses:
  (i) One of the most widespread uses of hybrid computer is in automated assembly lines. In radar and sonar applications, signals are received in the analog form and often need to be analyzed instantaneously so that the next signal can be interpreted.
  (ii) Other entities that use hybrid computer include the military and defense organisations of all the countries and some research labs. These military devices are a form of hybrid computer since they process analog signals with digital logical circuits.

1.8.1 Super Computers
- Super computer are one of the fastest computer currently available.
- Super computer are very expensive and are employed for specialized applications that require immense amounts of mathematical calculations (number crunching), like weather forecasting, scientific simulations, (animated) graphics, analysis of geological data etc.
- They are the best in terms of processing capacity and also the most expensive ones. These computer can process billions of instructions per second.
- Perhaps the best known super computer manufacturer is Cray Research. Some of the traditional companies which produce super computer are Cray, IBM and Hewlett-Packard.
- As of July 2009, the IBM Roadrunner, located at Los Alamos National Laboratory, is the fastest super computer in the world.

Fig. 1.62: Super computer

Advantages:
1. Super computer can solve bigger problems.
2. Run more problems in shorter time i.e. they are very fast.
3. They have very high storage capacity.

Disadvantages:
1. They require very high power.
2. Takes up a lot of space i.e. they are larger in size.
3. May only be good for specific applications.
4. They are more costly.
5. Maintenance cost is very high.
6. Difficult to assembly.
7. Air-conditioning is required.

Applications of Super computers:
1. The machine can be used in both scientific and business applications, but used mainly in scientific applications. Few large multinational banks and corporations are using small super computers.
2. Applications of super computer includes, special effects in film, collecting and processing of weather data, processing of geological data, processing of data regarding genetic decoding, aerospace (aerodynamics and structural designing), simulation, and mass destruction weapons.
3. The user include Film makers, National weather forecasting agencies, Geological data processing agencies, Genetics research organisations, Space agencies, Government agencies, Scientific laboratories, Research groups, Military and defence systems, Large time-sharing network, and Large corporations.

1.8.2 Mainframe Computers

- Mainframe computers, created in the early 1940s, initially were bulky machines that required cooling-sensitive rooms.
- Mainframe computer can also process data at very high speeds i.e., hundreds of million instructions per second and they are also quite expensive.
- Normally, they are used in banking, airlines and railways etc. for their applications.

- Mainframe is a very large in size and is an expensive computer capable of supporting hundreds, or even thousands, of user simultaneously.
- Mainframe executes many programs concurrently. Mainframes support many simultaneous programs execution.
- Examples of mainframe computer are DEC-1090, IBM 308-580 series, IBM 4300, ICIM 2904, etc.

Characteristics of mainframe computers:
1. Ability to run multiple operating systems.
2. Mainframes can add system capacity non disruptively and granularly.
3. Mainframes are designed to handle very high volume input and output (I/O) and emphasize throughput computing.
4. Mainframe Return On Investment (ROI), like any other computing platform, is dependent on its ability to scale, support mixed workloads, reduce labor costs, deliver uninterrupted service for critical business applications, and several other risk-adjusted cost factors.
5. Mainframes also have execution integrity characteristics for fault tolerant computing.

Fig. 1.63: Mainframe computer

Advantages:
1. Huge memory.
2. High speed compared to volume of data.
3. No virus attack so far reported in last 50-60 years.
4. Superb virtualization.
5. Huge data processing.

Disadvantages:
1. Cost of hardware is high.
2. Special operating systems/software require so higher cost.
3. Intense human attention required.
4. Intense space occupied.
5. More resource consumption.

Applications of mainframe computers:
1. Both e-business and e-commerce use mainframe computer to perform business functions and exchange money over the internet.

2. The military one of the first user of mainframe computer continues employing this technology in combat and for keeping the country's border secure. All branches of the armed forces use mainframes for communication among ships, planes and land; for prediction of weather patterns; and for tracking strategic locations and positions using a Global Positioning System (GPS).
3. Satellites that were once a science fiction fantasy continue to operate mainframe computer in their intelligence and spying efforts.
4. Public and private libraries, as well as colleges and universities, use mainframe computer for storage of critical data.

1.8.3 Mini Computers

- Mini computer are computer that are somewhere, in between a micro computer and a mainframe computer.
- Mini computer are lower to mainframe computer in terms of speed and storage capacity.
- They are also less expensive than mainframe computers. Some of the features of mainframes will not be available in mini computers. Hence, their performance also will be less than that of mainframes.
- Mini computer is a class of multi-user computer that lies in the middle range of computing spectrum, in between mainframe computer and micro computer.
- Mini computer are designed for single user.
- Examples of mini computer are Control Data's CDC 160A and CDC 1700, DEC PDP and VAX series, Data General Nova, Hewlett-Packard HP3000 series, Honeywell-Bull Level 6/DPS 6/DPS 6000 series, IBM midrange computers

Characteristics of mini computers:
1. Small in size and require small space.
2. More reliable and less power required.
3. Faster in speed.
4. Larger primary and secondary storage capacity.
5. Use for scientific and commercial use.
6. Standardization of high level language.

Fig. 1.64: Mini computer

Advantages:
1. They are faster and powerful than other computers.
2. Smaller in size.
3. Less power required.

4. Larger storage capacity.
5. Support high level language.
6. More reliable.
7. Support both scientific and commercial applications.
8. Support standardized high level languages.
9. Supports time sharing concept.

Disadvantages:
1. Air-conditioning required.
2. Cost is more than micro computer.

Applications of Minicomputers:
1. Mini computer were often used in manufacturing sector for process control. A mini computer used for process control has two primary functions. The first function of a process control minicomputer is data acquisition. The second function of a process control minicomputer is feedback, or, controlling a process.
2. Mini computer used for data management can be employed to acquire data, as in process control, generate data, or simply as a storage system for information.
3. Mini computer can be used as a communications tool in a larger system.

1.8.4 Micro Computers

- The invention of microprocessor (single chip CPU) gave birth to the much cheaper micro computers.
- Micro computer are also known as Personal Computer (PC).
- A PC can be defined as a small, relatively inexpensive computer designed for an individual user. PCs are based on the microprocessor technology that enables manufacturer to put an entire CPU on one chip.
- Businesses use personal computer for word processing, accounting, desktop publishing, and for running spreadsheet and database management applications. At home, the most popular use for personal computer is for playing games and surfing the internet.
- Some examples of micro computer are HP 9100 A, Altair 8800 etc.
- Microcomputer is the term coined in the 1970s for a personal computer. Until that point, computer had been bulky room-sized electronics; even the smallest models were the size of large cars.
- The microcomputer has many uses, especially in the home, in business and in the medical field.

Characteristics of micro computers:
1. Support Graphical User Interface (GUI).
2. Speed is faster and larger storage capacity.
3. More powerful.
4. Smaller in size and cheaper.
5. Uses standard high level programming.
6. Use for office and homes .
7. Less power required.

Types of Micro Computers:

(i) Desktop Computers:
- Today the Desktop computer are the most popular computer systems.
- The desktop computer are also known as personal computer or simply PCs.
- They are usually easier to use and more affordable. They are normally intended for individual user for their word processing and other small application requirements.

Fig. 1.65: Desktop computer

(ii) Laptop Computers:
- Laptop computer are portable computers.
- They are lightweight computer with a thin screen. They are also called as notebook computer because of their small size.
- They can operate on batteries and hence are very popular with travellers. The screen folds down onto the keyboard when not in use.

Fig. 1.66: Laptop computer

(iii) Handheld Computers:
- Handheld computer or Personal Digital Assistants (PDAs) are pen-based and also battery-powered.
- They are small and can be carried anywhere. They use a pen like stylus and accept handwritten input directly on the screen.
- They are not as powerful as desktops or laptops but they are used for scheduling appointments, storing addresses and playing games.
- They have touch screens which we use with a finger or a stylus to be operated by user.

Fig. 1.67: Handheld computer

Advantages:
1. Smaller in size.
2. Cheaper.
3. More powerful and easy for installation.
4. Air-conditioning not required.
5. Faster in speed.
6. Larger primary and secondary storage.
7. Sharing resources in networking.
8. Does not require manual assembly.
9. More reliable and less hardware failure.

Disadvantages:
1. Non-portable.
2. Single user oriented.
3. More maintenance.

Applications of Micro computers:
1. Families use microcomputer for education; software can hold thousands of book volumes worth of information. Also, the first portable video games were built for the microcomputers. The home microcomputer paved the way for the invention of laptops.
2. Businesses took a huge leap forward in book-keeping, inventory and communication when microcomputer were made readily available.
3. The first microcomputer was built specifically for storing medical records. Before microcomputer were available, medical records were stored in paper form.

General Purpose and Special Purpose Computers:
- General purpose computer are designed to solve a large variety of problems. That is they can be given different program to solve different types of problems.
- General purpose computer can process business data as readily as they process complex mathematical formulas.
- General purpose computer can store large amount of data and the programmes necessary to process them. Because general purpose computer are so versatile, most businesses today use them.
- Special purpose computer are often used as training simulators.
- A simulator is a computer-controlled device for training people under simulated, or artificially created, conditions.
- The computer creates test conditions the trainee must respond to it then records and evaluates the responses, providing these results to both trainee and supervisor.
- Special purpose computer are simpler and cheaper than general purpose computer but have more limited logical and computational capabilities.

Difference between a Micro computer and a Mini computer:

Micro computer	Mini computer
1. A micro computer is a standard desktop computer used at a home and in business.	1. Mini computer are mid-sized computer used in universities, research labs and small corporations.
2. A micro computer is a computer with a microprocessor as its CPU.	2. Mini computer are faster than micro-computers.
3. They are cheap, compact and can be easily accommodated on a study table.	3. They are expensive and larger than microcomputer.
4. Microcomputer is a single-user computer.	4. Minicomputer is a multi-user computer.
5. The two most common types of storage devices used with microcomputer are tapes and disks.	5. For secondary storage, most minicomputer use magnetic disks or tapes.
6. Micro computer is not powerful or as fast as minicomputer.	6. Mini computer is powerful than microcomputer but not as super computer and mainframe computer.
7. Examples are: Modern computers like desktop, laptop etc.	7. Examples are: IBM 9375, Motorola 68040 etc.

Comparison between a Mainframe and Super computers:

Mainframe computer	Super computer
1. Low speed than super computer.	1. Very high speed computers. It can process trillions of instructions in one second.
2. Low storage capacity.	2. High storage capacity.
3. A Mainframe computer is a large computer that is used in large companies like insurance companies or the government.	3. A super computer is the largest computer with extremely high speed. Companies like Nasa use super computers.
4. Cost is low.	4. Cost is very high.
5. Examples: (i) IBM4381 (ii) NEC 610 (iii) DEC 10 etc.	5. Examples: (i) CRAY-XP (ii) ETA-10 etc.

1.8.5 Laptop

- A laptop is a portable personal computer with a clamshell form factor, suitable for mobile use.
- A laptop has most of the same components as a desktop computer, including a display, a keyboard, a pointing device such as a touchpad (also known as a trackpad) and/or a pointing stick, and speaker into a single unit.

- A laptop is a battery or AC-powered personal computer that can be easily carried and used in a variety of locations.
- Many laptops are designed to have all of the functionality of a desktop computer, which means they can generally run the same software and open the same types of files.
- However, some laptops, such as netbooks, sacrifice some functionality in order to be even more portable.

Fig. 1.68

Classification of Laptops:
- The term "laptop" can refer to a number of classes of small portable computers:
    1. **Full-size Laptop:** A laptop large enough to accommodate a "full-size" keyboard (a keyboard with the minimum QWERTY key layout, which is at least 13.5 keys across that are on ¾ (0.750) inch centers, plus some room on both ends for the case). The measurement of at least 11 inches across has been suggested as the threshold for this class.
    2. **Netbook:** A smaller, lighter, more portable laptop. It is usually cheaper than a full-size laptop, but sometimes has fewer features and less computing power. The smaller keyboards of a netbook can be more difficult to operate. There is no sharp line of demarcation between netbooks and inexpensive small laptops; some 11.6" models are marketed as netbooks. Since netbook laptops are quite small in size and designed to be light and inexpensive they typically do not come with an internal optical drive. The Asus Eee PC launched this product class, while the term was coined later by Intel.
    3. **Tablet PC:** These have touch screens. There are "convertible tablets" with a full keyboard where the screen rotates to be used atop the keyboard, a "hybrid tablet" where the keyboard can be detached from the screen, and "slate" form-factor machines which are usually touch-screen only (although a few older models feature very small keyboards along the sides of the screen.)
    4. **Ultra-mobile PC:** An ultra-mobile PC (ultra-mobile personal computer or UMPC) is a small form factor version of a pen computer, a class of laptop whose specifications were launched by Microsoft and Intel in spring 2006. Sony had already made a first attempt in this direction in 2004 with its Vaio U series, which was only sold in Asia. UMPCs are smaller than subnotebooks, have a TFT display measuring (diagonally) about 12.7 to 17.8 cm, and are operated like tablet PCs using a touchscreen or a stylus. This term is commonly (if inaccurately) used for small notebooks and/or netbooks.

5. **Handheld PC:** A Handheld PC, or H/PC for short, is a term for a computer built around a form factor which is smaller than any standard laptop computer. It is sometimes referred to as a Palmtop. The first handheld device compatible with desktop IBM personal computer of the time was the Atari Portfolio of 1989. Other early models were the Poqet PC of 1989 and the Hewlett Packard HP 95LX of 1991. Other DOS compatible hand-held computer also existed.

Advantages of Laptops:
1. **Portability:** Portability is usually the first feature mentioned in any comparison of laptops versus desktop PCs. Portability means that a laptop can be used in many places - not only at home and at the office, but also during commuting and flights, in coffee shops, in lecture halls and libraries, at clients' location or at a meeting room, etc.
2. **Size:** Laptops are smaller than standard PCs. This is beneficial when space is at a premium, for example in small apartments and student dorms. When not in use, a laptop can be closed and put away.
3. **Low power consumption:** Laptops are several times more power-efficient than desktops. A typical laptop uses 10-30 W, compared to 60-300 W for desktops. This could be particularly beneficial for businesses (which run hundreds of personal computers, multiplying the potential savings) and homes where there is a computer running 24/7 (such as a home media server, print server, etc.)
4. **Quiet:** Laptops are often quieter than desktops, due both to better components (quieter, slower 2.5-inch hard drives) and to less heat production leading to use of fewer and slower cooling fans.
5. **Battery:** A charged laptop can run several hour in case of a power outage and is not affected by short power interruptions and brownouts. A desktop PC needs a UPS to handle short interruptions, brownouts and spikes; achieving on-battery time of more than 20-30 minutes for a desktop PC requires a large and expensive UPS.

Disadvantages of Laptops:
1. **Performance:** While the performance of mainstream desktops and laptops is comparable, laptops are significantly more expensive than desktop PCs at the same performance level. The upper limits of performance of laptops are lower, and "bleeding-edge" features usually appear first in desktops and only then, as the underlying technology matures, are adapted to laptops.
2. **Upgradeability:** Upgrade ability of laptops is very limited compared to desktops, which are thoroughly standardized. In general, hard drives and memory can be upgraded easily. Optical drives and internal expansion cards may be upgraded if they follow an industry standard, and all other internal components, including the CPU and graphics, are not intended to be upgradeable.
3. **Ergonomics and health:** Because of their small and flat keyboard and trackpad pointing devices, prolonged use of laptops can cause RSI. Usage of ergonomic keyboards and pointing devices is recommended to prevent injury when working for long periods of time; they can be connected to a laptop easily by USB or via a docking station. Some health standards require ergonomic keyboards at workplaces.

4. **Durability:** Due to their portability, laptops are subject to more wear and physical damage than desktops. Components such as screen hinges, latches, power jacks and power cords deteriorate gradually due to ordinary use. A liquid spill onto the keyboard, a rather minor mishap with a desktop system, can damage the internals of a laptop and result in a costly repair.
5. **Security:** Being expensive, common and portable, laptops are prized targets for theft. The cost of the stolen business or personal data and of the resulting problems (identity theft, credit card fraud, breach of privacy laws) can be many times the value of the stolen laptop itself. Therefore, both physical protection of laptops and the safeguarding of data contained on them are of the highest importance.
6. **Cost:** Cost of laptops are more than desktop.

Questions

1. What is computer? Explain generations of computer.
2. Define the following terms:
   (i) Computer, (ii) Software, and (iii) Hardware.
3. What is analog computer? Explain its applications.
4. With the help of diagram describe relation between computer hardware and software.
5. Compare analog and digital computer.
6. What are the types of computers? Explain two of them in detail.
7. Describe general and special purpose computer in detail.
8. Enlist advantages of computers.
9. What is digital computer? State its applications and advantages.
10. Explain limitations of computer.
11. Enlist various application of computer in various fields like banking, business, military etc.
12. Write short note on: Data organisation.
13. Describe generations of computer with their advantages and disadvantages.
14. What is super computer? State its advantages and disadvantages.
15. What is mini computer? State its advantages and disadvantages.
16. What is mainframe computer? State its advantages and disadvantages.
17. What is micro computer? State its advantages and disadvantages.
18. Distinguish between:
    (i) Mini and micro computers.
    (ii) Super and mainframe computers.
19. What are the types of micro computer?
20. Explain hybrid computer in detail.
21. Describe functional block diagram of computer.
22. Define data and information.
23. Explain the following terms:
    (i) Input unit, (ii) Storage unit, and (iii) Output unit.

24. What is input and output? Explain meaning of input and output device.
25. What is scanner? What are its types?
26. What are the types of printers? Explain two of them in detail.
27. What is monitor? What are its types?
28. Explain the term keyboard in detail.
29. With the help of diagram describe working of following:
    (i) Laser printer, (ii) Daisy wheel printer, and (iii) Dot matrix printer.
30. Compare impact and non impact printers.
31. What is OMR? How it works? Explain in brief.
32. Write short note on: Plotter.
33. With the help of diagram describe working of dot matrix printer.
34. Explain working of CRT and LCD diagrammatically.
35. Describe the term MICR in detail.
36. Explain working of inkjet printer in detail.
37. What are the types of line printers?
38. Distinguish between character printer and line printer.
39. Explain the following term:
    (i) Mouse and (ii) Drum printer.
40. What is MICR? State its advantages.
41. With the help of diagram describe keyboard.
42. Compare printer and plotter.
43. Distinguish between inkjet and laser printers.
44. Explain the following terms in short:
    (i) Digitizer, (ii) Joystick, (iii) Digital camera, and (iv) OCR.
45. Write short note on: Bar code reader.
46. What is computer memory?
47. What are the types of memory?
48. With the help of diagram describe floppy disk.
49. Explain memory organisation in detail.
50. What is meant by primary and secondary memory? Compare them.
51. What is hard disk? Explain its construction in detail.
52. What is RAM and ROM? State its characteristics.
53. Enlist characteristics of primary and secondary memory.
54. What is CD? How it works? Explain diagrammatically.
55. Differentiate between RAM and ROM.
56. What is floppy disk? How it works?
57. Compare hard disk and floppy disk.
58. Write short note on: DVD.
59. Describe magnetic tape in detail.
60. With the help of diagram describe classification of memory.
61. Distinguish between magnetic tape and magnetic disks.
62. What is meant by volatile and non-volatile memories?
63. Compare computer hardware and software.
64. Distinguish between harddisk and floppy disk.

■■■

Chapter 2...

System Concept

Contents ...

2.1 Introduction to System Analysis and Design
    2.1.1 What is a System?
    2.1.2 Definition of System
    2.1.3 Elements of System
2.2 Types of Systems
2.3 Characteristics of System
2.4 System Development Life Cycle (SDLC)
2.5 Prototyping
- Questions

2.1 Introduction to System Analysis and Design

- We are surrounded by systems. There are many systems such as transportation system, the distribution of goods and services system, education, manufacturing and almost every other human economic activity systems.
- Term system is derived from the Greek word 'Systema' which means an organized relationship among functioning units or components.
- We can define system as "A system is an orderly grouping of interdependent components linked together according to a plan to achieve a specific objective."
- Systems development can generally be thought of as having two major components: System analysis and Systems design.
    1. **System design** is the process of planning a new business system or one to replace or complement an existing system. Before this planning can be done the old system must be thoroughly understood before we can determine how computers can best be used (if at all) to make its operation more effective.
    2. **Systems analysis**, is then, the process of gathering and interpreting facts, diagnosing problems and using that information to recommend improvements to the system. This is the job of the systems analyst.
- System Analysis and Design (SAD) focus on systems, process and technology.
- In System Analysis and Design (SAD):
    - **System Analysis:** Understanding and specifying in detail what an information system should do.
    - **System Design:** Specifying the detail how the parts of an information system should be implemented.

2.1.1 What is a System?

- A system is a set or group of components that interact to accomplish some purpose. System around us. For example, complex nervous system which is made up of set of parts or components i.e. brain, spinal cord, nerves etc.
- Take another example of a publication firm that contains Authors, Proof readers, Typists, Editors are the set of components.
- Following are some points are related to the system.
   1. System interacts with their environment.
   2. System also interacts with their surrounding.
   3. The purpose of system is it's reason for existing.
   4. All system has acceptable level of standards.

2.1.2 Definition of System

- A system can be defined as a network of interrelated procedures that are joined together to perform an activity or to accomplish a specific objective.

OR

- A system is an orderly grouping of interdependent components linked together according to a plan to achieve a specific objective.

OR

- A collection of components that work together to realize some objectives forms a system. Basically there are three major components in every system, namely input, processing and output, (See Fig. 2.1).

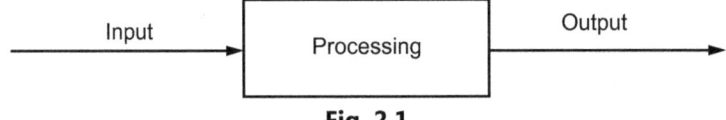

Fig. 2.1

2.1.3 Elements of System

- To reconstruct a system following are the elements of system to be considered as:
  Outputs and Inputs, Processors, Control, Feedback, Environment, Boundaries and Interfaces.

1. Outputs and Inputs:

A major objective of a system is to produce the output as per the user's requirement. The output could be in the form of goods (finished products), information as services. It must be done with expectations of intended user.

Inputs are elements that make the system to work in order to produce required output. Input could be material, human resources or information. Inputs are elements that enter the system for processing. Output is outcome of processing. It is important to point out that determining output is first step in specifying the nature, amount and regularity of input needed to operate a system. In system analysis, first concern is to determine user's requirement of a proposed system.

2. **Processors:**

   The processor is the element of a system that involves the actual transformation of Input into Output. The processor should be designed of such type that it can accept the input in the given form and can give output in desired format. It is the operational component of system. Processors may modify input totally or partially depending on specifications of output.

3. **Control:**

   The control elements guide the system. The control element controls the working of the system at all stages. It is necessary to control input, process and output, continuously, in order to get desired results. In a complete system operating system and accompanying software influence the behavior of system. Management support is required for screening control and supporting the objective of proposed change.

4. **Feedback:**

   Feedback is a method that helps to compare output produced with output expected and make necessary changes in the process or input in order to reduce the difference between output produced and output expected.

   Input information is fed back to input for deliberation. After the output is compared against performance standards, changes can result in input or output processing and output. Feedback may be positive or negative. Positive feedback reinforces the performance of system. Negative feedback generally provides controller with information for action. During system change the user may be told the problems in given application verify the initial concerns and justify the need for change.

5. **Environment:**

   All the things which are outside the system are called environment of the system. The environment do affect working or progress of the system. The system should be sensitive to the changes in its environment. It determines how a system must function.

6. **Boundaries and Interface:**

   The boundary indicates the extent or limit of the system. The boundary divides the things into the system and its environment. The things which are inside boundary are part of system otherwise which are outside boundary are its environment. It is very much essential to limit the system by its boundaries so that system's working can be controlled. Interface means interaction of different system parts with each other as interaction of the system with the system outside its boundaries.

   The system should be capable of dealing with the systems which are outside to it. Boundaries are the limits that identify its components, processes and interrelationships when it interfaces with another system.

2.2 Types of Systems

- Several types of systems are listed below:

1. Physical or Abstract system:

(a) Physical system:

- The physical system could be static or dynamic in nature. Static means which do not change as far as working or life of the system is concerned. On the other hand, dynamic system may change due to processing of the system.
- For example: In computer system the hardware parts are static, but the data which changes due to processing is dynamic. These both together form physical system along with programs controlling the data.

(b) Abstract system:

- The systems which are represented conceptually (i.e. nonexisting) non physical systems are called abstract system. The abstract systems are prepared for studying the physical system.
- The computer itself is a physical system and its block diagram is called as abstract system. A model is representation of real or planned system. The use of model makes it easier for analyst to visualize relationship in system under study.
- There are following types of models:

    (a) System model: The analyst begins by creating a model of reality i.e. facts, relationship, procedures etc. with which the system is concerned. Every computer system deals with real world. The analyst begins by modeling this reality before considering the function that system is to perform. Various business system models are used to show benefits of abstracting complete systems to model form. The, major of this type models are:

    (i) Schematic models: It shows a two dimensional depicting system elements and their linkages.

    (ii) Flow system models: It shows the flow of material, energy and information that hold system together. A widely used example is Program Evaluation and Review Technique (PERT).

    (iii) Static system models: This type of model exhibits are pair of relationship such as activity time or cost quantity.

    The example is Gantt chart. It gives a static picture of an activity time relationship.

    (iv) Dynamic system models: Business organizations are dynamic systems. It depicts constantly an ongoing constantly changing the system. It consists of:
    1. Inputs that enter the system.
    2. Processor through which transformation takes place.
    3. The programs required for processing.
    4. Output that results from processing.

2. Open or Closed System:

(a) Open system:

An open system is that interacts freely with outside environment and also it can be affected from environment. An open system is a one which does not provide for its own control or modification. It does not supervise itself so it needs to be supervised by people.

For example: If the high speed printer used with computer systems did not have a switch to sense whether paper is in the printer, then a person would have to notice when the paper runs out and signal the system (push a switch) to stop printing. It has many interfaces to its environment. It permits interaction across its boundary. Five important characteristics of open system are:

(i) **Inputs from outside:** Open systems are self adjusting and self regulating. When functioning properly an open system reaches a steady state. The response gives the firm a steady state.

(ii) **Entropy:** All dynamic system tends to run down over time resulting in entropy or loss of energy. Open system resist entropy by seeking new inputs or modifying the processes to return to a steady state.

(iii) **Process, Output and Cycle:** Open systems produce useful output and operate in cycle following a continuous path.

(iv) **Differentiation:** Open system have a tendency toward an increasing specialization of functions and greater differentiation of their components. This characteristic offers a completing reason for increasing value of concept of system in system analyst's thinking.

(v) **Equifinality:** This term implies that the goals are achieved through differing courses of action and a variety of paths.

(b) Closed system:

A closed system in one which automatically controls or modifies its own operation by responding to data generated by the system itself.

For example: High speed printers used with computer systems usually have a switch that senses whether there is paper in the printer. If the paper runs out, the switch signals to stop printing.

3. Manmade information system:

With the help of information system, we can define some standards for the working of the system. This we can try to make the system to work according to the standards defined. We can define information system as a set of devices, procedures, rules but most of the work performs manually. It provides instructions, commands and feedback. It determines nature of relationship among decision makers.

4. Formal information system:

A formal information system is represented by organization chart. It gives a representation of the different parts of system and flow of information among them.

Categories of information: There are three categories of information related to management levels and decision managers make.

(i) **Strategic Information:** The first level relates to long range planning policies that are of direct interest to upper management.

(ii) **Managerial Information:** The second level is of direct use of middle management and department heads for implementation and control.

(iii) **Operational Information:** The third level is short term, daily information is used to operate department and enforce day-to-day rules and regulations of information.

5. **Informal information system:**

    A formal information system is one which is shown on the chart, on the other hand, the informal information system is one which is working to meet requirements of employees. Thus, informal information system is related with what is happening practically rather than what is shown on paper, it is an employee based system designed to meet personnel and vocational needs and help work related problem.

6. **Computer-based Information System:**

    In manmade (manual) information system papers were used to hold the information. But toady entire world is of computer. Computer based information systems are faster, more accurate, more neat and attractive. It is possible to perform different operations easily. Security of data is possible in this system.

7. **Management Information System (MIS):**

    A MIS is a system that provides historical information, information on the current status. It is a communication process in which data are recorded and processed for further operational uses.

    A MIS is a system that collects, processes, stores and distributes information to help in decision making for the managerial functions of planning, organizing, directing, controlling and staffing a business organization.

MIS are built using:

(a) People, who are needed to operate the system.

(b) Data processing, which provides the needed speed for information sorting and classifying.

(c) Data communications which is required in order to keep the information flowing between the different parts of the system and the people using the system.

(d) Information storage and retrieval, which is required in order to store information in its proper format and to make sure that the information can be retrieved when it is needed.

(e) System planning which is required in order to integrate the people, the data processing, the data communication, the information storage and retrieval and the uses of the system into an overall meaningful and well organized management information system.

8. Decision Support Systems (DSS):

DSS systems make use of analytical planning modules (operation research model). DSS mostly used for assisting top-level management in decision making.

Using DSS better decision are taken. DSS reduces clerical work and overtime.

DSS also saves cost and time. It consists of decision making with support of other lower level systems (MIS). DSS systems used organizational data as well as external data collected from environment of the organization.

DSS uses two data's:

(i) Internal data: Internal data mostly used for studying the trends

(ii) External data: External data is mostly used for understanding the environment.

9. Expert Systems (ES):

ES operates with few rules. Effectiveness is a major goal of these types of systems. Human beings are experts in specific areas. ES are more flexible than other systems. ES increases output and productivity of the system.

ES gives effective manipulation of large knowledge based system. The output is selected with the opinion of many experts.

Expert system consist of following component:

(i) User interface.

(ii) Explanation facility.

(iii) Knowledge acquisition.

(iv) Knowledge base, facts rules.

(v) Knowledge refining system.

10. Execution Information Systems (EIS):

EIS systems operates continuously to keep management abreast of what is happening in all major areas.

EIS is structured tracking system. It provides rapid access to timely information and direct access to management reports.

EIS contains extensive graphics capabilities. It serves the information needs of top executives.

EIS gives quick and easy access to detailed information.

11. Transaction Processing System (TPS):

A Transaction Processing System (TPS) is a type of information system. TPSs collect, store, modify and retrieve the transactions of an organization.

A transaction is an event that generates or modifies data that is eventually stored in an information system.

A transaction processing system is a set of information which processes the data transaction in database system that monitors transaction programs. The system is useful when something is sold over the internet. It allows for a time delay between when an item is being sold to when it is actually sold.

An example is that of a sporting event ticket. While the customer is filling out their information to purchase the seat ticket; the transaction processing system is holding the ticket so that another customer cannot also buy it. It allows for a ticket not to be sold to two different customers.

2.3 Characteristics of a System

- According to definition of system some characteristics that are present in all systems.
- Following are the some important characteristics of a system:
    1. Organization
    2. Interaction
    3. Interdependence
    4. Integration
    5. Central objective.

1. Organization:

Organization implies structure and order of a system. Basically, organization means the arrangement of components that helps to achieve objectives. In the design of a college (polytechnic) system, the hierarchical relationship starting with the Chairman on top and leading downward to the blue-collar peon, represent the organization structure. Likewise, a computer system is designed around an input device, a central processing unit and an output device with one or more storage units, when linked together they work as a whole system for producing information.

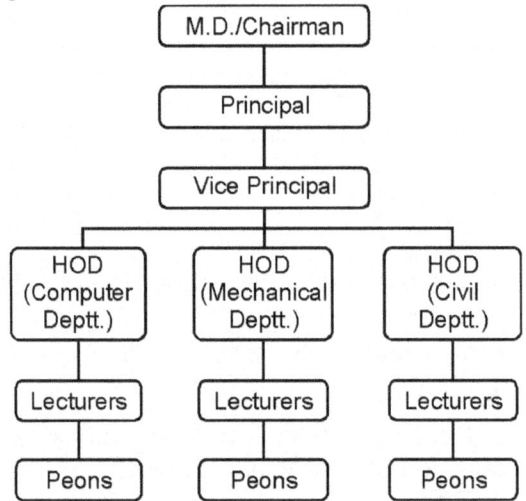

Fig. 2.2: Organization structure for college system

2. Interaction:

Interaction refers to the manner in which each component interacts with other components of the system. Thus, interaction means, it is the media, by means of which every component interact or communicate with other for proper functioning. In an organization, For example, purchasing must interact with production, advertising with sales and payrolls with personnel. In a computer system, the central processing must interact with input device to solve problem. In turn main memory holds programs and data that arithmetic unit uses for computation. The interrelationship between these components enables the computer to perform.

3. **Interdependence:**

   Interdependence means that parts of the organization depend on one another. They are co-ordinated and linked together according to plan. One subsystem depends on the input of another subsystem for proper functioning i.e. the output of one subsystem is the required input for another subsystem. In computer system, the three units Input, System unit, Output is interdependent for proper functioning. No subsystems can function in isolation because it is dependent on data (input) it receives from other subsystems to perform its required tasks.

   For example: A decision to computerize an application is initiated by user, analyzed and designed by analyst, programmed and tested by programmer and run by computer operator as shown in Fig. 2.3.

   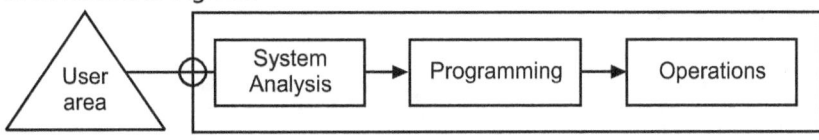

   Fig. 2.3

4. **Integration:**

   Integration is concerned with how a system is tied together in order to achieve common goal, thus forming integration. Integration refers to holism of system. Synthesis follows analysis to achieve the central objective of organization. It means that parts of system work together within system even though each part performs unique function.

5. **Central Objective:**

   The stated objective and real objective of the system could differ based on the policy of the company. The user should develop a central objective by taking into consideration real objective and stated objective. The important point is that the users must know the central objective of computer application in analysis for successful design and conversion. This means that the analyst must work around the obstacles to identify real objective of proposed change.

2.4 System Development Life Cycle (SDLC)

- The System Development Life Cycle (SDLC) is the overall process for developing information systems from planning and analysis through implementation and maintenance.
- The SDLC beings with a business need, followed by an assessment of the functions a system must have to satisfy the need and ends when the benefits of the system no longer outweigh its maintenance cost. This is why it is referred to as a 'lifecycle'.

- System life cycle is an organisational process of developing and maintaining systems. It helps in establishing a system project plan, because it gives overall list of processes and sub-processes required for developing a system.
- System development life cycle means combination of various activities. In other words we can say that various activities put together are referred as system development life cycle.
- In the system analysis and design terminology, the system development life cycle also means software development life cycle.
- It is a well defined process by which a system is planned, developed and maintained.
- Fig. 2.4 shows following activities involves in SDLC.
    1. Preliminary Investigation (Problem Identification).
    2. Feasibility study.
    3. System analysis.
    4. System designing.
    5. Development of software.
    6. System testing.
    7. Implementation and Evaluation
    8. Maintenance.

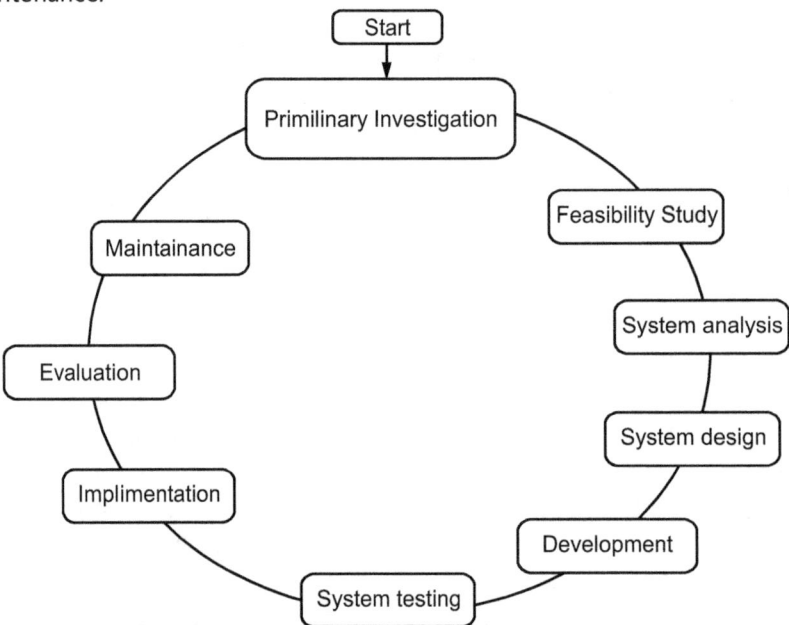

Fig. 2.4: System Development Life Cycle (SDLC)

Various phases of S.D.L. Card is listed below:

1. **Preliminary Investigation (Problem Identification):** One of most difficult task of the system analyst is identifying the real problem of the existing system. It defines the user requirements or what the user expects from the new system. This also includes the rough idea of the resource requirements as well as estimated time for completion and number of persons expected to be involve in each phase.

Problem identification helps in:
(i) Defining a problem,
(ii) Setting proper system goal, and
(iii) Determining the boundaries of the project by considering the limitations of available resources

2. **Feasibility study:** It determine the possibility of either improving the existing system or developing the complete new system. It helps to obtain an overview of the problem and to get rough assessment of whether physical solution exist. The purpose of feasibility study is to determine whether the requested system successfully realizable.

   There are four aspects of feasibility study as given below:

   (i) **Technical feasibility:** It involves the required and existing computer system, hardware, software and to what extent it can support the proposed application.

   It answers following questions:
   - Whether the system can be carried out with existing equipments?
   - Whether the existing software is enough?
   - If a new technology is required how best it can be implemented?

   (ii) **Economic feasibility:** It involves post benefit analysis to determine the benefit and savings that are expected from new system and compared with costs. It benefits out weight cost then decision is made to design and implement new system.

   (iii) **Operational feasibility:** It concerns with human, organisational and political aspects. It covers technical performance as well as acceptance within the organisation. It determines the general attitude and job skills of existing personals and whether any restructuring of jobs will be acceptable to the current user.

   (iv) **Behavioural feasibility:** It includes how strong the reaction of staff will be towards the development of new system that involves computer's use in their daily work. So resistant to change is identified.

3. **System analysis:** It involves detailed understanding of all important facts of the business area under investigation. This require data collection from a verity of sources such as questionnaires, forms, interviews, study of existing documents. It can be involved the direct observation in the organisation and collected documents to understand the whole existing system.

   The analysis phase involves analysing end-user business requirements and refining project goals into defined functions and operations of the intended system. A good start is essential and the organisational must be spend as much time, energy and resources as necessary to perform a detailed, accurate analysis.

The three primary activities involved in the analysis phase are:
(i) Gather business requirements,
(ii) Create process diagrams, and
(iii) Perform a buy versus build analysis.

4. **System designing:** In this process the primary object is to identify user requirements and to build a system that satisfies these requirements. Design of the system is mainly the logical design that can be sketch on a paper or on a computer. It includes physical design elements, describes the data to be inputted.

    The design phase involves describing the desired features and operations of the system including screen layouts, business rules, process diagrams, pseudo code and other documentation.

    The two primary activities involved in the design phase are:
    (i) Design the infrastructure, and
    (ii) Design system models.

    The process involved in manipulation of data and output design represents:
    (i) File structure, storage devices etc.,
    (ii) Database is also designed in this phase,
    (iii) Changes to be made in the organisational structure of the firm are outlines,
    (iv) Input, Output, files, forms and procedures are planned, and
    (v) Finally standards for testing, documentation, system control are designed.

5. **Development of software:** Development is a phase where detailed design is used to actually construct and build the system. In this phase the system is decided whether to buy commercial software or to develop new customized program with the help of the programmers. The choice depends upon the cost of software and cost of programming.

    The development phase involves taking all of the detailed design documents from the design phase and transforming them into the actual system. The two primary activities involved in the development phase are:
    (i) Develop the infrastructure, and
    (ii) Develop the database and programs.

6. **System testing:** Testing is a process of making sure that the program performs the intended task. Once the system is designed it should be tested for validity. During this phase the system is used experimentally to ensure that software does not fail and it will work according to its specification. It is tested with special test data.

    The testing phase involves bringing all the project pieces together into a special testing environment to test for errors, bugs and interoperability, in order to verify that the system meets all the business requirements defined in the analysis phase.

The two primary activities involved in the testing phase are:
(i) Write the test conditions, and
(ii) Perform the system testing.

7. **Implementation and Evaluation:** This is the final phase of development. It consists of installing hardware, programs, collecting data and organizing people to interact with and run the system. In this phase user actually starts using the system therefore it also involves training of users and provides friendly documentation.

    Evaluation is the process of verifying the capability of a system after it put into operation to see whether it meets the objective or not. It includes response time, overall reliability and limitations user behaviour.

    The implementation phase involves placing the system into production so users can begin to perform actual business operations with the system. The implementation phase is also referred to as 'delivery'. The implementation phase is comprised of two activities; training and conversion. Each of these activities include multiple part tasks such as writing detailed user documentation, determining the conversion method and providing training for system users. How and what time during the phase these tasks occur, often depends upon the conversion method selected. For example, for a plunge conversion, all training must take place prior to the conversion. Alternatively, during a parallel conversion, training can be offered at scheduled intervals as the new system is rolled out. Also, the complexity and comprehensive nature of the new system can dictate timing and steps necessary to deliver or implement the system. The two primary activities of the implementation phase include:
    (i) System training, and
    (ii) Implementation method.

8. **Maintenance:** It is process of incorporating changes in the implemented existing system. The maintenance phase involves performing changes, corrections, additions and upgrades to ensure the system continues to meet the business goals. This phase continues for the life of the system because the system must change as the business evolves and its needs change, demanding constant monitoring, supporting the new system with frequent minor changes (for example, new reports or information capturing) and reviewing the system to be sure it is moving the organisation toward its strategic goals. Once a system is in place, it is must change as the organisation changes. The three primary activities involved in the maintenance phase are:
    (i) Build a help desk to support the system users.
    (ii) Perform system maintenance.
    (iii) Provide an environment to support system changes.

    This phase provides following functions:

    (a) Enhancement: Adding new functions or additional capability of the system.

    (b) Adaptation: Customizing the software to run in a new environment.

    (c) Correction: Correcting the bugs in the existing software.

2.5 Prototyping

- Prototyping is the process of building a model system. In terms of an information system prototype are employed to help system designers build an information system that intuitive and easy to manipulate end users.
- Prototyping is an iterative process that is part of analysis phase of system development of life cycle.
- Prototyping is the process that enables the developer to create a working model of an information system application. It allows developer to create a model to the software that must be built.
- The model can take one of the three forms:
    1. A paper prototypes or PC-based model.
    2. A working prototype.
    3. An existing program.
- Prototype just gives the idea about the system. It does not contain all features or perform all the necessary functions of the final system. Customer evaluates the prototype and then suggest what changes needed in the system. That's why prototyping is an interactive process as it is revised to satisfy the needs of the customer.
- It does not require lot of cost to build. It can be prepared by pen and pencil or computer software like green generators, report generators and application generators. The sequence of events for the prototyping are illustrated in Fig. 2.5.

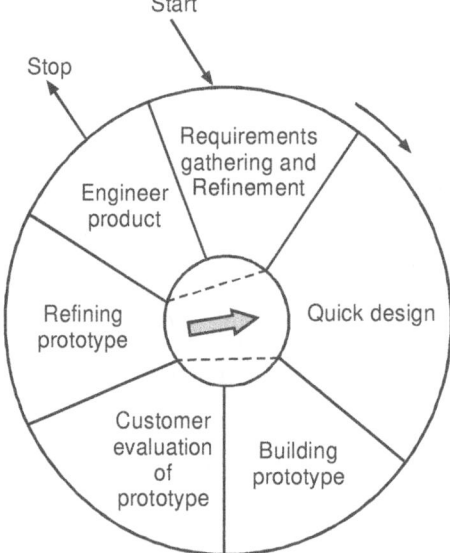

Fig. 2.5: Prototyping model

- Let us see all the steps in prototyping in detail.
    1. **Requirement gathering and Refinement:** Prototyping begins with the requirement gathering. In this step both developer i.e. system analyst and customer [user] work together and define the overall objectives for the software. They both together identify the requirement to be fulfilled.
    2. **Quick design:** This focuses on the representation of those aspects of the software that will be visible to the user. Analyst estimates a prototyping cost and gives this idea to management.
    3. **Building prototype:** The quick design leads to the construction of prototype. A prototype is constructed using several tools. Prototypes are prepared to represent input screen formats and output formats.
    4. **Customer evaluation of prototype:** The prototype is evaluated by the customer or user and is used to refine requirements for the software to be developed. User or customer works on the prototype to evaluate its features and operations.
    5. **Review prototype:** The prototype is refined, after getting information from user about what they want and what they do not want. Developer should understand the need of the customer properly for making modifications in the prototypes.
    6. **Repeat as needed:** The process is repeated till both the users and developers find all the necessary features are fulfilled and there is no benefit of repeating the steps. At last user gets engineer product with his/her specifications.

Advantages:
1. Prototype reduce the development time.
2. It reduce the development cost.
3. It requires the users involvement.
4. Its results are higher user satisfaction.
5. Prototype are an active, not passive, model that end user can see, touch and feel.
6. Prototyping can increase creativity because it allows for quicker user feedback which can lead to better solutions.

Disadvantages:
1. Prototyping often leads to premature commitment to a design.
2. Prototyping can reduce creativity in designs.
3. Not suitable for large applications.
4. Structure of system can be damaged since many changes could be made.
5. Developer misunderstanding of user objectives.

Questions

1. What is a system?
2. Define system.
3. Give characteristics of a system.
4. List out elements of a system with their brief description.
5. Explain different types of system.
6. With the help of diagram describe SDLC.
7. What is feasibility study? Explain its types.
8. What is prototyping? State its advantages and disadvantages.
9. Define the following terms:
   (i) System analysis, and
   (ii) System design.
10. Explain prototyping diagrammatically.
11. Write short note on: Types of Systems.

■■■

Chapter 3...

Operating System and Services in Operating System

Contents ...

3.1 Introduction
    3.1.1 Definition
    3.1.2 Objectives
    3.1.3 Characteristics
    3.1.4 Features
    3.1.5 Need
    3.1.6 Advantages
    3.1.7 Disadvantages
    3.1.8 Types
3.2 Introduction to DOS
    3.2.1 DOS History
3.3 Files and Directories
    3.3.1 Files
    3.3.2 Directories
3.4 Internal and External Commands of DOS
    3.4.1 Internal DOS Commands
    3.4.2 External DOS Commands
3.5 Batch Files
    3.5.1 Creating Batch Files
    3.5.2 Batch File Commands
3.6 Types (Examples) of Operating Systems
- Questions

3.1 Introduction

- An Operating System (OS) is a software program that enables the computer hardware to communicate and operate with the computer software.
- Without a computer operating system, a computer and software programs would be useless.
- An operating system is a program that acts as an interface between the software and the computer hardware.

- OS is an integration set of specialised programs that are used to manage overall resources and operations of the computer.
- An operating system is a collection of software that manages computer hardware resources and provides common services for computer programs.
- Most popular operating systems are Windows 7, Windows XP, Windows 8, Macintosh OSX, Linux, Unix, Windows Vista, Debian, Xandros Linux, Android, Solaris, etc.

3.1.1 Definition

- An operating system is a computer program that manages the resources of a computer.

OR

- An operating system is software that communicates with the hardware and allows other programs to run.

OR

- An operating system is a program that controls the execution of application programs and acts as an interface between the user of a computer and the computer hardware. In other words "the software that controls the hardware".

3.1.2 Objectives

- Objectives of operating system are listed below:
    1. To provide users a convenient interface to use the computer system.
    2. Manage the resources of a computer system.
    3. Making a computer system convenient to use in an efficient manner.
    4. The efficient and fair sharing of resources among users and programs.
    5. To hide the details of the hardware resources from the users.
    6. Keep the track of who is using which resource, granting resource requests, according to resource using and mediating conflicting requests from different programs and users.
    7. To act as an intermediary between the hardware and its users and making it easier for the users to access and use other resources.

3.1.3 Characteristics

- The operating system have the following characteristics:
    1. Operating system is a collection of programs those are responsible for the execution of other programs.
    2. Operating system is that which is responsible for controlling all the input and output devices those are connected to the system.
    3. Operating system is that which is responsible for running all the application software's.
    4. Operating system is that which provides scheduling to the various processes means allocates the memory to various process those want to execute.
    5. Operating system is that which provides the communication between the user and the system.

6. Operating system is stored into the BIOS means in the Basic Input and Output System means when a user starts his system then this will read all the instructions those are necessary for executing the system means for running the operating system, operating system must be loaded into the computer this will use the floppy or hard disks which stores the operating system.

3.1.4 Features
- Some of the features of operating systems are detailed here:
    1. **Software and hardware management:** The operating system is the bridge between computer hardware and software and makes the communication between them possible. Also communication between different softwares in the computer is also taken care by operating system.
    2. **Constant API:** Application Program Interface (API) is a software that allows different applications that run on a computer to work on other computers also. But they should have same operating system. So it is very vital to have consistent API in the operating system.
    3. **Execution of programs:** Programs running in the computer are completely dependent on the operating system. But program execution is a tough process. The multitasking and multithreading features of the operating system are dependent upon the type of program execution feature of operating system.
    4. **Interruptions:** Interruption may happen at any time while using the computers. So the operating system should allow and handle many numbers of interrupts. Whenever, an interruption occurs, the operating system should respond to it by saving and stopping the current execution and work on the new execution. This is the most hard-hitting process for the operating system.
    5. **Managing memory:** The operating system provides the memory for the programs those are executed at any moment. So the operating system should have good memory allocation facility to execute the programs smoothly. The prioritization and allocation of memory to the applications running should be taken care by the operating systems.
    6. **Networking:** Today computers are nothing without internet connection or some network connection. This is the age of networking. So if computers are connected to a network, the there should be definitely communication between one computer and another. So the operating system is what makes it possible for one computer to communicate with other computers.
    7. **Security:** Security is the important feature that should be looked for in an operating system. An operating system in the computer takes care of all security issues of computer and data in it. Log in passwords, firewall settings, and every such aspect related to security depends on the ability of the operating system. Some of the computers in network may involve in file sharing, and other data sharing. So it is important in such cases to have powerful secured operating systems.

3.1.5 Need

- An operating system is an essential component of a computer system.
- The primary objectives of an operating system are to make computer system convenient to use and utilizes computer hardware in an efficient manner.
- Some of the important reasons why do we need an operating system are as follows:
    1. Operating system provides an environment for running user programs.
    2. Operating system provides an interface to the user to communicate with the system.
    3. User interacts with the computer through operating system in order to accomplish his/her task since it is his primary interface with a computer.
    4. It helps the user in understand the inner functions of a computer very closely.
    5. Operating system executes user programs and to make solving user problems easier.
    6. Operating system provides an overall control to the system.
    7. Many concepts and techniques found in operating system have general applicability in other applications.
    8. Operating system manages the computer resources in an efficient manner.
    9. Operating system uses hardware of the system in efficient manner.
- The positioning of operating system in overall computer system is shown in Fig. 3.1.

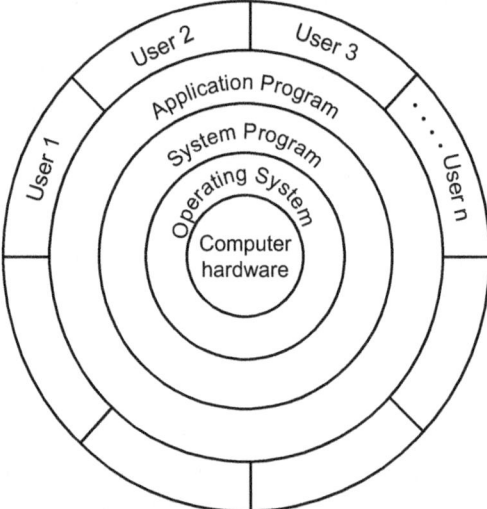

Fig. 3.1: Positioning of operating system in overall computer system

3.1.6 Advantages

- Operating system consists of following advantages:
    1. Operating system provides direct hardware access.
    2. Fast in speed because it provides direct access of computer hardware.
    3. Easy and complete memory use, and
    4. Efficiency use of computer hardware.

3.1.7 Disadvantages

- Disadvantages of operating systems are given below:
  1. No back-up available.
  2. Unrestricted access.
  3. Deadlock problems, and
  4. Problems of memory data loss.

3.1.8 Types

- Various types of operating system are listed below:

1. Batch Operating System:

- In old days the computers were large systems run from a console. The common input devices were card readers and tape drives and output devices were line printers, tape drives and card punches.
- The computer system did not directly interact with the users instead the computer users used to prepare a format that consisted of the programs, the data and some control information about the nature of the job and submitted it to the computer operator.
- The job was usually in the form of punch cards. The process as a whole took a lot of time and was slow. To speed up the processing jobs with similiar needs were batched together and were run through the computer as a group.
- Fig. 3.2 shows the memory layout for a simple batch system.

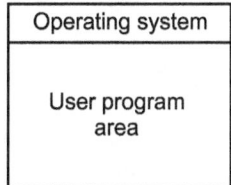

Fig. 3.2: Memory layout for a simple batch system

- A batch operating system, normally reads a stream of separate jobs, each with its own control cards that predefine what the job does. When the job is complete, its output is usually printed.
- The important feature of a batch system is lack of interaction between the user and the job while that job is being executed. The job is prepared and submitted and at some later time, the output appears.
- In a batch processing system, a job is described by a sequence of control statements stored in a machine-readable form.
- The operating system can read and execute a series of such jobs without human intervention except for such functions as tape and disk mounting. The order in which the jobs are selected and executed can be scheduled using appropriate algorithms.
- A batch is a sequence of user jobs.
- The batch monitor is responsible for:
  - Accepting command from the system operator,
  - Initiate the processing of a batch,

- Sets up the processing of the first job,
- At end of the job, terminates process and initiate execution of the next job,
- At end of the batch, terminates batch and awaits initiation of the next batch by the operator.

Advantages of batch operating system:
(i) Move much of the work of the operator to the computer.
(ii) Increased performance since it was possible for job to start as soon as the previous job finished.

Disadvantages of batch operating system:
(i) Turn around time can be large from user standpoint.
(ii) Difficult to debug program.
(iii) Due to lack of protection scheme, one batch job can affect pending jobs.
(iv) A job could corrupt the monitor, thus affecting pending jobs.
(v) A job could enter an infinite loop.

Spooling Technique:
- In the batch operating system execution environment, the CPU is often idle. This idleness occurs because the speeds of the mechanical I/O devices are slower than those of electronic devices.
- As time passed, improvements in technology resulted in faster I/O devices and CPU speeds increased even faster, so the problem was not only unsolved but also increased.
- In the disk technology rather than the cards being read from the card reader directly into memory, and then the job being processed, cards are read directly from the card reader onto the disk.
- The location of the card images is recorded in a table kept by the operating system. When a job is executed, the operating system satisfied its request for card reader input by reading from the disk.
- Similarly, when the job requests the printer to output a line, that line is copied into a system buffer and is written to the disk. When the job is completed, the output is actually printed. This form of processing is called spooling.
- Spooling is used for data processing of remote sites. The CPU sends the data via communication paths to a remote printer. The remote processing is done at its own speed, with no CPU intervention.

Advantages of spooling:
(i) Spooling overlaps the I/O of one job with the computation of other jobs.
(ii) Spooling has a direct beneficial effect on the performance of the system.
(iii) Spooling can keep both the CPU and the I/O devices working at much higher rates.
(iv) Spooling operating uses a disk as a very large buffer.

2. Multiprogramming:
- Multiprogramming is a technique to execute number of programs simultaneously by a single processor.
- In multiprogramming number of processes reside is main memory at a time and the operating system picks and begins executing one of the jobs in the main memory.

Advantages of multiprogramming are:
  (i) Efficient memory utilization.
  (ii) CPU never sits idle, so it increases the CPU performance.
  (iii) Throughput of the CPU increases.
  (iv) In non-multiprogramming environment (mono programming) the user/ program has to wait for CPU much time. But waiting time is limited in multiprogramming.

3. **Multiprocessing (Multiprocessor) System:**
- Multiprogramming allows running a program on more than one CPU simultaneously.
- This system is similar to multiprogramming system, except that there is more than one CPU available.
- In most multiprocessor systems, the processors share a common memory. Thus, the user can view the system as if it were a powerful single processor.
- Below are some examples of multiprocessing operating systems.
  - Linux,
  - Unix, and
  - Windows 2000.

Advantages of multiprocessor systems:
  (i) Increases throughput: by increasing the number of processors, more work done in a shorter period of time.
  (ii) Multiprocessors can also save money compared to multiple single systems, because the processors can share peripherals, cabinets and power supplies.
  (iii) It increases reliability: if functions can be distributed properly among several processors, then the failure of one processor will not halt the system, but rather will only slow it down.
  (iv) Minimum hardware is required.

4. **Multithreading:**
- Multithreading is a technique in which a process executing an application is divided into threads that can run concurrently.
  (i) Thread: A dispatchable unit of work. It includes a processor context (which includes the program counter and stack pointer) and its own data area for stack.(to enable subroutine branching). A thread executes sequentially and is interruptable so that the processor can turn to another thread.
  (ii) Process: A collection of one or more threads and associated system resources. (Such as memory containing both code and data, open files and devices).
- Operating systems that would fall into this category are:
  - Linux
  - Unix
  - Windows 2000.
- Multithreading refers to the ability of an operating system to support multiple threads of execution per process. The traditional approach of a single thread of execution per process is referred to as a single threaded approach.

Advantages of multithreading:
   (i) The efficiency of multithreading system is evident in multiprocessor system where parallel processing of thread is possible.
   (ii) Thread switching is faster than process switching.
   (iii) Threads are also useful for structuring processes that are part of the kernel.

Disadvantages of multithreading:
   (i) Multithreading is a complicated concept due to which operating system maintainability and designing are time consuming and expensive.
   (ii) It is still evolving and requires multiprocessor machines, increased machine speed, high speed network attachments and increased size and variety of memory storage devices.

5. **Multitasking or Time Sharing:**
- Time sharing or multitasking, is a logical extension of multiprogramming. Multiple jobs are executed by the CPU switching between them, but the switches occur so frequently that the users may interact with each program while running.
- Time sharing systems were developed to provide interactive use of a computer at reasonable cost.
- A time shared operating system uses CPU scheduling and multiprogramming to provide each user with a small portion of a time-shared computer. Each user has atleast one separate program in memory.
- A program that is loaded into memory and is being executed is commonly referred to as a process.
- Below are some examples of multitasking operating systems.
   o Unix
   o Windows 2000.
- A time shared operating system allows many uses to share the computer simultaneously. Since each action or command in, in a time-shared system tends to be short, only a little CPU time is needed for each user.
- Time sharing operating systems are even more complex than a multiprogrammed operating systems.

6. **Distributed Systems:**
- A distributed system is a collection of processors that do not share memory or a clock. Instead, each processor has its own local memory, and the processors communicate with each other through various communication lines.
- The purpose of distributed system is to provide an efficient and convenient environment for this type of sharing of resources.
- A distributed operating system allows a more complex type of network organization. This kind of operating system manages hardware and software resources, so that the user views the entire network as a simple system.
- The user is unaware of which machine on the network is actually running a program or storing data.

Advantages of distributed systems are:
   (i) Resource sharing,
   (ii) Reliability,
   (iii) Computation speed-up,
   (iv) Communication, and
   (v) Incremental growth.

7. **Real Time Operating System (RTOS):**
- Real Time Operating Systems are used to control machinery, scientific instruments and industrial systems.
- An RTOS typically has very little user-interface capability, and no end-user utilities, since the system will be a sealed box when delivered for use.
- A very important part of an RTOS is managing the resources of the computer so that a particular operation executes in precisely the same amount of time, every time it occurs.
- In a complex machine, having a part move more quickly just because system resources are available may be just as catastrophic as having it not move at all because the system is busy.

3.2 Introduction to DOS

- DOS (Disk Operating System) was the first widely-installed operating system for personal computers.
- The first personal computer version of DOS, called PC-DOS, was developed for IBM by Bill Gates and his new Microsoft Corporation. He retained the rights to market a Microsoft version, called MS-DOS.
- PC-DOS and MS-DOS are almost identical and most users have referred to either of them as just "DOS."
- DOS was (and still is) a non-graphical line-oriented command- or menu-driven operating system, with a relatively simple interface but not overly "friendly" user interface. Its prompt to enter a command looks like this:

```
C:\>
```

3.2.1 DOS History

- MS-DOS is a non-graphical command line operating system derived from 86-DOS that was created for IBM compatible computers.
- MS-DOS originally written by Tim Patersonand introduced by Microsoft in August 1981 and was last updated in 1994 when MS-DOS 6.22 was released.
- Today, MS-DOS is no longer used; however, the command shell, more commonly known as the Windows command line is still used by many users.

- Fig. 3.3 shows DOS window.

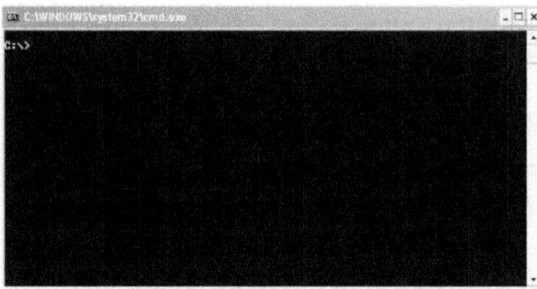

Fig. 3.3

- Following table shows brief history of DOS:

Year	Event
1981	Microsoft buys the rights for QDOS from Seattle Computer Products (SCP) for $25,000 on July 1981.
1981	MS-DOS 1.0 was released August, 1981.
1982	MS-DOS 1.25 was released August, 1982.
1983	MS-DOS 2.0 was released March, 1983.
1984	Microsoft introduces MS-DOS 3.0 for the IBM PC AT and MS-DOS 3.1 for networks.
1986	MS-DOS 3.2 was released April, 1986.
1987	MS-DOS 3.3 was released April, 1987.
1988	MS-DOS 4.0 was released July, 1988.
1988	MS-DOS 4.01 was released November, 1988.
1991	MS-DOS 5.0 was released June, 1991.
1993	MS-DOS 6.0 was released August, 1993.
1993	MS-DOS 6.2 was released November, 1993
1994	MS-DOS 6.21 was released March, 1994
1994	MS-DOS 6.22 was released April, 1994

3.3 Files and Directories

3.3.1 Files

- A file is a collection of data that is stored on disk and that can be manipulated as a single unit by its name.
- We can define file as "a collection of logically related records".
- The way records are physically arranged on a storage device is termed as file organisation.
- File organisation refers to the arrangement of records within a database.
- The organisation of a given file may be sequential, relative, or indexed.

1. **Sequential File Organisation:**
   - In these file organisation, records are arranged sequentially.
   - A sequentially organized file may be stored on either a serial–access or direct access storage medium.
   - Sequential files may be recorded in variable-length of fixed-length record form. If a file consists of variable-length records, each logical record is preceded by control information that indicates the size of the logical record.
   - Sequential files are normally created and stored on magnetic tape using batch processing method.

   Advantages:
   (i) Simple and easy to understand and implement.
   (ii) Easy and simple to maintain and organize.

   Disadvantages:
   (i) Data redundancy is high.
   (ii) Very low activity rate stored.
   (iii) Impossible to handle random enquiries.

   Index Sequential file organisation:
   - In index this file organisation, the records are stored in the key sequence order usually in ascending order. Some index tables are also created and maintained with the file.
   - Index table in this organisation provide to identify the groups of records in the file. When an indexed file is accessed randomly, the programmers control the sequence on which the records are accessed by specifying the value of a data item called record key.

   Advantages:
   (i) Random access is possible.
   (ii) Updating is easily accommodated.

2. **Direct/Random File Organisation:**
   - In this file organisation, records are placed randomly throughout the file.
   - Records need not be in sequence because they are updated directly and rewritten back in the same location.
   - New records in this organisation are added at the end of the file or inserted in specific locations based on software commands.
   - In this organisation records are accessed by addresses that specify their disk locations. An address is required for locating a record, for linking records, or for establishing relationships.

   Advantages:
   (i) Very easy and simple to handle random enquiries.
   (ii) Transaction need not be sorted.
   (iii) Several files can be simultaneously updated during transaction processing.
   (iv) Existing records can be amended or modified.

Disadvantages:
   (i) Expensive hardware and software are required.
   (ii) Risk of loss of accuracy and breach of security.
   (iii) High complexity in programming.

3. Indexed Files:
- An indexed file, which must be allocated in the execution activity to more than two random mass storage files is organized such that each record is uniquely identified by the value of key within the record.
- In index file an index is a data structure that organizes data records on disk to optimize certain file operations and it allows us to efficiently search or retrieve all records. Using an index, we can achieve a fast search of data records.
- In order to create and maintain index files a computer create a data file and an index file. The data file contains the actual contents (data) of the record and index file contains the index entries. The one field in a file is the primary key, which identifies a record uniquely.
- Files are organized in the following ways:
   (i) The data file is stored in the order of the primary key values.
   (ii) The index file contains two fields: the key value and the pointer to the data record.
   (iii) One record in the index file thus, consists of a key value and a pointer to the corresponding data record. The pointer points to the first entry within the range of data records.

3.3.2 Directories

- A directory is a file that acts as a folder for other files. A directory can also contain other directories (subdirectories); a directory that contains another directory is called the parent directory of the directory it contains.
- A directory tree includes a directory and all of its files, including the contents of all subdirectories. (Each directory is a "branch" in the "tree.") A slash character alone (`/`) is the name of the root directory at the base of the directory tree hierarchy; it is the trunk from which all other files or directories branch.
- Shows an abridged version of the directory hierarchy.

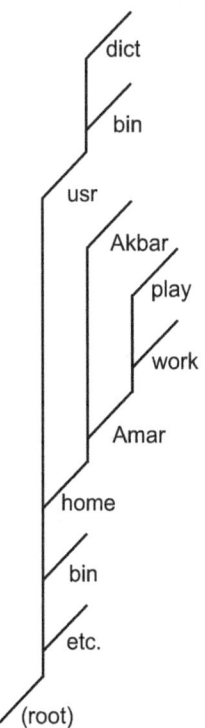

Fig. 3.4

- To represent a directory's place in the file hierarchy, specify all of the directories between it and the root directory, using a slash ('/') as the delimiter to separate directories. So the directory 'dict' as it appears in the preceding illustration would be represented as '/usr/dict'.
- Each user has a branch in the '/home' directory for their own files, called their home directory. The hierarchy in the previous illustration has two home directories:'Amar' and 'Akbar', both subdirectories of '/home'.
- When you are in a shell, you are always in a directory on the system, and that directory is called the current working directory. When you first log in to the system, your home directory is the current working directory.
- Whenever specifying a file name as an argument to a tool or application, you can give the slash-delimited path name relative to the current working directory. For example, if '/home/Amar' is the current working directory, you can use work to specify the directory '/home/Amar/work', and work/schedule to specify 'schedule', a file in the '/home/Amar/work' directory.
- Every directory has two special files whose names consist of one and two periods: '..' refers to the parent of the current working directory, and '.' refers to the current working directory itself. If the current working directory is '/home/Amar', you can use '.' to specify '/home/Amar' and '..' to specify '/home'. Furthermore, you can specify the '/home/Akbar' directory as ../Akbar.
- Another way to specify a file name is to specify a slash-delimited list of all of the directory branches from the root directory ('/') down to the file to specify. This unique, specific path from the root directory to a file is called the file's full path name, (When referring to a file that is not a directory, this is sometimes called the absolute file name).
- You can specify any file or directory on the system by giving its full path name. A file can have the same name as other files in different directories on the system, but no two files or directories can share a full path name. For example, user Amar can have a file 'schedule' in his '/home/Amar/work' directory and a file 'schedule' in his '/home/Amar/play' directory. While both files have the same name ('schedule'), they are contained in different directories, and each has a unique full path name--- '/home/Amar/work/schedule' and '/home/Amar/play/schedule'.
- However, you don't have to type the full path name of a tool or application in order to start it. The shell keeps a list of directories, called the *path*, where it searches for programs. If a program is "in your path," or in one of these directories, you can run it simply by typing its name.
- By default, the path includes '/bin' and '/usr/bin'. For example, the who command is in the '/usr/bin' directory, so its full path name is /usr/bin/who. Since the '/usr/bin' directory is in the path, you can type who to run /usr/bin/who, no matter what the current working directory is.

What is Directory?

- Files contain text or data. Directories contain files. Directories should be organized in hierarchical manner.
- A directory is a named group of related files that are separated by the naming convention from other groups of files.
- A directory is file system cataloging structure in which references to other computer files, and possibly other directories, are kept.
- The following extensions have become accepted standards.

Extension	Meaning
EXE	DOS executable file.
COM	DOS command file.
BAT	DOS Batch file.
SYS	DOS operating system file.
BAK	Back up file.
TXT	Text or word processing file.
DOC	A document file.
BAS	File containing Basic Program.
PAS	File containing Pascal Program.

- Files (program or data file) are usually stored on disks. DOS organizes these files by grouping related files into lists called directories. In addition to directories, DOS use an area called the File Allocation Table (FAT). When a disk is formatted (see FORMAT command explained later), this table is copied onto the disk and an empty directory, called root directory, is created.
- On every storage disk, files are stored in directories and File Allocation Table keeps the information about their location on the disk surface. The root directory is represented by the backslash character '\'.
- A pathname is a sequence of directory names followed by a filename. Each directory name is separated from the previous one by a backslash.
- A path is similar to pathname except that it does not include a filename. The pathname is specified in the following form:
    [\dir_name] [\dir_name ...] \filename
  For example, the pathname for RAVI's ABC.PAS file is,
    \STUDENT\RAVI\ABC.PAS

3.4 Internal and External Commands of DOS

- To be functional, each DOS command should be entered in a particular way. This command entry structure is known as the command's "syntax." Syntax notation is a way to reproduce a command syntax in print.
- For example, optional items can be determined by looking at the information printed inside square brackets. The notation [d:], for example, indicates an optional drive designation. The command syntax, on the other hand, is how you enter a command to make it work.

Elements of Command Syntax:
1. **Command Name:** The DOS command name is the name one enters into start a DOS program. A few of the DOS commands can be entered using shortcut names. DOS command name is always entered first. It should be kept in mind that one can enter command names in both lowercase and uppercase, or a mix of both.
2. **Drive Designation:** Drive designation (d:) is an option for many DOS commands. However, some commands are not related to disk drives and, therefore, do not require a drive designation. Whenever you enter a DOS command, it deals with disk drives. If you are already working in the drive in question, you do not have to enter the drive designator. For example, if you are working in drive A (when the DOS prompt A> is showing at the left side of the screen) and you want to use DIR command to display a directory listing of that same drive, you do not have to enter the drive designation. If you do not enter a drive designation, DOS always assumes you are referring to the drive you are currently working in.
3. **Filename:** A filename is the name of a file stored on disk. A filename can be of eight or fewer letters or other legal characters.
4. **Pathname:** A pathname (path) refers to the path you want DOS to follow in order to act on the DOS command. It indicates the path from the current directory or subdirectory to the files that are to be acted upon.
5. **Colon:** When referring to a drive in a DOS command, you should always follow the drive designator with a colon (:). This is how DOS recognizes it as a drive designation.
6. **Space:** One should always leave a space after command name.
7. **Brackets:** Items enclosed in square brackets are optional. In other words, a command will work in its basic form without entering the information inside the brackets.
8. **Filename Extension:** A filename extension is a string of characters added to the end of a filename. It is done usually to help specify what kind of information the file contains, or to distinguish between different versions of a file with the same name. A filename extension can follow the filename to further identify it. The extension follows a period and can be of three or fewer characters. A user does not actually have to type a filename extension.
9. **Ellipses:** Ellipses (...) indicate that an item in command syntax can be repeated as many times as needed.
10. **Switches:** The characters in command syntax that are represented by letters or numbers and preceded by forward slash (for example, "/P") are known as switches. Use of these options activates special operations as part of a DOS command's functions.
11. **Vertical Bar:** When items are separated by a vertical bar (|), it means that you are entering one of the separated items. For example, ON|OFF means that you can enter either ON or OFF, not both.

3.4.1 Internal DOS Commands

1. **BUFFERS Command:**
   It is used in the CONFIG.SYS file to set the number of disk buffers (number) that will be available for use during data input. It is also used to set a value for the number of sectors to be read in advance (read-ahead) during data input operations.
   ```
   BUFFERS = (number), (read-ahead number)
   ```

2. **CALL Command:**
   It calls another batch file and then returns to current batch file to continue.
   ```
   CALL [d:][path] batch filename [options]
   ```

3. **CLS Command:**
   It clears (erases) the screen.
   ```
   CLS
   ```

4. **CHOICE Command:**
   It is used to provide a prompt so that a user can make a choice while a batch program is running.
   ```
   CHOICE [/C [:] keys] [/N][/S][/T [:] c, nn] [text]
   ```

5. **CHCP Command:**
   It displays the current code page or changes the code page that DOS will use.
   ```
   CHCP (code page)
   ```

6. **CHDIR Command:**
   It displays working (current) directory and/or changes to a different directory.
   ```
   CHDIR (CD) [d:] path
   CHDIR (CD)[..]
   ```

7. **COPY Command:**
   It copies and appends files.
   ```
   COPY    [/Y|-Y]    [/A][/B]    [d:][path]    filename    [/A][/B]
   [d:][path][filename] [/V]
   OR
   COPY    [/Y|-Y][/A][/B]    [d:][path]    filename+[d:][path]    filename
   [...][d:][path][filename] [/V]
   ```

8. **CTTY Command:**
   It changes the standard I/O (Input/Output) device to an auxiliary device.
   ```
   CITY (device)
   ```

9. **DATE Command:**
   It displays and/or sets the system date.
   ```
   DATE mm-dd-yy
   ```

10. **COUNTRY Command:**
    It is used in the CONFIG.SYS file to tell DOS to use country-specific text conventions during processing.
    ```
    COUNTRY=country code, [code page][,][d:][filename]
    ```

11. **DIR Command:**
    It displays directory of files and directories stored on disk.
    ```
    DIR     [d:][path][filename]     [/A:(attributes)]     [/O:(order)]
    [/B][/C][/CH][/L][/S][/P][/W]
    ```
12. **DEL (ERASE) Command:**
    It deletes (erases) files from disk.
    ```
    DEL (ERASE) [d:][path] filename [/P]
    ```
13. **DEVICEHIGH Command:**
    Like DEVICE, DEVICEHIGH is used in the CONFIG.SYS file to tell DOS which device driver software to use for devices. However, this option is used to install the device driver into the upper memory area.
    ```
    DEVICEHIGH=(driver name)
    ```
14. **DEVICE Command:**
    It is used in the CONFIG.SYS file to tell DOS which device driver to load.
    ```
    DEVICE=(driver name)
    ```
15. **DOS Command:**
    It is used in the CONFIG.SYS file to specify the memory location for DOS. It is used to load DOS into the upper memory area and to specify whether or not the upper memory blocks will be used.
    ```
    DOS = [high|low], [umb|noumb]
    ```
16. **ECHO Command:**
    It displays messages or turns on or off the display of commands in a batch file.
    ```
    ECHO on|off
    ECHO (message)
    ```
17. **DRIVPARM Command:**
    It is used in the CONFIG.SYS file to set parameters for a disk drive.
    ```
    DRIVPARM= /D:(number) [/C] [/F:(form factor)] [/H:(number)]
    [/I][/N][/S:(number)] [/T:(tracks)]
    ```
18. **EXIT Command:**
    It exits a secondary command processor.
    ```
    EXIT
    ```
19. **FILES Command:**
    It is used in the CONFIG.Sys file to specify the maximum number of files that can be open at the same time.
    ```
    FILES=(number)
    ```
20. **FOR Command:**
    It performs repeated execution of commands (for both batch processing and interactive processing).
    ```
    FOR %%(variable) IN (set) DO (command)
    or (for interactive processing)
    FOR %(variable) IN (set) DO (command)
    ```

21. FCBS Command:
It is used in the CONFIG.SYS file to specify the number of file-control blocks for file sharing.
```
FCBS=(number)
```
22. GOTO Command:
It causes unconditional branch to the specified label.
```
GOTO (label)
```
23. INCLUDE Command:
It is used in the CONFIG.SYS file to allow one to use the commands from one CONFIG.SYS block within another.
```
INCLUDE= block name
```
24. IF Command:
It allows for conditional operations in batch processing.
```
IF [NOT] EXIST filename (command) [parameters]
IF [NOT] (string1)==(string2) (command) [parameters]
IF [NOT] ERRORLEVEL (number) (command) [parameters]
```
25. INSTALL Command:
It is used in the CONFIG.SYS file to load memory-resident programs into conventional memory.
```
INSTALL=[d:][\path] filename [parameters]
```
26. LASTDRIVE Command:
It is used in the CONFIG.SYS file to set the maximum number of drives that can be accessed.
```
LASTDRIVE=(drive letter)
```
27. LOADFIX Command:
It ensures that a program is loaded above the first 64K of conventional memory, and runs the program.
28. LOADHIGH Command:
It loads memory resident application into reserved area of memory (between 640K-1M).
```
LOADHIGH (LH) [d:][path]filename [parameters]
```
29. MENUCOLOR Command:
It is used in the CONFIG.SYS file to set the colors that will be used by DOS to display text on the screen.
```
MENUCOLOR=textcolor,[background]
```
30. MENUDEFAULT Command:
It is used in the CONFIG.SYS file to set the startup configuration that will be used by DOS if no key is pressed within the specified timeout period.
```
MENUDEFAULT=blockname, [timeout]
```

31. MENUITEM Command:
It is used in the CONFIG.SYS file to create a start-up menu from which you can select a group of CONFIG.SYS commands to be processed upon reboot.

```
MENUITEM=blockname, [menutext]
```

32. MKDIR/ MD Command:
It creates a new subdirectory.

```
MKDIR (MD) [d:]path
```

33. MOVE Command:
It moves one or more files to the location you specify. Can also be used to rename directories.

```
MOVE    [/Y|/-Y]    [d:][path]filename[,[d:][path]filename[...]] destination
```

34. NUMLOCK Command:
It is used in the CONFIG.SYS file to specify the state of the NumLock key.

```
NUMLOCK=on|off
```

35. PATH Command:
It sets or displays directories that will be searched for programs not in the current directory.

```
PATH;
PATH [d:]path[;][d:]path[...]
```

36. PAUSE Command:
It suspends execution of a batch file until a key is pressed.

```
PAUSE [comment]
```

37. PROMPT Command:
It changes the DOS command prompt.

```
PROMPT [prompt text] [options]
```

38. REM Command:
It is used in batch files and in the CONFIG.SYS file to insert remarks (that will not be acted on).

```
REM [comment]
```

39. RENAME (REN) Command:
It changes the filename under which a file is stored.

```
RENAME (REN) [d:][path]filename [d:][path]filename
```

40. SET Command:
It inserts strings into command environment. Programs can use the set values later.

```
SET (string1)=(string2)
```

41. SHELL Command:
It is used in the CONFIG.SYS file to specify the command interpreter that DOS should use.

```
SHELL=[d:][path]filename [parameters]
```

42. **SHIFT Command:**
    It increases number of replaceable parameters to more than the standard ten for use in batch files.
    ```
    SHIFT
    ```
43. **STACKS Command:**
    It is used in the CONFIG.SYS file to set the number of stack frames and the size of each stack frame.
    ```
    STACKS=(number),(size)
    ```
44. **SUBMENU Command:**
    It is used in the CONFIG.SYS file to create a multilevel menu from which you can select start-up options.
    ```
    SUBMENU=blockname, [menutext]
    ```
45. **SWITCHES Command:**
    It is used in the CONFIG.SYS file to configure DOS in a special way; for example, to tell DOS to emulate different hardware configurations.
    ```
    SWITCHES= [/K][/F][/N][/W]
    ```
46. **TIME Command:**
    It displays current time setting of system clock and provides a way for you to reset the time.
    ```
    TIME hh:mm[:ss][.cc][A|P]
    ```
47. **TYPE Command:**
    It displays the contents of a file.
    ```
    TYPE [d:][path]filename
    ```
48. **VER Command:**
    It displays the DOS version number.
    ```
    VER
    ```
49. **VERIFY Command:**
    It turns on the verify mode; the program checks all copying operations to assure that files are copied correctly.
    ```
    VERIFY on|off
    ```
50. **VOL Command:**
    It displays a disk's volume label.
    ```
    VOL [d:]
    ```

3.4.2 External DOS Commands

1. **APPEND Command:**
   It displays or sets the search path for data files. DOS will search the specified path(s) in case the file is not found in the current path.
   ```
   APPEND;
   APPEND [d:] path [;][d:] path [...]
   APPEND [/X: on |off][/path: on |off] [/E]
   ```

2. **BACKUP Command:**
   It makes a backup copy of one or more files. In DOS Version 6, this program is stored on DOS supplemental disk.
   ```
   BACKUP d: [path][filename] d: [/S][/M][/A][/F:(size)] [/P][/D:
   date] [/T: time] [/L: [path] filename]
   ```
3. **ASSIGN Command:**
   It redirects disk drive requests to a different drive.
   ```
   ASSIGN x=y [...] /sta
   ```
4. **ATTRIB Command:**
   It sets or displays the read only, archive, system and hidden attributes of a file or directory.
   ```
   ATTRIB [d:][path] filename [/S]
   ATTRIB [+R|-R] [+A|-A] [+S|-S] [+H|-H] [d:][path] filename [/S]
   ```
5. **BREAK Command:**
   It is used from the DOS prompt, or in a batch file, or in the CONFIG.SYS file to set (or display) whether or not DOS should check for a Ctrl + Break key combination.
   ```
   BREAK = on|off
   ```
6. **CHKDSK Command:**
   It checks a disk and provides a file and memory status report.
   ```
   CHKDSK [d:][path][filename] [/F][/V]
   ```
7. **COMP Command:**
   It compares two groups of files to find information that does not match. (See FC command).
   ```
   COMP [d:][path][filename] [d:][path][filename]
                                    [/A][/C][/D][/L][/N:(number)]
   ```
8. **COMMAND Command:**
   It starts a new version of the DOS command processor, the program that loads the DOS Internal programs.
   ```
   COMMAND    [d:][path]    [device]    [/P][/E:(size)]    [/MSG][/Y    [/C
   (command)|
   /K (command)]
   ```
9. **DBLSPACE Command:**
   It is a program available with DOS 6.0 that allows you to compress information on a disk.
   ```
   DBLSPACE / automount=drives
   DBLSPACE /chkdsk [/F] [d:]
   DBLSPACE /compress d: [/newdrive=host:] [/reserve=size] [/F]
   DBLSPACE /create d: [/newdrive=host:] [/reserve=size] [/size=size]
   DBLSPACE /defragment [d:] ]/F]
   DBLSPACE /delete d:
   DBLSPACE /doubleguard=0|1
   ```

```
DBLSPACE /format d:
DBLSPACE [/info] [d:]
DBLSPACE /list
DBLSPACE /mount[=nnn] host: [/newdrive=d:]
DBLSPACE /ratio[=ratio] [d:] [/all]
DBLSPACE /size[=size] [/reserve=size] d:
DBLSPACE /uncompress d:
DBLSPACE /unmount [d:]
```

10. DEBUG Command:

It is an MS-DOS utility used to test and edit programs.

```
DEBUG [pathname] [parameters]
```

11. DEFRAG Command:

It optimizes disk performance by reorganizing the files on the disk.

```
DEFRAG [d:] [/F][/S[:]order] [/B][/skiphigh [/LCD|/BW|/GO] [/H]
DEFRAG [d:] [/V][/B][/skiphigh] [/LCD]|/BW|/GO] [/H]
```

12. DELOLDOS Command:

It deletes all files from previous versions of DOS after a 5.0 or 6.0 installation.

```
DELOLDOS [/B]
```

13. DISKCOMP Command:

It compares the contents of two diskettes.

```
DISKCOMP [d:] [d:][/1][/8]
```

14. DELTREE Command:

It deletes (erases) a directory including all files and subdirectories that are in it.

```
DELTREE [/Y] [d:] path [d:] path [...]
```

15. DOSKEY Command:

It loads the DOSKEY program into memory which can be used to recall DOS commands so that you can edit them.

```
DOSKEY [reinstall] [/bufsize=size][/macros][/history]
                   [/insert|/overstrike] [macroname=[text]]
```

16. DISKCOPY Command:

It makes an exact copy of a diskette.

```
DISKCOPY [d:] [d:][/1][/V][/M]
```

17. DOSSHELL Command:

It initiates the graphic shell program using the specified screen resolution.

```
DOSSHELL [/B] [/G: [resolution][n]]|[/T: [resolution][n]]
```

18. EMM386 Command:

It enables or disables EMM386 expanded-memory support on a computer with an 80386 or higher processor.

```
EMM386 [on|off|auto] [w=on|off]
```

19. EXE2BIN Command:
It converts .EXE (executable) files to binary format.
```
EXE2BIN [d:][path] filename [d:][path] filename
```

20. EDIT Command:
It starts the MS-DOS editor, a text editor used to create and edit ASCII text files.
```
EDIT [d:][path] filename [/B][/G][/H][/NOHI]
```

21. FC Command:
It displays the differences between two files or sets of files.
```
FC  [/A][/C][/L][/Lb  n][/N][/T][/W][number]  [d:][path]  filename [d:][path]
```
filename or (for binary comparisons)
```
FC [/B][/number] [d:][path] filename [d:][path] filename
```

22. FASTOPEN Command:
It keeps track of the locations of files for fast access.
```
FASTOPEN d: [=n][/X]
```

23. FASTHELP Command:
It displays a list of DOS commands with a brief explanation of each.
```
FASTHELP [command][command] /?
```

24. EXPAND Command:
It expands a compressed file.
```
EXPAND [d:][path] filename [[d:][path] filename [. . .]]
```

25. FDISK Command:
It prepares a fixed disk to accept DOS files for storage.
```
FDISK [/status]
```

26. FIND Command:
It finds and reports the location of a specific string of text characters in one or more files.
```
FIND [/V][/C][/I][/N] òstringó [d:][path] filename [...]
```

27. GRAFTABL Command:
It loads a table of character data into memory (for use with a color/graphics adapter).
```
GRAFTABL [(code page)]
GRAFTABL [status]
```

28. FORMAT Command:
It formats a disk to accept DOS files.
```
FORMAT d: [/1][/4][/8][/F:(size)] [/N:(sectors)]
              [/T:(tracks)][/B|/S][/C][/V:(label)] [/Q][/U][/V]
```

29. HELP Command:
It displays information about a DOS command.
```
HELP [command] [/B][/G][/H][/NOHI]
```

30. **GRAPHICS Command:**
    It provides a way to print contents of a graphics screen display.
    ```
    GRAPHICS [printer type][profile] [/B][/R][/LCD][/PB:(id)]
                                              [/C][/F][/P (port)]
    ```
31. **JOIN Command:**
    It allows an access to the directory structure and files of a drive through a directory on a different drive.
    ```
    JOIN d: [d:path]
    JOIN d: [/D]
    ```
32. **INTERSVR Command:**
    It starts the interlink server.
    ```
    INTERSVR    [d:][...][/X=d:][...]    [/LPT:    [n|address]]    [/COM:
    [n|address]][/baud: rate] [/B][/V] INTERSVR /RCOPY
    ```
33. **INTERLINK Command:**
    It connects two computers via parallel or serial ports so that the computers can share disks and printer ports.
    ```
    INTERLINK [client [:]=[server][:]]
    ```
34. **LABEL Command:**
    It creates or changes or deletes a volume label for a disk.
    ```
    LABEL [d:][volume label]
    ```
35. **KEYB Command:**
    It loads a program that replaces the support program for U. S. keyboards.
    ```
    KEYB [xx][,][yyy][,][d:][path]filename [/E][/ID:(number)]
    LOADFIX [d:][path]filename [parameters]
    ```
36. **MEM Command:**
    It displays an amount of installed and available memory including extended, expanded and upper memory.
    ```
    MEM [/program|/debug|/classify|/free|/module(name)] [/page]
    ```
37. **MEMMAKER Command:**
    It starts the MemMaker program, a program that lets you optimize your computer's memory.
    ```
    MEMMAKER [/B][/batch][/session][/swap:d][/T][/undo][/W:size1,size2]
    ```
38. **MIRROR Command:**
    It saves disk storage information that can be used to recover accidentally erased files.
    ```
    MIRROR [d:]path [d:] path [...]
    MIRROR [d1:][d2:][...] [/T(drive)(files)] [/partn][/U][/1]
    ```
39. **MODE Command:**
    It sets mode of operation for devices or communications.
    ```
    MODE n
    MODE LPT#[:][n][,][m][,][P][retry]
    MODE [n],m[,T]
    MODE (displaytype,linetotal)
    ```

```
MODE COMn[:]baud[,][parity][,][databits][,][stopbits][,][retry]
MODE LPT#[:]=COMn [retry]
MODE CON[RATE=(number)][DELAY=(number)]
MODE (device) CODEPAGE PREPARE=(codepage) [d:][path]filename
MODE (device) CODEPAGE PREPARE=(codepage list) [d:][path]filename
MODE (device) CODEPAGE SELECT=(codepage)
MODE (device) CODEPAGE [/STATUS]
MODE (device) CODEPAGE REFRESH
```

40. MORE Command:
It sends output to console, one screen at a time.
```
MORE < (filename or command)
(name)|MORE
```

41. MSAV Command:
It scans your computer for known viruses.
```
MSAV [d:] [/S|/C][/R][/A][/L][/N][/P][/F][/video][/mouse]
MSAV /video
```

42. MSBACKUP Command:
It is used to backup or restore one or more files from one disk to another.
```
MSBACKUP [setupfile] [/BW|/LCD|/MDA]
```

43. MSCDEX Command:
It is used to gain access to CD-ROM drives (new with DOS Version 6).
```
MSCDEX  /D:driver  [/D:driver2. . .]  [/E][/K][/S][/V][/L:letter]
[/M:number]
```

44. MSD Command:
It provides detailed technical information about your computer.
```
MSD [/B][/I]
MSD [/I] [/F[d:][path]filename [/P[d:][path]filename
                                    [/S[d:][path]filename
```

45. NLSFUNC Command:
It is used to load a file with country-specific information.
```
NLSFUNC [d:][path]filename
```

46. POWER Command:
It is used to turn power management on and off, report the status of power management, and set levels of power conservation.
```
POWER [adv:max|reg|min]|std|off]
```

47. PRINT Command:
It queues and prints data files.
```
PRINT [/B:(buffersize)] [/D:(device)] [/M:(maxtick)] [/Q:(value)]
[/S:(timeslice)][/U:(busytick)]
[/C][/P][/T] [d:][path][filename] [...]
```

48. RECOVER Command:

It resolves sector problems on a file or a disk. (Beginning with DOS Version 6, RECOVER is no longer available).
```
RECOVER [d:][path]filename
RECOVER d:
```

49. REPLACE Command:

It replaces stored files with files of the same name from a different storage location.
```
REPLACE [d:][path]filename [d:][path] [/A][/P][/R][/S][/U][/W]
```

50. RESTORE Command:

It restores to standard disk storage format files previously stored using the BACKUP command.
```
RESTORE d: [d:][path]filename [/P][/S][/B:mm-dd-yy]
[/A:mm-dd-yy][/E:hh:mm:ss]
[/L:hh:mm:ss] [/M][/N][/D]
RMDIR (RD) (Internal) - Removes a subdirectory.
RMDIR (RD) [d:]path
```

51. SCANDISK Command:

It starts the Microsoft ScanDisk program which is a disk analysis and repair tool used to check a drive for errors and correct any problems that it finds.
```
SCANDISK [d: [d: . . .]|/all][/checkonly|/autofix[/nosave]|/custom]
[/surface][/mono][/nosummay]
SCANDISK   volume-name[/checkonly|/autofix[/nosave]|/custom][/mono]
[/nosummary]
SCANDISK /fragment [d:][path]filename
SCANDISK /undo [undo-d:][/mono]
```

52. SELECT Command:

It formats a disk and installs country-specific information and keyboard codes (starting with DOS Version 6, this command is no longer available).
```
SELECT [d:] [d:][path] [country code][keyboard code]
```

53. SETVER Command:

It displays the version table and sets the version of DOS that is reported to programs.
```
SETVER [d:]:path][filename (number)][/delete][/quiet]
```

54. SHARE Command:

It installs support for file sharing and file locking.
```
SHARE [/F:space] [/L:locks]
```

55. SORT Command:

It sorts input and sends it to the screen or to a file.
```
SORT [/R][/+n] < (filename)
SORT [/R][/+n] > (filename2)
```

56. SUBST Command:

It substitutes a virtual drive letter for a path designation.
```
SUBST d: d:path
SUBST d: /D
```

57. SYS Command:

It transfers the operating system files to another disk.
```
SYS [source] d:
```

58. TREE Command:
It displays directory paths and (optionally) files in each subdirectory.
```
TREE [d:][path] [/A][/F]
```

59. UNDELETE Command:
It restores files deleted with the DELETE command.
```
UNDELETE [d:][path][filename] [/DT|/DS|/DOS]
UNDELETE [/list|/all|/purge[d:]|/status|/load|/U|/S[d:]|
                                                 /Td:[-entries]]
```

60. UNFORMAT Command:
It is used to undo the effects of formatting a disk.
```
UNFORMAT d: [/J][/L][/test][/partn][/P][/U]
```

61. VSAFE Command:
VSAFE is a memory-resident program that continuously monitors your computer for viruses and displays a warning when it finds one.
```
VSAFE [/option [+|-]...] [/NE][/NX][Ax|/Cx] [/N][/D][/U]
```

62. XCOPY Command:
It copies directories, subdirectories and files.
```
XCOPY [d:][path]filename [d:][path][filename] [/A][/D:(date)]
[/E][/M][/P][/S][/V][/W][Y\-Y]
```

3.5 Batch Files

- Batch file is the name given to a type of script file, a text file containing a series of commands to be executed by the command interpreter.
- A batch file may contain any command the interpreter accepts interactively at the command prompt. A batch file may also have constructs (IF, GOTO, Labels, CALL, etc.) that enable conditional branching and looping within the batch file.
- A file that contains a sequence, or batch, of commands. Batch files are useful for storing sets of commands that are always executed together because you can simply enter the name of the batch file instead of entering each command individually.
- In DOS systems, batch files end with a .BAT extension.
- MS-DOS allows you to put this command sequence into a special file called a batch file, and then run the whole sequence of commands by simply typing the name of the batch file.
- A batch file is simply a text file that contains one or more DOS commands and/or the names of application programs. Batch files are sometimes called batch commands. When batch command is executed, DOS locates that command on disk, reads the list of commands it contains, and executes them one at a time in the order in which they appear in the file.

- After the last command is executed, DOS is ready to accept another command. By using a batch file, we have to remember to type one command, instead of several. Thus, batch files allow us to extend and enhance the capabilities of DOS.

3.5.1 Creating Batch Files

- To create batch files, you will need to use a word processor or text editor. Batch files can also be created by using EDLIN, the MS-DOS editor, or by using simply the copy command.
- In this topic, we use the COPY command to create batch files. Suppose, we wish to create a batch file named TODAY.BAT to perform the following operations:
    1. Clear the screen (CLS command)
    2. Verify the date (DATE command), and
    3. Verify the time (TIME command)
- To do this simply follow the steps given below:
    1. Type the following

        A> COPY CON TODAY.BAT ↵

        This command instructs MS-DOS to copy the information from the console (keyboard) to the file TODAY.BAT.
    2. Now, type the following commands

        CLS ↵

        DATE ↵

        TIME ↵
    3. At the end of last command (in this example, TIME) press CONTROL - Z and then press ↵ (RETURN KEY) to save the batch file. DOS then displays the message:

        1 FILE(s) copied

        to indicate that it created the file.
    4. To execute the created batch file simply type the following command

        A> TODAY ↵

- When this batch file command is executed, DOS executes, in order, each command the batch contains. In this example, DOS will first execute CLS clearing the display screen. Next it executes the second command DATE displaying current date and allowing you to change the date, if required. Finally, it executes TIME command displaying current time and giving a chance to change the time, if the displayed time is incorrect. This shows that the result is same as if the commands in the .BAT file were typed from the keyboard as individual commands.

Dummy Parameters:

- We discussed how to create a batch file. We can also create a batch file that takes parameters and does different operations depending upon the values of parameters at the execution time. This can be accomplished by using dummy parameters in the lines in the batch file.

- Each time the batch file is executed, DOS replaces the dummy parameters used in the batch file by the parameters used in the batch file by the parameter values expressed at the command line. For instance, let's consider a batch file named TEST.BAT having following lines in it:

    DIR %1

    CHKDSK %1

    TREE %1

- '%1' used in this batch file represents a dummy parameter. Dummy parameters are sometimes called replaceable parameters. Every dummy parameter consists of the percent sign (%) followed by a numeral. A batch file may have upto nine dummy parameters, '%1' through '%9'. The '%0' parameter always contains the name of the batch file. The remaining nine parameters receive command line values/arguments. Specifically, the '%1' parameter is replaced by the first command line argument, '%2' is replaced by the second argument, and so on. If the batch file TEST.BAT in our example is executed as:

    A> TEST C: ↵

    then the DOS substitutes the parameter value (argument) 'C:' for the dummy parameter '%1' for its every occurrence in the batch file. This execution will result as if we entered the following commands:

    DIR C: ↵

    CHKDSK C: ↵

    TREE C: ↵

- Executing the batch file TEST.BAT with no parameter value at command line will result in the substitution of null parameter in place of '%1'.
- While using batch file parameters following rules must be observed:
    1. There are ten dummy parameters, '%0' through '%9'.
    2. The ith argument (parameter value) in a batch file command relates to the dummy parameter '%i'.
    3. Executing batch file command results in temporarily replacing each dummy parameter with the corresponding argument. The batch file remains unchanged after its execution.
    4. Generally, the count of command line arguments and dummy parameters should be the same. If less number of arguments are specified while executing the batch file, null parameters are substituted for the excess dummy parameters.
- If a batch file command is to be terminated while it is running, press CONTROL + C keys. On pressing CONTROL + C, DOS displays a message asking you to confirm that you want to terminate the batch process. If you respond with the Y key (yes), DOS abandons the batch file and gives you next prompt. If you respond with the N key (NO), DOS continues with the next command in the batch file.

3.5.2 Batch File Commands

- MS-DOS supports several batch file commands that add power and flexibility to the batch files. Since several commands are included in a batch file, it is somewhat similar to programs.
- Table 3.1 shows the list of batch file commands.

Table 3.1: Batch File Commands

Command	Purpose
REM	Includes a remark in a batch file.
ECHO	Displays a message on the screen and can also be used to prevent screen output.
PAUSE	Temporarily suspends execution of a batch file.
CALL	Calls another batch file.
IF	Performs conditional execution of a command.
GOTO	Transfers execution of a batch file to a specified place in the file.
FOR	Allows a command sequence to be repeated.
SHIFT	Increase the number of command line arguments.

1. **REM:** The REM command allows you to place remarks or comments within batch file to explain the batch file processing. DOS does not execute lines containing the RPM command; instead, DOS simply ignores the line and continues the batch file's execution with next line.

   Syntax: REM [comment]

   where:

   comment - is string of characters of the length upto 123 characters.

   Example: The following statements can be included in a batch file to add comment about the creation and purpose of a batch file.

   ```
   REM Filename     :  TODAY.BAT
   REM Purpose      :  To display current date and time and clear the
                       display screen.
   REM Created By   :  Mohankumar Zade
   REM Date         :  08-16-1995
   REM
   ```

   The fifth REM statement in above example adds spaces to increase the readability.

2. **ECHO:** The ECHO command is used in batch files to display or suppress batch command messages. Normally, commands in a batch file are displayed/ echoed on the display screen when they are executed by MS-DOS. This feature can be controlled through the ECHO - ON/OFF options. Moreover, many batch files use ECHO to display messages to the user.

Syntax: `ECHO [ON | OFF | message]`

where:

`ON` : enables display of batch commands as they are executed.

`OFF` : prevents displays of batch commands as they are executed.

`message` : text line to be displayed to the user.

Example: To prevent each command in a batch file from being displayed, use the following command in a batch file:

`ECHO OFF`

Likewise, to cause commands to be displayed once again, use

   `ECHO ON`

The following example shows how to use display user message in the batch file.

   `@ ECHO OFF`
   `ECHO This batch file`
   `ECHO displays today's`
   `ECHO date and time.`

3. **PAUSE:** The PAUSE command temporarily stops execution of a batch file. When the DOS encounters a PAUSE command within a batch file, it temporarily suspends the execution of a batch file and prints the message "strike a key when ready". On pressing any key, the execution of batch file resumes on the next command within the batch file. If you respond with CONTROL + C or CONTROL + BREAK, the batch file is terminated.

   Syntax: `PAUSE [message]`

   where:

   `message` : is a text upto 123 characters that is displayed by PAUSE when batch processing is suspended.

   Example: In a batch processing, to instruct the user to insert a new disk in drive B, use the command:

   PAUSE Insert a new disk in drive B

   On encountering the above command, DOS will suspend batch processing, display the message, and will wait for user to strike any key to resume batch processing.

   Similarly, the following command can be included in a batch file to suspend batch file processing without any user message:

   `PAUSE`

4. **CALL:** The CALL command is used to execute one batch file from within another. When the called batch file is executed, the calling batch file resumes execution at the line immediately following the CALL command.

   Syntax: `CALL [drive] [path] batch filename [argument(s)]`

   where:

   `batch filename` : is the name of a batch file to be called.

   `argument(s)` : is the command line parameters(s) for the called batch file.

Example: Let's assume that, we are writing a batch file named DISKINFO.BAT to format a floppy disk and display information about the disk. To display today's date and time, we can include a call to the batch file TODAY.BAT by using the statement as:

```
CALL TODAY
```

5. **IF:** The IF command is used to perform a specific command in a batch file based on the result of a condition.

   Syntax: `IF condition command`

   where:

   `condition`   : can have one of the following three forms:

   `command`   : any DOS command.

   ERRORLEVEL value is true if the previous program's exit status code is equal to, or greater than, value.

   EXIST filename   is true if specified file exists.

   string1 == string2 true if both strings are same.

   Example: The following command determines the existence of a file named INFO.TXT and displays a message if file is not found in the current directory:

   ```
   IF NOT EXIST INFO.TXT ECHO File not found
   ```

   Here NOT parameter is used before the condition to negate the result of the condition, i.e., ECHO command will be performed when the condition is false.

6. **GOTO:** The GOTO command transfers the execution to a specific place within the batch file. The GOTO command instructs the DOS to process commands starting with the line after the specified label. If the specified label does not exist, the execution of batch file is terminated.

   Syntax: `GOTO [:] label`

   where:

   `label` a character string, may include spaces, but not other separators such as ; or =.

   Example: In the following example the existence of a file REPORT.DOC is checked. If the file exist it is displayed on the display screen, otherwise, a message is displayed on the screen.

   ```
   @ ECHO OFF
   IF NOT EXIST REPORT.DOC GOTO LBL1
   TYPE REPORT.DOC
   GOTO LBL2
   : LBL1
   ECHO REPORT.DOC not found
   : LBL2
   ECHO BATCH EXECUTION IS OVER
   ```

In the above example LBL1 and LBL2 are the labels. Note that any line that start with a colon (:) is ignored during batch processing.

Creating AUTOEXEC.BAT File:
- While working with DOS, one may find that several commands are always performed each time the system starts. For instance, defining the system prompt and setting the path for the most commonly used commands or applications.
- DOS lets you include such commands into a special batch file called AUTOEXEC.BAT. When computer is switched on, DOS searches the root directory of default disk drive for AUTOEXEC.BAT file. If AUTOEXEC.BAT file is found, DOS automatically executes it, by passing the date and time prompt. However, if AUTOEXEC.BAT file is not present, DOS automatically prompts for date and time.
- An example, let's create a AUTOEXEC.BAT file to perform:
  1. DATE command
  2. TIME command, and
  3. Set the PROMPT to display current drive and directory information.
  4. Clear display screen.
- To do so, follow the steps listed below:
  1. Enter the following command
     ```
     A> COPY CON AUTOEXEC.BAT ←
     ```
  2. Include the required commands with appropriate options as below:
     ```
     DATE ←
     TIME ←
     PROMPT $P$G ←
     CLS ←
     ```
  3. Press CONTROL - Z and press ENTER key to copy the commands in step 2 into the AUTOEXEC.BAT file.
- Now, whenever you restart your computer, DOS will automatically locate AUTOEXEC.BAT file and executes it.

3.6 Types (Examples) of Operating Systems

1. Microsoft Windows:
- Microsoft Windows is a series of graphical interface operating systems developed, marketed, and sold by Microsoft.
- Microsoft introduced an operating environment named Windows on November 20, 1985 as a graphical operating system shell for MS-DOS in response to the growing interest in graphical user interfaces (GUI). Microsoft Windows came to dominate the world's personal computer market with over 90% market share, overtaking Mac OS, which had been introduced in 1984.
- As of April 2013, the most recent versions of Windows for personal computers, mobile devices, server computers and embedded devices are respectively Windows 8, Windows Phone 8, Windows Server 2012 and Windows Embedded 8.

Fig. 3.5: Microsoft Window 7

Fig. 3.6: Microsoft Window 8

Advantages of using Windows:
- **(i) Ease of use:** Users familiar with earlier versions of Windows will probably also find the more modern ones easy to work with.
- **(ii) Available software:** There is a huge selection of software available for Windows. This is both due to and the reason for Microsoft's dominance of the world market for PC computer operating systems and office software.
- **(iii) Backwards compatibility:** If you are currently using an older version of Windows and need something more up to date, but you don't want to loose the use of some older programs that are only available for Windows and are critical to your business needs, the chances are good (although not a certainty) that those programs will also work with a newer version of Windows.
- **(iv) Support for new hardware:** Virtually all hardware manufacturers will offer support for a recent version of Windows when they go to market with a new product. Again, Microsoft's dominance of the software market makes Windows impossible for hardware manufacturers to ignore. So, if you run off to a store today any buy some random new piece of computer hardware, you will find that it will probably work with the latest version of Windows.

(v) Plug and Play: As an operating system for the average home user, Windows still has an edge over the competition in the area of Plug & Play support for PC hardware. As long as the right drivers are installed, Windows will usually do a good job at recognising new hardware. Other operating systems also offer Plug & Play functionality, but to a lesser degree and more frequently require manual intervention.

Disadvantages of using Windows:

(i) **High resource requirements:** As opposed to the makers of other operating systems, Microsoft requires its customers to invest the most in their computer hardware: a faster processor (the CPU), more internal memory and a larger hard disk.

(ii) **Virus susceptibility:** The susceptibility of any of Microsoft's operating systems to computer viruses has always been pronounced; nearly all computer viruses target Windows computers and regularly wreak newsworthy havoc.

(iii) **Extortionist prices:** In the past, when Microsoft was asked on numerous occasions why it was raising the price of its Windows licenses yet again, the standard reply was that it was necessary to offset the development costs of their latest version.

(iv) **Poor stability:** For people who are used to dealing with Windows, rebooting and re-installing are such a regular occurance that most don't even give it a second thought. However, that is by no means an excuse for such poor performance: Windows should not freeze up and reboot simply because Word or Internet Explorer was being used.

(v) **Backwards incompatible file formats:** A well-known drawback of using Microsoft applications such as Office (Word, Excel, etc.), is that their file formats are not backwards compatible.

2. Mac Operating System:

- Mac operating system is a series of graphical user interface-based operating systems developed by Apple Inc. for their Macintosh line of computer systems.
- The original version was the integral and unnamed system software first introduced in 1984 with the original Macintosh, and referred to simply as the "System" software. The System was renamed to Mac OS in 1996 with version 7.6. The System is credited with popularizing the graphical user interface concept.
- Mac OS releases have existed in two major series. Up to major revision 9, from 1984 to 2000, it is historically known as Classic Mac OS. Major revision 10 (revisioned minorly, such as 10.0 through 10.9), from 2001 to present, has had the brand name of Mac OS X and now OS X. Both series share a general interface design and some shared application frameworks for compatibility, but also have deeply different architectures.

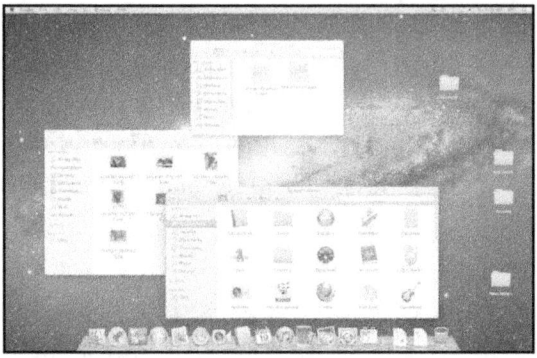

Fig. 3.7

Advantages:
   (i) Easier to use for the non technical.
   (ii) Content creation is its strength.
   (iii) More secure than Windows due to its UNIX base
   (iv) More stable than Windows due to Apple's tighter control over the configuration options and its UNIX base.
   (v) Almost no spyware or virus applications.
   (vi) More powerful than Windows due to its UNIX base.
   (vii) You have almost complete access to the enormous library of free open source applications.

Disadvantages:
   (i) More expensive upfront than other choices.
   (ii) Less support. You have to goto Apple for all your hardware problems.
   (iii) Less hardware choices than Windows.
   (iv) More complex than Windows due to its UNIX base.

3. Linux:
- Linux is an operating system that evolved from a kernel created by Linus Torvalds when he was a student at the University of Helsinki.
- Generally, it is obvious to most people what Linux is. However, both for political and practical reasons, it needs to be explained further. To say that Linux is an operating system means that it's meant to be used as an alternative to other operating systems, Windows, Mac OS, MS-DOS, Solaris and others.
- Linux is not a program like a word processor and is not a set of programs like an office suite. Linux is an interface between computer/server hardware, and the programs which run on it.

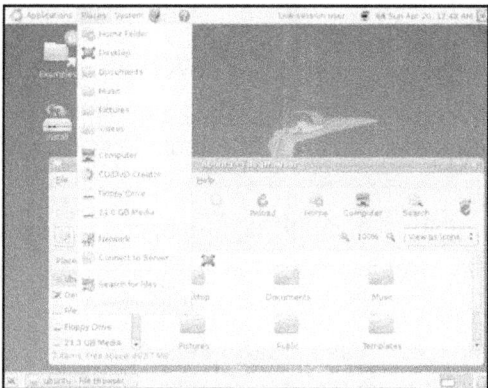

Fig. 3.8

Advantages:

(i) The main advantage of Linux is that it is very flexible and it is highly adaptable for any kind of device.

(ii) Linux is a free open source operating system. So it can be said, there is no license fee for buying or using Linux.

(iii) Easy to use. In the past, they said that Linux is a difficult operating system,and only devoted to the hackers. But now, this opinion is wrong. Linux is easy to use and can be said that's almost as easy as using Windows.

(iv) Almost all applications included in Windows, there have been alternative in Linux. We can access the Open Source website as Alternative to obtain useful fairly complete information about alternative of Windows applications on Linux.

(v) Security is more superior than Windows.

(vi) Linux is relatively stable. Computers that run on UNIX operating system is known to run stable indefinitely. Linux is a variant of UNIX, also inherits this stability.

(vii) Linux is cheaper in cost as compare to windows.

Disadvantages:

(i) The hardware support from certain vendors are not too good to Linux.

(ii) The installation process of the software / application that is not as easy as in Windows. Installing software in Linux will be easier when connected to internet or if you have a CD / DVD repository.

(iii) For the system administrators who are not familiar with Unix-like systems (like Linux), inevitably have to learn more about this. So the requirements to become an administrator is a person who likes to learn new things and continually learning.

(iv) Linux does not have as much of a corporate backing as alternative operating systems.

4. Unix:

- UNIX is an operating system which was first developed in the 1960s, and has been under constant development ever since. By operating system, we mean the suite of programs which make the computer work. It is a stable, multi-user, multi-tasking system for servers, desktops and laptops.

- The Unix system is a multi-user, multi tasking operating system which means that it allows a single or multiprocessor computer to simultaneously execute several programs by one or several users.

- Unix has one or several command interpreters (shell) as well as a great number of commands and many utilities (assembler, compilers for many languages, text processing, email, etc.). Furthermore, it is highly portable, which means that it is possible to implement a Unix system on almost all hardware platforms.

- Currently, Unix systems have a strong foothold in professional and university environments thanks to their stability, their increased level of security and observance of standards, notably in terms of networks.

Advantages:

(i) Full multitasking with protected memory. Multiple users can run multiple programs each at the same time without interfering with each other or crashing the system.

(ii) Very efficient virtual memory, so many programs can run with a modest amount of physical memory.

(iii) Access controls and security. All users must be authenticated by a valid account and password to use the system at all. All files are owned by particular accounts. The owner can decide whether others have read or write access to his files.

(iv) A rich set of small commands and utilities that do specific tasks well -- not cluttered up with lots of special options. Unix is a well-stocked toolbox, not a giant do-it-all Swiss Army Knife.

(v) Ability to string commands and utilities together in unlimited ways to accomplish more complicated tasks -- not limited to preconfigured combinations or menus, as in personal computer systems.

(vi) A powerfully unified file system. Everything is a file: data, programs, and all physical devices. Entire file system appears as a single large tree of nested directories, regardless of how many different physical devices (disks) are included.

(vii) A lean kernel that does the basics for you but doesn't get in the way when you try to do the unusual.

(viii) Available on a wide variety of machines - the most truly portable operating system.

(ix) Optimized for program development, and thus for the unusual circumstances that are the rule in research.

Disadvantages:

(i) The traditional command line shell interface is user hostile -- designed for the programmer, not the casual user.

(ii) Commands often have cryptic names and give very little response to tell the user what they are doing. Much use of special keyboard characters - little typos have unexpected results.

(iii) To use Unix well, you need to understand some of the main design features. Its power comes from knowing how to make commands and programs interact with each other, not just from treating each as a fixed black box.

(iv) Richness of utilities (over 400 standard ones) often overwhelms novices. Documentation is short on examples and tutorials to help you figure out how to *use* the many tools provided to accomplish various kinds of tasks.

5. Android:

- Operating Systems have developed a lot in last 15 years. Starting from black and white phones to recent smart phones or mini computers, mobile OS has come far away.
- Especially for smart phones, Mobile OS has greatly evolved from Palm OS in 1996 to Windows pocket PC in 2000 then to Blackberry OS and Android.
- One of the most widely used mobile OS these days is ANDROID. Android is a software bunch comprising not only operating system but also middleware and key applications.
- Android Inc was founded in Palo Alto of California, U.S. by Andy Rubin, Rich miner, Nick sears and Chris White in 2003. Later Android Inc. was acquired by Google in 2005. After original release there have been number of updates in the original version of Android.

Advantages of Android:

(i) Android is open, because it is linux based open source so it can be developed by anyone.

(ii) Easy access to the Android App Market: Android owners are people who love to learn the phone, with Google's Android App Market you can download applications for free.

(iii) Populist Operating System: Android Phones, different from the iOS is limited to the iphone from Apple, then Android has many manufacturers, with their respective flagship gadget from HTC to Samsung.

(iv) USB full facilities. You can replace the battery, mass storage, DiskDrive, and USB tethering.

(v) Easy in terms of notification: The operating system is able to inform you of a new SMS, Email, or even the latest articles from an RSS Reader.

Android 1.1 Feb 2009	• Support for saving attachments for MMS • MArquee in layouts • API changes
Android 1.5 Cupcake April 2009	• Bluetooth A2DP and AVRCP support • Uploading videos to YouTube and pictures to Picasa
Android 1.6 Donut Sep. 2009	• WVGA screen revolution support • Google free turn by turn support
Android 2.0/1 Eclair Oct. 2009	• HTML5 file support • Microsoft exchange server • Bluetooth 2.1
Android 2.2 Froyo May 2010	• USB tethering and Wi-Fi hotspot functionality • Adobe flash 10.1 support
Android 2.3 Gingerbird Dec. 2010	• Multi touch software keyboard • Support for Extra Large screen sizes and resolution
Android 3.0 Honeycomb May 2011	• Optimized tablet support with a new user interface • 3D desktop • Video chat and Gtalk support

Fig. 3.9: Android versions

(vi) Supports all Google services: Android operating system supports all of google services ranging from Gmail to Google reader. All google services can you have with one operating system, namely Android.

(vii) Install ROM modification: There are many custom ROM that you can use on Android phones, and the guarantee will not harm your device.

Disadvantages of Android:

(i) Connected to the Internet: Android can be said is in need of an active internet connection. At least there should be a GPRS internet connection in your area, so that the device is ready to go online to suit our needs.

(ii) Sometimes slow device company issued an official version of Android your own.

(iii) Android Market is less control of the manager, sometimes there are malware.

(iv) As direct service providers, users sometimes very difficult to connect with the Google.

(v) Sometimes there are ads: because it is easy and free, sometimes often a lot of advertising. In appearance it does not interfere with the performance of the application itself, as it sometimes is in the top or bottom of the application.

(vi) Wasteful Batteries, This is because the OS is a lot of "process" in the background causing the battery quickly drains.

Android applications:

1. Android applications are composed of one or more application components (activities, services, content providers, and broadcast receivers).
2. Each component performs a different role in the overall application behavior, and each one can be activated individually (even by other applications).
3. The manifest file must declare all components in the application and should also declare all application requirements, such as the minimum version of Android required and any hardware configurations required.
4. Non-code application resources (images, strings, layout files, etc.) should include alternatives for different device configurations (such as different strings for different languages).

Questions

1. What is meant by operating system? List its features.
2. State advantages and disadvantages of operation system.
3. Define the following terms:
    (i) File
    (ii) Directory
4. Enlist various characteristics of operating system.
5. What are the types of operating systems? Explain two of them in detail.
6. Write short note on: Batch files.
7. What is DOS? Explain its history in detail.
8. Explain the following terms and state its advantages and disadvantages:
    (i) Linux
    (ii) Unix
    (iii) Android
    (iv) Windows
9. Explain following DOS commands with examples:
    (a) Break
    (b) CHDIR
    (c) MKDIR
    (d) CLS
    (e) COPY
    (i) ECHO
    (j) EDIT
    (k) EXIT
    (l) GOTO
    (m) FORMAT

(f)	DATE	(n)	MORE
(g)	DEBUG	(o)	MOVE
(h)	DIR	(p)	SORT.

10. Describe external commands of DOS.
11. Which different files make up the DOS Operating System?
12. What is file and file organisation? Explain its types.
13. Enlist various types of operating system.

■■■

Chapter **4**...

Introduction to R.D.B.M.S.

Contents ...
- 4.1 Introduction
- 4.2 Introduction to R.D.B.M.S.
  - 4.2.1 Definition
  - 4.2.2 Characteristics
  - 4.2.3 Features
  - 4.2.4 Components of R.D.B.M.S.
  - 4.2.5 Difference between D.B.M.S. and R.D.B.M.S.
  - 4.2.6 Examples of D.B.M.S. and R.D.B.M.S. Softwares
  - 4.2.7 Advantages of R.D.B.M.S.
  - 4.2.8 Disadvantages of R.D.B.M.S.
  - 4.2.9 Keys of R.D.B.M.S.
- 4.3 Normalization
  - 4.3.1 Purpose of Normalization
  - 4.3.2 Steps of Normalization
  - 4.3.3 Advantages
  - 4.3.4 Disadvantages
  - 4.3.5 Normal Forms
    - 4.3.5.1 First Normal Form (1NF)
    - 4.3.5.2 Second Normal Form (2NF)
    - 4.3.5.3 Third Normal Form (3NF)
- 4.4 Entity Relationships
  - 4.4.1 Features
  - 4.4.2 Components
  - 4.4.3 Examples
- 4.5 Use of Simple SQL Commands
  - 4.5.1 Introduction to SQL
  - 4.5.2 Data Types
  - 4.5.3 SQL Languages and their Commands
    - 4.5.3.1 Data Definition Language (DDL)
    - 4.5.3.2 Data Manipulation Language (DML)
    - 4.5.3.3 SQL Queries
- Questions

4.1 Introduction

- Data is the collection of facts stored in the database.
- Data is a representation of facts, concepts, or instructions in a formalized manner suitable for communication, interpretation, or processing by humans or by automated means.
- The term data can be defined as "a set of isolated and unrelated raw facts with an implicit meaning".
- Database is a collection of data.
- A database is a collection of interrelated data that are stored in controllable and retrievable form. The collection represents static information of a group of related data that collectively makes sense. In this way, the information can be stored and retrieved quickly with ease using databases.
- The database is used to store information useful to an organization. Database contains information about one particular enterprise or an organization.
- A database is a collection of related data elements such as, Tables (entities), Columns (fields or attributes), Rows (records).

Definition of Database:

- A database is an application that manages data and allows fast storage and retrieval of that data.

OR

- A database is a data structure that stores organized information.

OR

- A database is a collection of information that is organized so that it can easily be accessed, managed, and updated.
- Databases are organized by fields, records and files. These are described briefly as follows:
    1. **Fields:** It is the smallest unit of the data that has meaning to its users and is also called data item or data element. Name, Address and Telephone number are examples of fields. These are represented in the database by a value.
    2. **Records:** A record is a collection of logically related fields and each field possesses a fixed number of bytes and is of fixed data type.
    3. **Files:** A file is a collection of related records.

Database Management System (D.B.M.S.):

- A Database Management System (D.B.M.S.) is an integrated set of programs used to create and maintain a database.
- A D.B.M.S. is a collection of interrelated data and a set of programs to access those data. The collection of data is usually referred as the database, contains information relevant to an enterprise.

- The primary goal of a D.B.M.S. is to provide a way to store and retrieve the database information in convenient and efficient manner.
- A Database Management System (D.B.M.S.) is a computer program for managing a permanent, self-descriptive repository of data. This repository of data is called a database and is store in one or more files.

Examples:
1. **Manufacturing company:** Which stores product_id, name, price etc., data.
2. **Bank:** Which stores customers banking data such as cust_name, balance, acc_no. etc.
3. **Hospital:** Which stores data such as Dr_name, Patient_name, Admit_date, discharge_date etc.
4. **University:** Which stores data such as college_name, address, courses, staff-details etc.

- Some of the popular relational database management systems include:
    1. Microsoft Access,
    2. Microsoft SQL Server,
    3. MySQL, and
    4. Oracle.

Definition of D.B.M.S.:
- A Database Management System [D.B.M.S.] is a software system that allows user to define, manipulate and process the data in a database, in order to produce meaningful information.

OR

- D.B.M.S. is a collection of data (database) and programs to access that data. The goal of D.B.M.S. is to store, retrieve, and display information (attribute).

OR

- A database management system (D.B.M.S.) is system software used to manage the organization, storage, access, security and integrity of data in a structured database.

Functions of a D.B.M.S.:
1. Data definition - How data is to be stored and organised.
2. Database Creation - Storing data in a defined database
3. Data Retrieval - Querying and reporting
4. Updating - Changing the contents of the database.
5. Programming user facilities for system development.
6. Database revision and restructuring
7. Database Integrity control
8. Performance monitoring.

Applications of D.B.M.S.:
1. **Banking:** For customer information, accounts loans and banking transactions.
2. **Airlines:** For reservations and schedule information. Airlines were among the first to use database in a geographically disturbed manner-terminals situated around the world accessed the central database system through phone lines and other data networks.
3. **Universities:** For student information, course registrations and grades.
4. **Credit card transactions:** For purchases on credit cards and generation of monthly statements.
5. **Telecommunications:** For keeping records of calls made, generating monthly bills, maintaining balances on prepaid calling cards and storing information about the communication networks.
6. **Finance:** For storing information about holdings, sales and purchase of financial instruments such as stocks and bonds.
7. **Sales:** For customer, product and purchase information.
8. **Manufacturing:** For management of supply chain and for tracking production of items in factories, inventories of items in warehouses/stores and orders for items.
9. **Human Resources:** For information about employees, salaries, payroll taxes and benefits and for generation of paychecks.
10. **Web Based Services:** For taking web users feedback, responses, resource sharing etc.
11. **E-commerce:** Integration of heterogeneous information sources (for example, catalogs) for business activity such as online shopping, booking of holiday package, consulting a doctor, etc.
12. **Education:** Schools and colleges use databases for course registration, result, and other information.

4.2 Introduction to R.D.B.M.S.

- R.D.B.M.S. stands for **R**elational **DataB**ase **M**anagement **S**ystem.
- R.D.B.M.S. is the basis for SQL, and for all modern database systems like MS SQL Server, IBM DB2, Oracle, MySQL, and Microsoft Access.
- A Relational database management system (R.D.B.M.S.) is a database management system (D.B.M.S.) that is based on the relational model as introduced by E. F. Codd.

4.2.1 Definition

- A simple definition of R.D.B.M.S. is "a database management system where the data are organized as tables of data values and all the operations on the data work on the these tables".

OR

- A relational database management system is a database management system used to manage relational databases.

OR

- R.D.B.M.S. is a type of database management system (D.B.M.S.) that stores data in the form of related tables.

4.2.2 Characteristics

- Various characteristics of R.D.B.M.S. are:
    1. **Data abstraction:** Relational abstraction enhances program-data independence.
    2. **Self-describing data:** Metadata describing structure of data stored together with data.
    3. **Concurrency:** Supporting shared concurrent access (transactions).
    4. **Support for multiple views:** External users can be provided with different views of the data.
    5. **Security:** Privacy/Confidentiality, Integrity, Availability, Accountability.

4.2.3 Features

- Features of R.D.B.M.S. are listed below:
    1. Provides data to be stored in tables.
    2. Persists data in the form of rows and columns.
    3. Provides facility primary key, to uniquely identify the rows.
    4. Creates indexes for quicker data retrieval.
    5. Provides a virtual table creation in which sensitive data can be stored and simplified query can be applied, (views).
    6. Sharing a common column in two or more tables (primary key and foreign key).
    7. Provides multi user accessibility that can be controlled by individual users.

4.2.4 Components of R.D.B.M.S

- Various components of R.D.B.M.S. are as shown in Fig. 4.1.

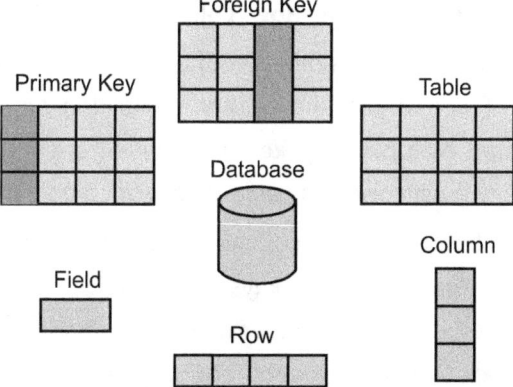

Fig. 4.1: Relational database components

- A **Table** is a basic storage structure of an R.D.B.M.S. and consists of columns and rows. A table represents an entity. For example, the E_DEPT table stores information about the departments of an organization.

- A record, also called a row of data, is each individual entry that exists in a table. A **Row** is a combination of column values in a table and is identified by a primary key. Rows are also known as **records**. For example, a row in the table E_DEPT contains information about one department.
- A column is a vertical entity in a table that contains all information associated with a specific field in a table. A **Column** is a collection of one type of data in a table. Columns represent the attributes of an object. Each column has a column name and contains values that are bound by the same type and size. For example, a column in the table E_DEPT specifies the names of the departments in the organization.
- Every table is broken up into smaller entities called fields. A **Field** is an intersection of a row and a column. A field contains one data value. If there is no data in the field, the field is said to contain a NULL value.

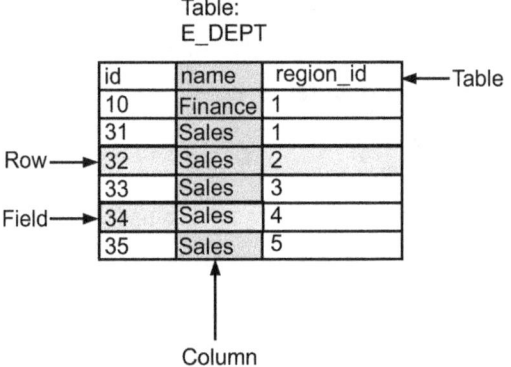

Fig. 4.2: Table, Row, Column and Field

- A **Primary key** is a column or a combination of columns that is used to uniquely identify each row in a table. For example, the column containing department numbers in the E_DEPT table is created as a **primary key** and therefore, every department number is different. A primary key must contain a value. It cannot contain a NULL value.
- A **Foreign key** is a column or set of columns that refers to a primary key in the same table or another table. You use foreign keys to establish principle connections between, or within, tables. A foreign key must either match a primary key or else be NULL. Rows are connected logically when required. The logical connections are based upon conditions that define a relationship between corresponding values, typically between a primary key and a matching foreign key. This relational method of linking provides great flexibility as it is independent of physical links between records.

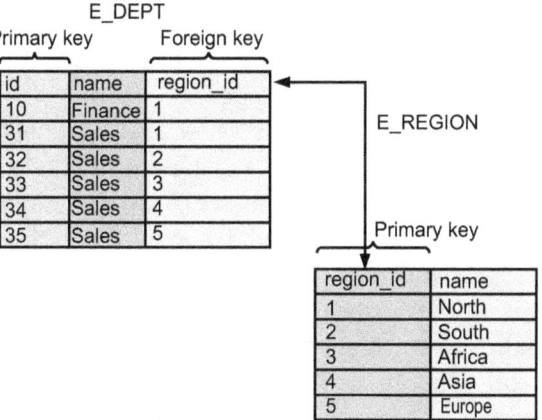

Fig. 4.3: Primary and Foreign key

4.2.5 Difference between D.B.M.S. and R.D.B.M.S.

D.B.M.S.	R.D.B.M.S.
1. D.B.M.S. stands for DataBase Management System.	1. R.D.B.M.S. stands for Relational DataBase Management System.
2. In D.B.M.S. no relationship concept.	2. It is used to establish the relationship concept between two database objects, i.e. tables.
3. It supports single user only.	3. It supports multiple users.
4. It treats Data as files internally.	4. It treats data as Tables internally.
5. It supports 3 rules of E.F. Codd out off 12 rules.	5. It supports minimum 6 rules of E.F. Codd.
6. It requires low software and hardware requirements.	6. It requires high softwares and hardware requirements.
7. D.B.M.S. is used for simpler business applications.	7. R.D.B.M.S. is used for more complex applications.
8. In D.B.M.S. normalization process will not be present.	8. R.D.B.M.S. fully supports normalization.
9. FoxPro, IMS are examples.	9. SQL-Server, Oracle are examples.

4.2.6 Examples of D.B.M.S. and R.D.B.M.S. Softwares

- Various D.B.M.S. and R.D.B.M.S. softwares are listed below:
    1. **FoxPro:** FoxPro is a database management system. It means that using this software we can handle the data in different way.
    2. **Microsoft Access:** Microsoft Access is a database management system from Microsoft that combines the relational Microsoft Jet Database Engine with a graphical user interface and software-development tools.

3. **MySQL:** MySQL is a fast, easy-to-use R.D.B.M.S. used being used for many small and big businesses. MySQL handles a large subset of the functionality of the most expensive and powerful database packages.,
4. **Microsoft SQL Server:** Microsoft SQL Server is a relational database management system developed by Microsoft. As a database, it is a software product whose primary function is to store and retrieve data as requested by other software applications, be it those on the same computer or those running on another computer across a network (including the Internet).
5. **Oracle:** Oracle is a fourth generation relational database management system. In general, a database management system (D.B.M.S.) must be able to reliably manage a large amount of data in a multi-user environment so that many users can concurrently access the same data. All this must be accomplished while delivering high performance to the users of the database.
6. **FileMaker Pro:** FileMaker Pro is easy to use database software for the Mac, Windows and other platforms. It is particularly useful to Mac users because the Access database program is not part of Microsoft Office for the Mac.
7. **IBM DB2:** IBM's DB2 is a relational database management system, DB2 is a collection of computer software programs that perform this particular type of task. DB2 is designed to make the storage and analysis of data easier.
8. **Ingres:** Ingres is open source relational database management system that helps in reducing down the various IT costs and on the other hand provides the class features that can be expected from the high level database.
9. **SQlite:** SQLite is an embedded relational database engine. Its developers call it a self-contained, serverless, zero-configuration and transactional SQL database engine. SQLite is used in Solaris 10 and Mac OS operating systems, iPhone or Skype.

4.2.7 Advantages of R.D.B.M.S.

- Advantages of R.D.B.M.S. are listed below:
    1. **Data Structure:** The table format is simple and easy for database users to understand and use. R.D.B.M.S.s provide data access using a natural structure and organization of the data. Database queries can search any column for matching entries.
    2. **Multi-User Access:** R.D.B.M.S.s allow multiple database users to access a database simultaneously. Built-in locking and transactions management functionality allow users to access data as it is being changed, prevents collisions between two users updating the data, and keeps users from accessing partially updated records.
    3. **Privileges:** Authorization and privilege control features in an R.D.B.M.S. allow the database administrator to restrict access to authorized users, and grant privileges to individual users based on the types of database tasks they need to perform. Authorization can be defined based on the remote client IP address in combination with user authorization, restricting access to specific external computer systems.

4. **Network Access:** R.D.B.M.S. provide access to the database through a server daemon, a specialized software program that listens for requests on a network, and allows database clients to connect to and use the database. Users do not need to be able to log in to the physical computer system to use the database, providing convenience for the users and a layer of security for the database. Network access allows developers to build desktop tools and Web applications to interact with databases.

5. **Speed:** The relational database model is not the fastest data structure. R.D.B.M.S. advantages, such as simplicity, make the slower speed a fair trade-off. Optimizations built into an R.D.B.M.S. and the design of the databases, enhance performance, allowing R.D.B.M.S. to perform more than fast enough for most applications and data sets. Improvements in technology, increasing processor speeds and decreasing memory and storage costs allow systems administrators to build incredibly fast systems that can overcome any database performance shortcomings.

6. **Maintenance:** R.D.B.M.S. feature maintenance utilities that provide database administrators with tools to easily maintain, test, repair and back up the databases housed in the system. Many of the functions can be automated using built-in automation in the R.D.B.M.S., or automation tools available on the operating system.

7. **Language:** R.D.B.M.S. support a generic language called "Structured Query Language" (SQL). The SQL syntax is simple, and the language uses standard English language keywords and phrasing, making it fairly intuitive and easy to learn. Many R.D.B.M.S. add non-SQL, database-specific keywords, functions and features to the SQL language

8. **Consistency:** Data is guarantees to be consistent. Irrespective of the number of Custom Web Design simultaneously accessing it. An R.D.B.M.S. always implements suitable locking mechanisms to prevent data inconsistency. A transaction either goes through fully or not at all i.e. it is either "committed "or "rolled back".

9. **Recoverability:** Irrespective of the type of failure, it is always possible to recover the data base upto the most recent consistent state. This means that if recovery measures are correctly implemented you would not lose all days work. And thus no need to reenter.

10. **Distributability:** Database can be distributed in more than one physical location. Irrespective of this, application's view of the database remains same as though it is in a single location. Applications need not undergo any change if the distribution of the data changes.

11. **Support for IV (4th) generation languages:** R.D.B.M.S. support 4GL. Today, there is even a standard 4GL in the structured query Language (SQL) form. The main difference between 4GLs and 3GLs is that in the former the user needs to specify what is required and not how it has to be done.

4.2.8 Disadvantages of R.D.B.M.S.

- R.D.B.M.S. disadvantages are listed below:
    1. Possibility of poor design and implementation.
    2. Relational databases do not have enough storage area to handle data such as images, digital and audio/video.
    3. The requirement that information must be in tables where relationships between entities are defined by values.
    4. **Cost:** One disadvantage of relational databases is the expensive of setting up and maintaining the database system. In order to set up a relational database, you generally need to purchase special software so it increases cost
    5. **Abundance of Information:** Advances in the complexity of information cause another drawback to relational databases. Relational databases are made for organizing data by common characteristics. Complex images, numbers, designs and multimedia products defy easy categorization leading the way for a new type of database called object-relational database management systems. These systems are designed to handle the more complex applications and have the ability to be scalable.
    6. **Structured Limits:** Some relational databases have limits on field lengths. When you design the database, you have to specify the amount of data you can fit into a field. Some names or search queries are shorter than the actual, and this can lead to data loss.
    7. **Isolated Databases:** Complex relational database systems can lead to these databases becoming "islands of information" where the information cannot be shared easily from one large system to another. Often, with big firms or institutions, you find relational databases grew in separate divisions differently.

4.2.9 Keys of R.D.B.M.S.

- Every table must have some columns or combination of columns which uniquely identify each row in the table. For that we require a key.
- A key is simply a field used to identify a record. In other words, a key is relation of subset of attributes with following properties:
    1. The value of key is unique for each tuple.
    2. No data redundancy.

1. Primary Key:

- The candidate key that you choose to identify each row uniquely is called the primary key. In the table Employee, if you choose Empid# to identify rows uniquely, Empid# is the primary key.

Employee

Empid#	Empname	Salary
1437	Kalaiselvi	5000
1337	Meena	5000
1137	Diana	5000

2. Candidate Key:

- The attribute which posses the unique identification property in a relation is called as candidate key.
- We can define "an attribute in a table that uniquely identifies a row is called a candidate key".
- There can be more than one candidate keys in a relation. Candidate key should have following things:

    (a) It must be unique

    (b) A candidate key's value must exist. It cannot be null.

    (c) The value of the candidate key must be stable. It's value cannot change outside the control of the system. In customer table, various employees were working and having unique identification number called as social security number (SSN)

Customer name	SSN	Basic
John	001-256	₹ 14,000
Martin	005-123	₹ 2,000
Paster	008-200	₹ 1,000
Mary	101-401	₹ 18,000
Johns	102-030	₹ 48,000

Candidate key

3. Alternate Key:

- A candidate key that is not chosen as a primary key is an alternate key. In the table Purchase If you choose Serial# as the primary key, Itemcode is the alternate key. It is important that you understand that a primary key is the only sure way to identify the rows of a table.
- Hence, an alternate key may have the value NULL. A NULL value is not to be permitted in a primary key since it would be difficult to uniquely identify rows containing NULL values.

Purchase

Serial#	Itemcode	Price
01437	1454	500
01438	1667	500
01439	1777	500

4. Composite Key:

- In certain tables, a single attribute cannot be used to identify rows uniquely and a combination of two or more attributes is used as a primary key. Such keys are called composite keys.
- Consider the following table, customer, which is used to maintain the purchase made by various customers.

Customers

Custcode	Productcode	Quantity
c0147	P454	50
c0148	P777	55
c0147	P777	20

- You can see all values are not unique for any of the attributes. However, a combination of Custcode and Productcode results in all unique values. Hence, the combination can be used as a composite primary key.

5. Foreign Key:

- If any key in a given relation has reference to the value of a primary key of some other relation then it is called as foreign key.
- Foreign key can have duplicate values it is used to search a record from two relations.

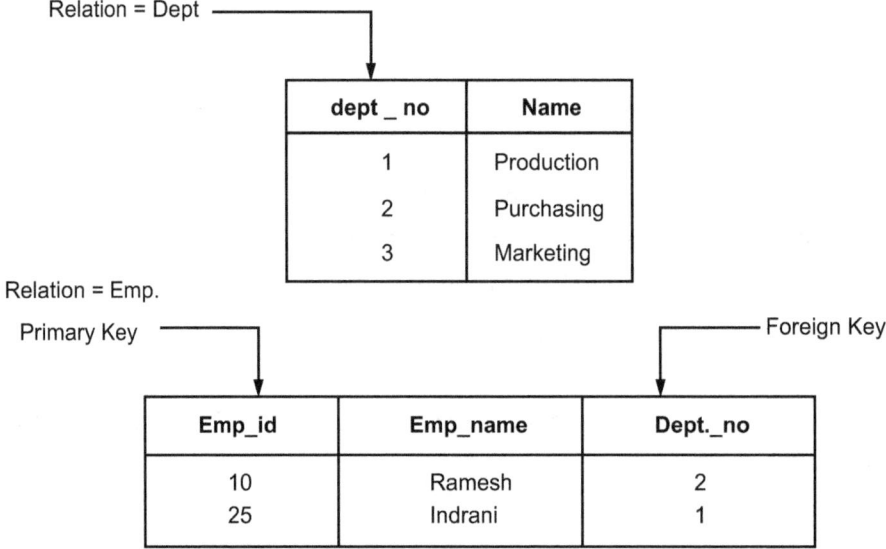

6. Super Key:

- Super key is a set of one or more attributes which taken collectively allows us to identify uniquely an entity in the entity set.

Integrity Rules:

- Data integrity ensures that the data entered into the database by the user is checked for its correctness as is the data that is supposed to go into the database.
- Thus, the data gets automatically validated when it is entered as per the instructions or commands of the designer and by this way R.D.B.M.S. ensures that the application is of a high degree of data security and integrity.
- R.D.B.M.S. ensures data integrity through automatic validation of data using integrity constraints. The integrity constraints are non-procedural constructs and by just specifying those, the designer can automate the validation process at the time of data entry.
- Popular integrity constraints are NOT NULL, UNIQUE, PRIMARY KEY, FOREIGN KEY and CHECK constraints.
- Data integrity falls into the following categories:
    1. **Entity integrity:** Entity integrity ensures that each row can be uniquely identified by an attribute called the primary key. The primary key cannot have a NULL value.
    2. **Domain integrity:** Domain integrity refers to the range of valid entries for a given column. It ensures that there are only valid entries in the column.
    3. **Referential integrity:** Referential integrity ensures that for every value of a foreign key, there is matching value of the primary key.

4.3 Normalization

- Data normalization is a process of refining database structures to improve the speed at which data can be accessed and to increase database integrity.
- Normalization is the process of efficiently organizing data in a database.
- There are two goals of the normalization process:
    1. Eliminating redundant data (for example, storing the same data in more than one table) and
    2. Ensuring data dependencies.
- Normalization is a technique that can be applied to data to ensure that a set of tables is derived that contains no redundant data.
- Normalization is a process of simplifying the relationship between data elements in a record. It is the transformation of complex data stores to a set of smaller, stable data structures.
- Normalized data structures are simpler, more stable and are easier to maintain. Normalization can therefore be defined as a process of simplifying the relationship between data elements in a record.

4.3.1 Purpose of Normalization

- We normalize the relational database management system because of the following reasons:

    1. To structure the data so that there is no repetition of data, this helps in saving space.
    2. To permit simple retrieval of data in response to query and report requests.
    3. To simplify the maintenance of the data through updates, insertions and deletions.
    4. To reduce the need to restructure or reorganize data when new application requirements arise.
    5. Minimize data redundancy i.e. no unnecessarily duplication of data.
    6. To make database structure flexible i.e. it should be possible to add new data values and rows without reorganizing the database structure.
    7. Data should be consistent throughout the database i.e. it should not suffer from following anomalies.

        (i) **Insert Anomaly:** Due to lack of data i.e., all the data available for insertion such that null values in keys should be avoided. This kind of anomaly can seriously damage a database

        (ii) **Update Anomaly:** It is due to data redundancy i.e. multiple occurrences of same values in a column. This can lead to inefficiency.

        (iii) **Deletion Anomaly:** It leads to loss of data for rows that are not stored else where. It could result in loss of vital data.

4.3.2 Steps of Normalization

- Systems analysts should be familiar with the steps in normalization, since this process can improve the quality of design for an application.
- Starting with a data store developed for a data dictionary the analyst normalizes a data structure in three steps. Each step involves an important procedure to simplify the data structure.
- It consists of basic three steps:

    1. First Normal form, which decomposes all data, groups into two-dimensional records.
    2. Second Normal Form, which eliminates do not fully depend on the primary key of the record.
    3. Third Normal Form, which eliminates any relationships that, contain transitive dependencies.

- Fig. 4.4 shows steps of normalization.

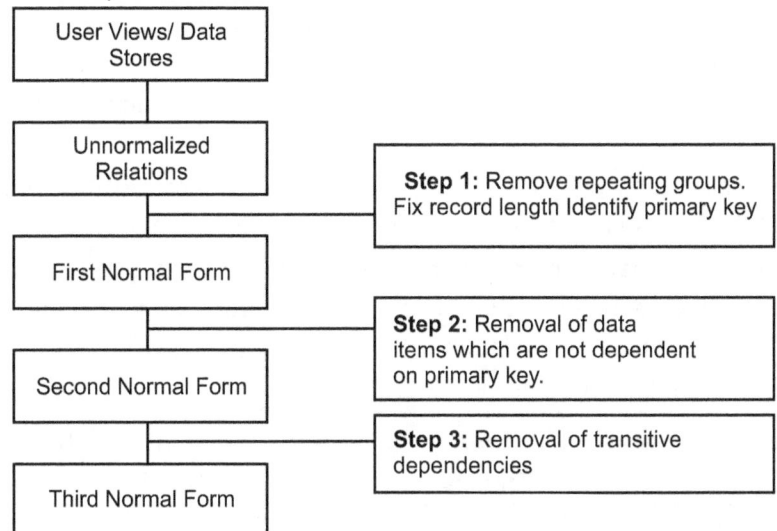

Fig. 4.4: Steps of normalization

4.3.3 Advantages
- Advantages of normalization are listed below:
    1. Avoids data modification (INSERT/DELETE/UPDATE) anomalies
    2. Greater flexibility in getting the expected data in atomic granular
    3. Fewer null values and less opportunity for inconsistency
    4. A better handle on database security
    5. Increased storage efficiency
    6. Easier to maintain data structure i.e. it is easy to perform operations and complex queries can be easily handled.
    7. Normalization minimizes data duplication.

4.3.4 Disadvantages
- Disadvantages of normalization are listed below:
    1. Requires much more CPU, memory, and I/O to process thus normalized data gives reduced database performance
    2. Requires more joins to get the desired result.
    3. Maintenance overhead. The higher the level of normalization, the greater the number of tables in the database.

4.3.5 Normal Forms
4.3.5.1 First Normal Form (1NF)
- **Definition:** "A relation is said to be in 1NF if the values in the domain of each attribute of the relation are atomic i.e. only one value associated with each attribute. A database system is in 1NF if every relation in the system is in 1NF".

- The first rule of data normalization states that you should make a separate table for each set of related columns and give each table a primary key. Databases that hold to this first rule of normalization are said to be in the First Normal Form (1NF).
- The first rule of data normalization is to eliminate repeating groups of data in a data table.
- The basic improvement the analyst should make to such a record structure is to design the record structure so that all records in the file are of fixed length.
- A repeating group, that is, the reoccurrence of a data item or group of data items within a record, is actually another relation. This is removed from the record and treated as an additional record structure, or relation.
- First Normal Form -Employee Record:

Emp. No.	Name	Emp. Details	Salary	Bank Details	Income Tax Details
A01	Jose				
A02	Joseph				

Emp. No.	MMYY	Net Paid
A01	195	3600
A01	196	3800
A01	197	3600
A01	198	3500
A02	199	6000

- As mentioned above the first normal form is carried out by removing the repeating group. In this case we remove the Annual salary earned items and include them in anew file or relation called Annual Salary earned record. Employee number is still the primary key in the employee record. A combination of employee number and MMYY is the primary key in the annual salary earned record.
- We thus form two record structures of fixed length: Employee record consisting of Employee no., employee name, employee details (department code, grade, date of joining, exit code and exit date), bank details (bank c ode, bank name, address, employees A/C no).
- Annual salary earned record consisting of - employee no., month & year (MMYY) and net paid.

- In the attributes mentioned above, the firstNormal form must not contain repeated groups. Here the repeated groups are products. When the Invoice Attribute is in 1st Normal Form, the tables would be:

Invoice_Master	Invoice_Item
Invoice_code	**Invoice_No**
Inv_date	**item_code**
Order_code	ORD_qty
Order_qty	Cust
Cust_code	Ord_value
Cust_name	description
Address	
Invoice_value	

- The attributes that are indicated as bold denote primary key.

4.3.5.2 Second Normal Form (2NF)

- **Definition:** "A relation r is in Second Normal Form (2NF) if and only if it is in 1NF and every non-key attribute (non prime attribute) is fully functionally dependent on the primary key".
- The second rule of data normalization states that if a column depends only on part of a multivalued key, you remove it to a separate table.
- The second normal form is achieved when every data item in a record that is not dependent on the primary key of the record should be removed and used to forma separate relation.
- The PF department ensures that only one employee in the state is assigned a specific PF number. This is called a one-to-one relation. The PF number uniquely identifies a specific employee; an employee is associated with one and only one PF number.
- Thus, if you know the Employee no., you can determine the PF number. This is functional dependency. Therefore a data item is functionally dependant if its value is uniquely associated with a specific data item.
- **Employee Record:**

Emp. No.	Name	Emp. Details	Salary	A/c. No.	Bank Code	Income Tax Details
A01	Jose			SB2152	01	
A02	Joseph			SB3212	03	

Annual Safety Earned Record

Emp. No.	MMYY	Net Paid
A01	195	3600
A01	196	3800
A01	197	3600
A01	198	3500
A02	199	6000

Bank Record

Code	Name	Address
01	SBI	Chennai
03	Canara	Madurai

- The three record structures that are created are:
  1. **Employee record** consisting of: _Employee no., employee name employee details (department code, grade, date of joining, exit code and exit date), bank details (bank code, bank name, address, employees A/C no.)
  2. **Annual salary earned record** consisting of - employee no., month & year (MMYY) and net paid
  3. **Bank record** consisting of: bank c ode, bank name and bank address. All the attributes of this relation are **fully dependent** on Bank c ode.
- A table in Second Normal Form must indicate that all the attributes, which are not dependent of primary key, must be removed. The table in Second Normal Form will be

Invoice_Master	Invoice_Item	Item_Master
Invoice_code	Invoice_No	Item_code
Inv_date	Item_code	description
Order_code	Rate	
Cust_code	Ord_value	
Cust_name		
Address		
Invoice_value		

- There are no changes in the Invoice details.

4.3.5.3 Third Normal Form (3NF)

- "A relation is in third normal for (3NF) if and only if it is in 2NF and every nonkey attribute (non prime attribute) is non-transitively dependent dependent on the primary key. Transitivity means if $\alpha \to \beta$ holds and $\beta \to \gamma$ holds, then $\alpha \to \gamma$ holds. No transitive dependencies implies no mutual dependencies i.e. none of the attributes are functionally dependent on any combination of the other attributes. Such independence implies that each can be updated independently of all the rest.

- The third rule of data normalization states that if a column does not fully describe the index key, that column should be moved to a separate table. In other words, if the columns in your table do not really need to be in this table, they probably need to be somewhere else. Databases that follow this rule are known to be in the Third Normal Form (3NF) i.e. Eliminate Columns Not Dependent on the Primary Key.
- The third normal form indicates that there must not be any dependency between non-key attributes. Resolving the above we get

Invoice_Master	Invoice_Item	Item_Master
Invoice_code	Invoice_No	Item_code
Inv_date	Item_code	description rate
Order_code	description	
Invoice_value	Ord_qty	
	Ord_value	

Order_Cust	Customer_Master
Order_code	cust_code
Cust_code	cust_name
Order_date	address

- Third normal form is achieved when transitive dependencies are removed from a record design. Some of the non-key attributes are dependent not only on the primary key but also on a non-key attribute. This is referred to as a transitive dependency.

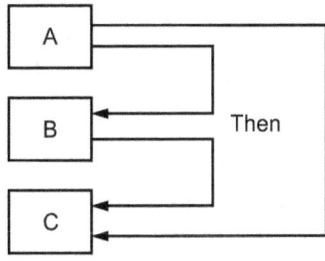

Fig. 4.5

- Conversion to third normal form removes transitive dependence by splitting the relation into two relations.

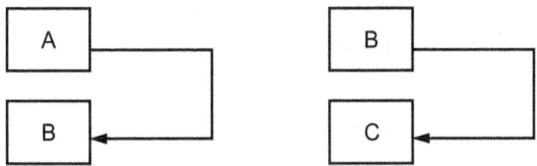

Fig. 4.6

- Reason for concern. When there is a transitive dependence, deleting A will cause deletion of B and C as well.
    - A, B and C are three data items in a record.
    - If C is functionally dependent on B and.
    - B is functionally dependent on A.
    - Then C is functionally dependent on A.
    - Therefore, a transitive dependency exists.
- There are no transitive dependencies, so it is also in third normal form.

4.4 Entity Relationships

- Entity Relationship (E–R) modeling is a design tool. It is a graphical representation of the database system which provides a high-level conceptual data model and supports the user's perception of the data.
- The overall logical structure of a database can be expressed graphically by an E–R diagram.

4.4.1 Features

1. The E-R diagram used for representing E-R Model can be easily converted into Relations (tables) in Relational Model.
2. The E-R Model is used for the purpose of good database design by the database developer so to use that data model in various D.B.M.S..
3. It is helpful as a problem decomposition tool as it shows the entities and the relationship between those entities.
4. It is inherently an iterative process. On later modifications, the entities can be inserted into this model.
5. It is very simple and easy to understand by various types of users and designers because specific standards are used for their representation.

4.4.2 Components

- The overall logical structure of a database can be expressed graphically by an E–R diagram, which is built up from the following components.
    1. **Rectangles** (▭) : Which represents entity sets
    2. **Ellipse** (⬭) : Which represents attributes
    3. **Diamonds** (◇) : Which represents relationships among entity sets.
    4. **Lines** (─────) : Which link attributes to entity sets and entity sets to relationships.

1. **Entities:**
- An entity is any object in the system that we want to model and store information about database.
- Individual objects are called entities. An entity instance is a specific value of an entity.
- Entities are the basic building blocks of relational database design.
- An entity defines any person, place, thing or concept for which data will be collected. Some examples of entities include the following:
    - **Person**: student, teacher
    - **Place:** classroom, building
    - **Thing:** computer, lab equipment
- Groups of the same type of objects are called entity types or entity sets.
- Entities are represented by rectangles.

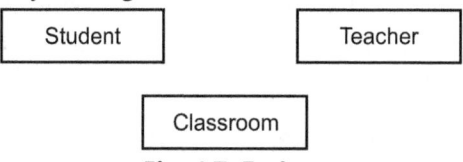

Fig. 4.7: Entity

- There are two types of entities ; weak and strong entity.

2. **Entity set:**
- Entity set is a set of entities of the same type that share the same properties or attributes.
- Entity sets need not be disjoint.
- The set of all students is defined as entity set student.

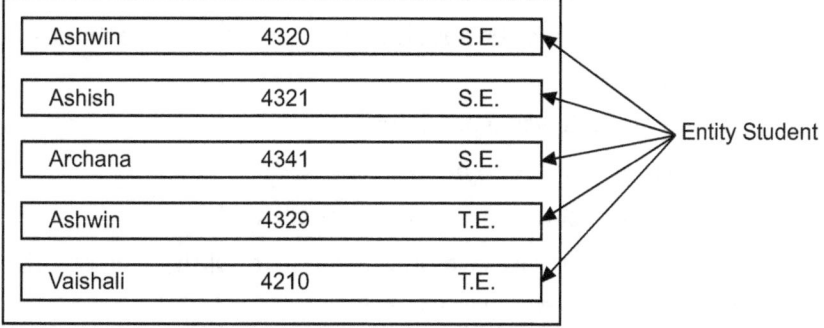

Student entity set

Fig. 4.8: Entity set

3. **Attributes:**
- All the data relating to an entity is held in its attributes.
- An attribute is a property of an entity.
- Each attribute can have any value from its domain.

- An attribute is a property of an entity that differential if from other entities and provides information about the entity. An attribute type is a property of an entity type.
- For example, the attributes of the entity Student are Course Name, Course Number and Gender. In an ER diagram, you represent attributes as ellipses and label them with the name of the attribute.

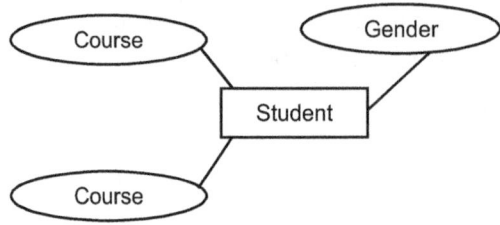

Fig. 4.9: Attributes

- The second major data-modelling concept that you must understand is that of attributes.
- Attributes are additional characteristics or information defined for an entity.
- Each entity within an entity type:
    o May have any number of attributes.
    o Can have different attribute values than that in any other entity.
- Have the same number of attributes. Attributes can be:

(i) Simple and composite attribute:
   o Simple attribute that consist of a single atomic value.
   o A composite attribute is an attribute that can be further subdivided. For example the attribute ADDRESS can be subdivided into street, city, state and zip code.
   o A simple attribute cannot be subdivided. For example, the attribute age, sex, etc. are simple attributes.
   o In composite attribute value not atomic.

(ii) Single valued and multi valued attributes:
   o A single valued attribute can have only a single value.
   o For example, a person can have only one 'date of birth', 'age' etc. That is a single valued attribute can have only single value.
   o But it can be simple or composite attribute. That is 'date of birth' is a composite attribute, 'age' is a simple attribute. But both are single valued attributes.
   o Multivalued attribute can have multiple values for instance a person may have multiple phone numbers, multiple degrees etc.
   o Multivalued attributes are shown by a double line connecting to the entity in the E-R diagram.

(iii) Derived attributes:

- The value for the derived attribute is derived from the stored attribute.
- For example, 'Date of birth' of a person is a stored attributed. The value for the attribute 'AGE' can be derived by subtracting the 'Date of Birth' (DOB) from the current date. Stored attribute supplies a value to the related attribute.
- An attribute that's value is derived from a stored attribute is called as derived attribute. Example: age, and its value is derived from the stored attribute Date of Birth.

(iv) Null attribute:

- Null value is used when an entity does not have a value for an attribute.
- Null can also designate that an attribute is unknown i.e. missing or not known.
- All attributes are shown in Fig. 4.10.

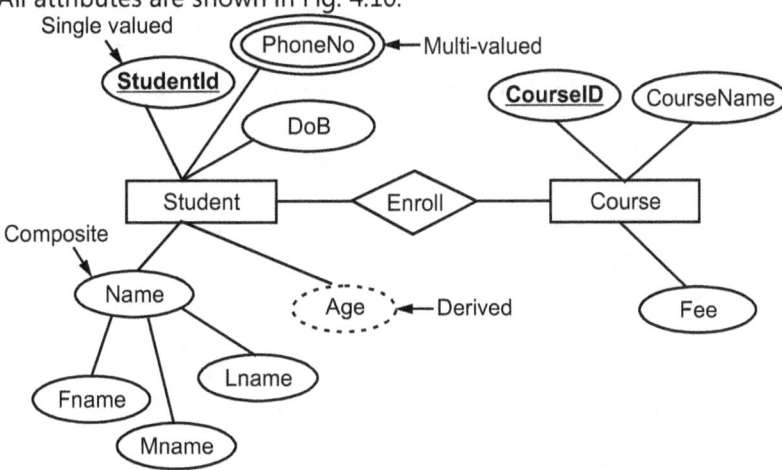

Fig. 4.10: E-R diagram with types of attributes

4. Weak and Strong Entity Sets:

- The entity sets that does not have sufficient attributes to define the primary key are called weak entity sets.
- The entity sets that have sufficient attributes to define the primary key are called strong entity sets.
- In such case the weak entity sets has to be dependent on strong entity sets.
- Strong entity is also called identifying or owner entity set. The relationship that is associating weak entity set with strong entity set is called identifying relationship.
- The identifying relationship is many to one from the weak entity set to the identifying entity set and the sharing of the weak entity set in the relationship is total.
- The weak entity does not have any primary key but a discriminator (set of attributes) in weak entity set is used to distinguish among the rows.
- The primary key of weak entity set is combination of primary key of strong entity set and discriminator of weak entity set.

- The weak entity is denoted by double rectangle ▭.
- The identifying relationship is denoted by double diamond ◇.
- The total participation of weak entity set is denoted by double line ══.
- The discriminator is underlined by dash line - - - - - - - -.
- For example, consider the relation loan (loan no, amount) and payment (pno, pdate, pamt).

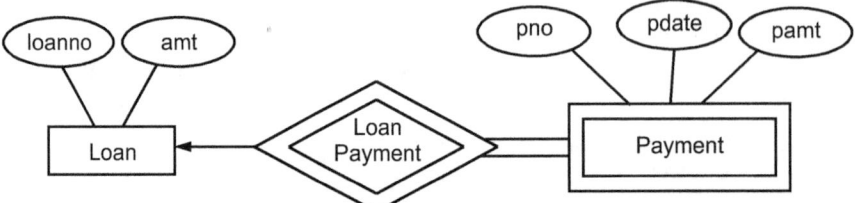

Fig. 4.11: E-R diagram with a weak entity set

5. **Keys:**
- A key is a data item that allows us to uniquely identify individual occurrences or an entity type.
- A candidate key is an attribute or set of attributes that uniquely identifies individual occurrences or an entity type.
- An entity type may have one or more possible candidate keys, the one which is selected is known as the **primary key**.
- A composite key is a candidate key that consists of two or more attributes.
- The name of each primary key attribute is underlined.

6. **Relationships:**
- A relationship type is a meaningful association between entity types.
- A relationship is an association of entities where the association includes one entity from each participating entity type.
- Relationship types are represented on the E-R diagram by a series of lines.
- The relationship is placed inside a diamond, For example, managers manage employees:

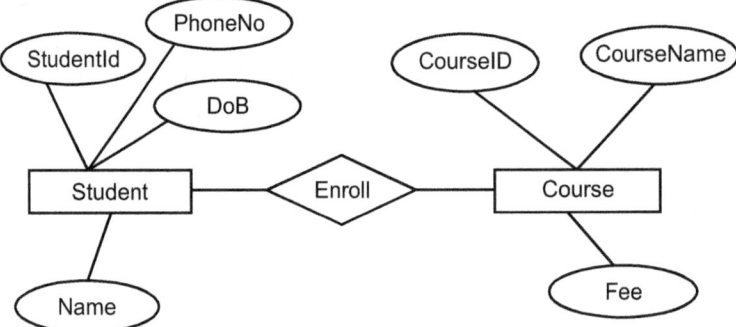

Fig. 4.12: Notation for relationships

7. Relationship Set:
- It is a set of relationships of same type.
- Formally, it is mathematical relation on n ≥ 2 (possibly non distinct) entity sets.
  If $E_1, E_2, ..., E_n$ are entity sets, then a relationship set R is a subset of $\{(e_1, e_2, ..., e_n) \mid e_1 \in E_1, e_2 \in E_2, e_n \in E_n\}$ where $(e_1, e_2, ..., e_n)$ is a relationship.
  Consider the following two entity sets.
  Account = {acc_no., balance, type}
  Customer = {name, city, social_security}

Cust_Acc Relationship Set

1721	10,000	SA	Ajay	Pune	234-1795
3251	25,000	CA	Ankita	Mumbai	174-2932
6220	50,200	RA	Nikita	Aurangabad	281-3942
3512	30,020	SA	Raj	Nagpur	321-4210
4210	10,000	CA			

Fig. 4.13: Relationship Set

- Binary Relationship Set relates two entity sets. n-ary Relationship Set relates 'n' number of entity sets. n-ary relationship set can be replaced by binary relationship set.

8. Degree of a Relationship:
- The number of participating entities in a relationship is known as the degree of the relationship.
- If there are two entity types involved it is a binary relationship type as shown in Fig. 4.14.

Fig. 4.14: Binary Relationships

- If there are three entity types involved it is a ternary relationship type as shown in Fig. 4.15.

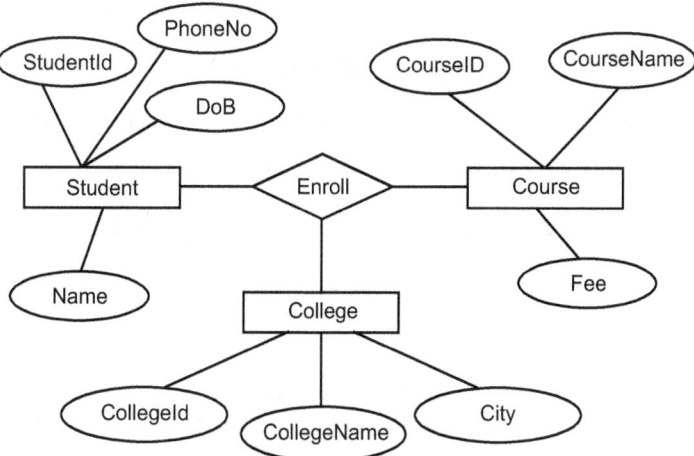

Fig. 4.15: Ternary relationship

- It is possible to have a n-ary relationship (For example, quaternary or unary).
- Unary relationships are also known as a recursive relationship as shown in Fig. 4.16.

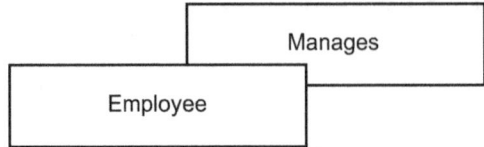

Fig. 4.16: Recursive relationship

- It is a relationship where the same entity participates more than once, in different roles.
- In the example above we are saying that employees are managed by employees.
- If we wanted more information about who manages whom, we could introduce a second entity type called manager.

9. **Mapping Cardinalities:**

- Mapping cardinality or cardinality ratio expresses the number of entities to which another entity can be associated via a relationship set. Mapping cardinalities are most useful in describing binary relationship sets.

    1. **One-to-One:** An entity in 'A' is associated with at most one entity in 'B' and an entity in 'B' is associated with at most one entity in 'A'.

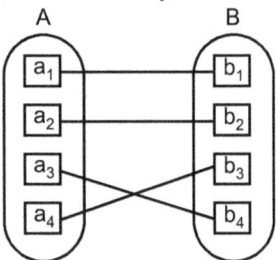

Fig. 4.17: One-to-One

One Customer has an account in the bank and account belongs to only one customer, so it is a one to one (1:1) relationship as shown in Fig. 4.18.

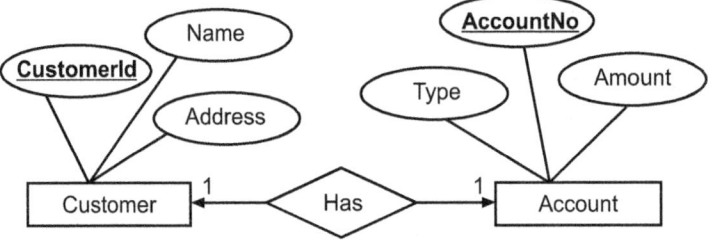

Fig. 4.18: One-to-one relationship example

2. **One-to-Many:** An entity in 'A' is associated with any number of entities in 'B'. An entity in 'B' however, can be associated with at most one entity in 'A'.

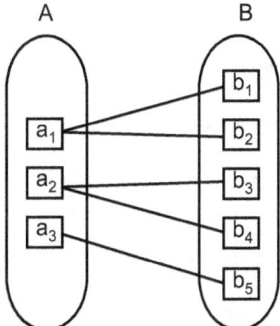

Fig. 4.19: One-to-Many

One customer has many accounts of different types in the bank, but each account has only one customer, so it is a one to many (1:m) relationship as shown in Fig. 4.20.

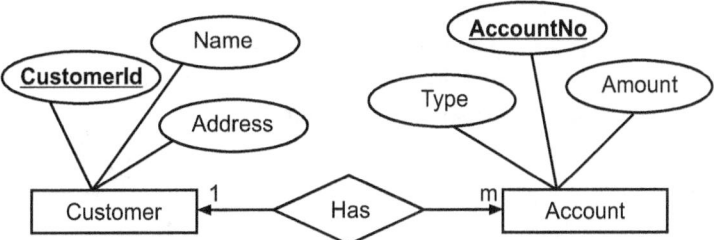

Fig. 4.20: One-to-many relationship example

3. **Many-to-One:** An entity in 'A' is associated with atmost one entity in 'B'. An entity in 'B' however can be associated with any number of entities in 'A'.

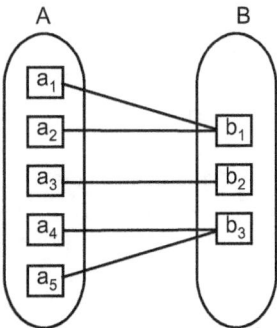

Fig. 4.21: Many-to-One

Many customers may have same account type, so it is a many to one (m:1) relationship as shown in Fig. 4.22.

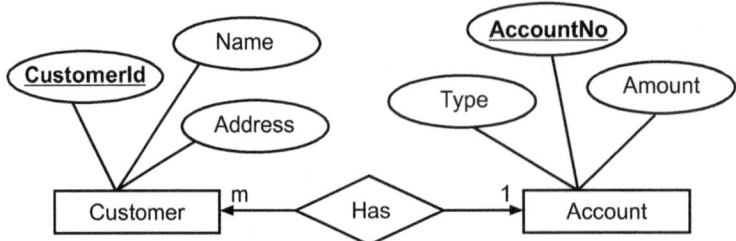

Fig. 4.22: Many-to-one relationship example

4. **Many-to-Many:** An entity in 'A' is associated with any number of entities in 'B' and an entity in 'B' is associated with any number of entities in 'A'.

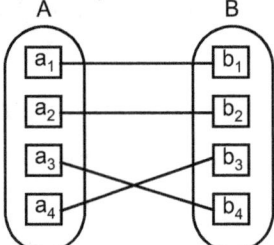

Fig. 4.23: Many-to-many

One customer has many accounts and account belongs to many customers, so it is a many to many (m:m) relationship as shown in Fig. 4.24.

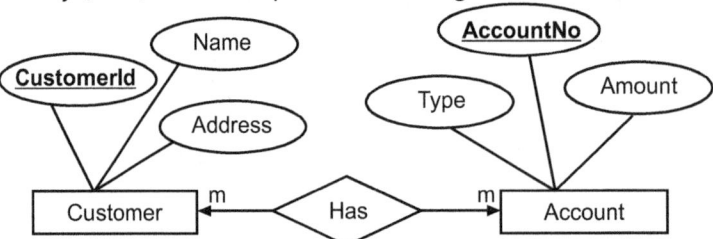

Fig. 4.24: Many-to-many relationship example

4.4.3 Examples

Example 1: *Draw an E-R diagram for order processing system where a person can give order for many items by specifying its quantity.*

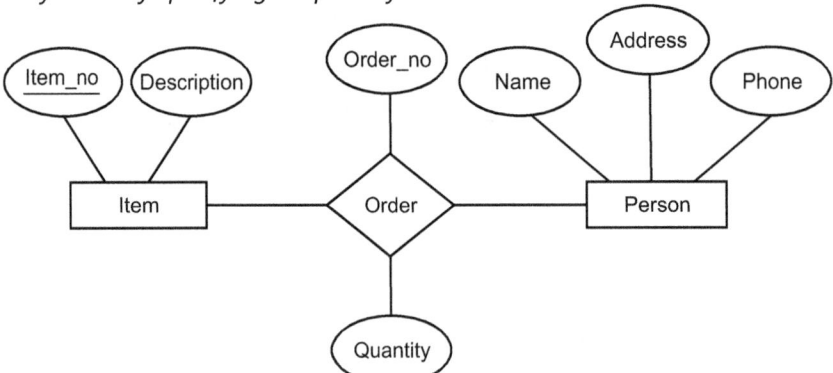

Example 2: *Assume you are to compose database requirements of a wholesale dealer for audio, video consumer equipment from different manufacturers. Customers are the various retail outlets (Retailers). Wholesaler extends credit to old customers (retailers). Draw E-R model.*

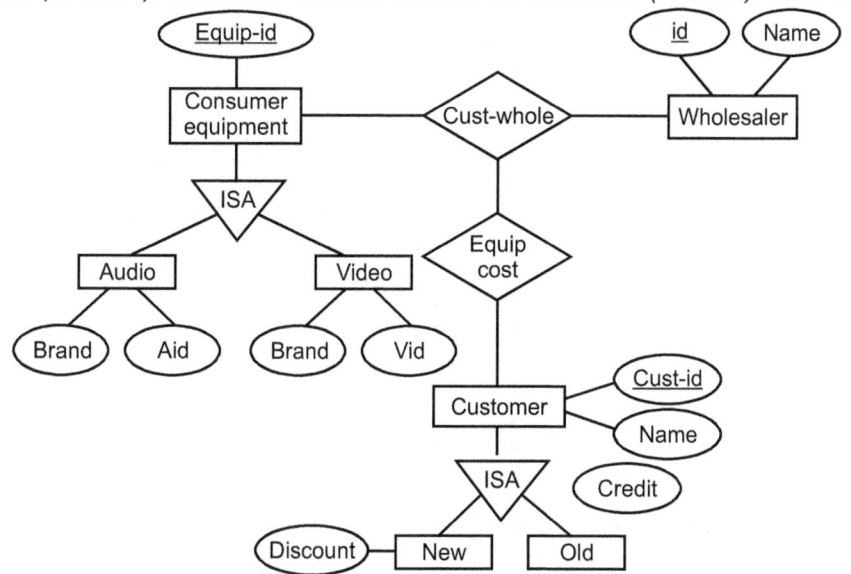

Example 3: *Consider a trucking company which is responsible for picking up shipments for warehouses of a retail chain and delivery the shipments to the individual store location. A truck may carry several shipments in a single trip and deliver it to multiple stores. Draw an E-R diagram for truck-shipment system.*

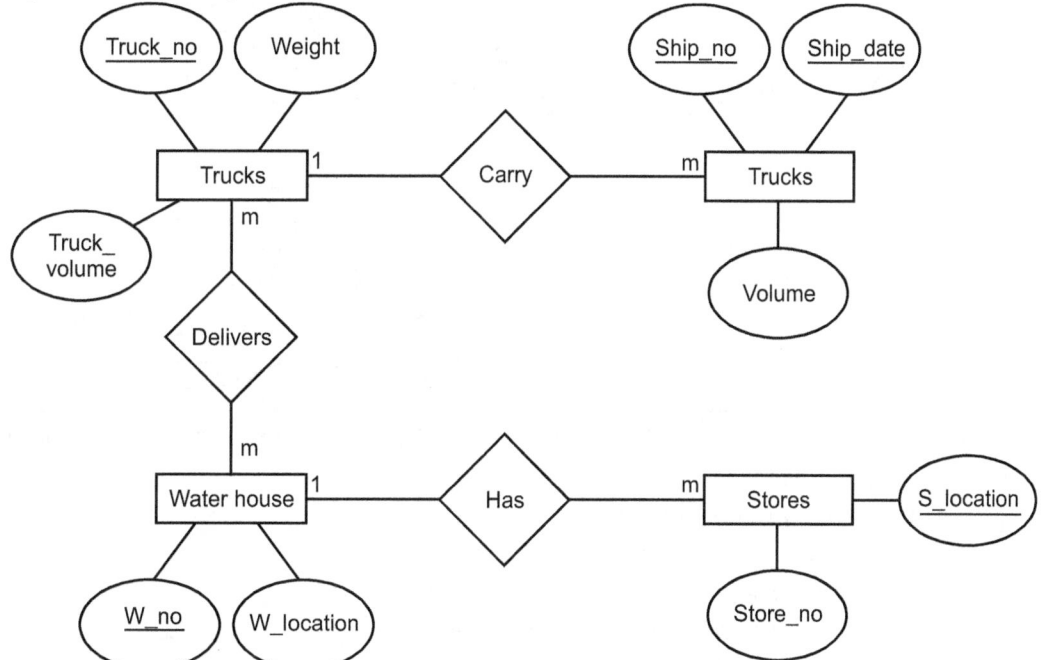

Example 4: *Draw an E-R diagram for airlines reservation system. Here a passenger can book ticket from personal for a flight on some date.*

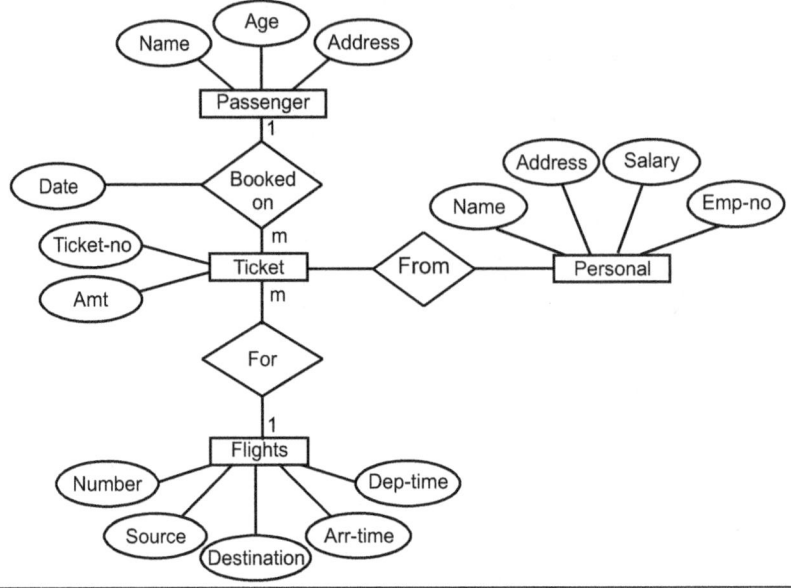

Example 5: *Construct an E-R diagram for a car insurance company that has a set of customers. Each customer owns one or more cars. Each are has associated with more cars. Each can has associated with zero to any number of recorded accidents.*

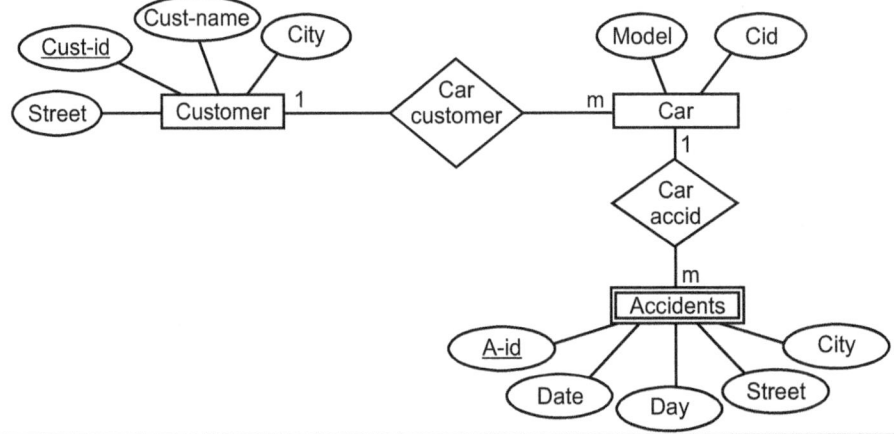

Example 6: *A movie studio wishes to institute a database to manage their files of movies actors and directors. The following facts are relevant.*

(i) *Each actor has appeared in many movies.*
(ii) *Each director has directed many movies.*
(iii) *Each movie has one director and one or more actors.*
(iv) *Each actor and director may have several addresses.*
Draw E-R diagram.

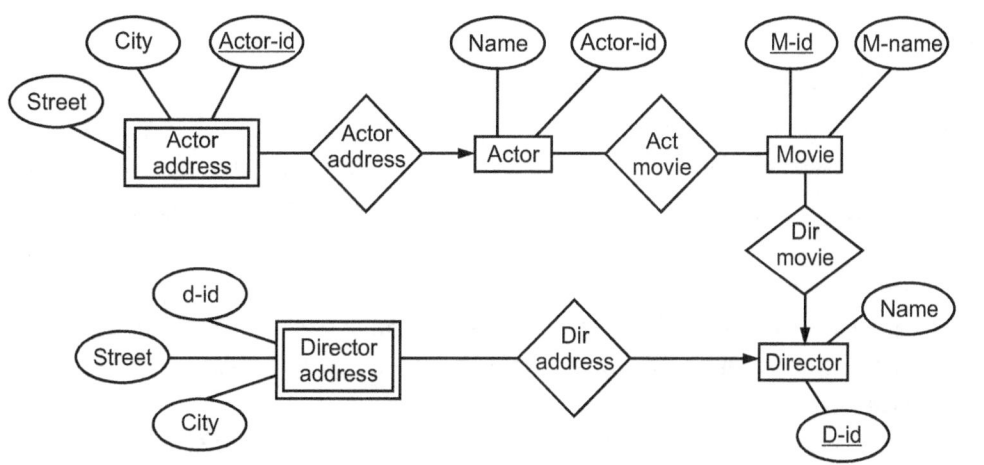

Example 7: *Construct an E-R diagram for a hospital with a set of patients and a set of medical doctors. Associate with each patient a log of the various tests and examination conducted.*

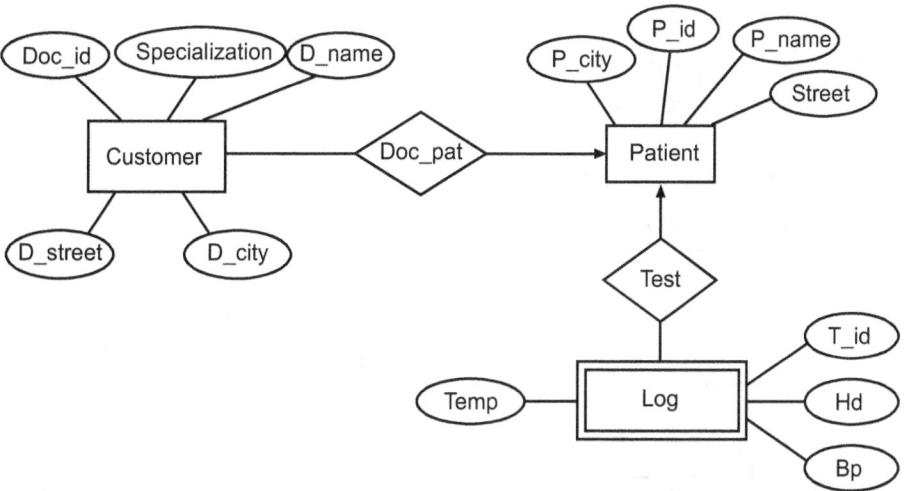

4.5 Use of Simple SQL Commands

4.5.1 Introduction to SQL

- SQL (Structured Query Language) is a database language for querying and modifying relational databases.
- It was developed by IBM Research in the mid 1970's and standardized by ANSI in 1986. It is also pronounced as "Sequel".
- SQL is a Structured Query Language and is the industry standard language to define and manipulate the data in Relational Database Management System.

Why SQL?

- SQL allow users to access data in relational database management systems.
- SQL allow users to describe the data.
- SQL allow users to define the data in database and manipulate that data.
- SQL allow to embed within other languages using SQL modules, libraries & pre-compilers.
- SQL allow users to create and drop databases and tables.
- SQL allow users to create view, stored procedure, functions in a database.
- SQL allow users to set permissions on tables, procedures, and views

SQL Architecture:

- When you are executing an SQL command for any R.D.B.M.S., the system determines the best way to carry out your request and SQL engine figures out how to interpret the task.
- There are various components included in the process. These components are Query Dispatcher, Optimization engines, Classic Query Engine and SQL query engine etc. Classic query engine handles all non-SQL queries but SQL query engine won't handle logical files.
- Fig. 4.25 shows SQL architecture.

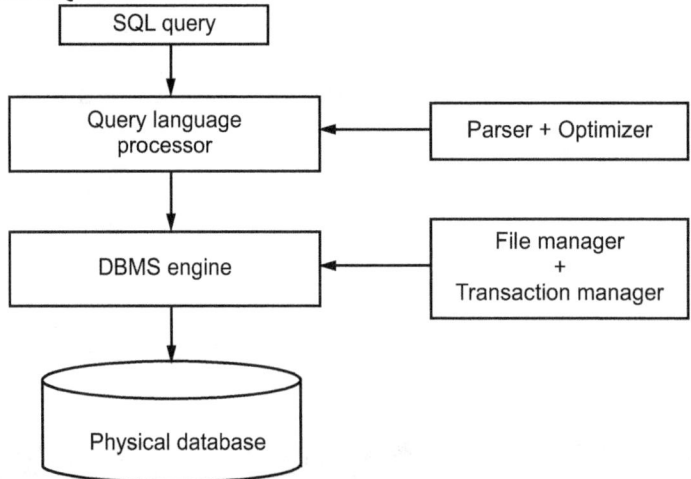

Fig. 4.25: SQL architecture

Types of SQL Languages:

Sr. No.	Classifications	Description	Commands
1.	DDL (Data Definition Language)	Is used to define the structure of a table, or modify the structure.	CREATE, ALTER, DROP, TRUNCATE, RENAME
2.	DML (Data Manipulation Language)	Is used to manipulate with the data.	INSERT, UPDATE, DELETE

contd. ...

3.	DCL (Data Control Language)	Is used to restrict or grant access to tables.	GRANT, REVOKE
4.	TCL (Transaction Control Language)	Is used to complete fully or undo the transactions.	COMMIT, SAVEPOINT, ROLLBACK.
5.	Queries	Is used to select records from the tables or other objects.	SELECT.

4.5.2 Data Types

- Each literal or column value manipulated by Oracle has a datatype. A value's datatype associates a fixed set of properties with the value.

1. **Character Datatypes:**

    (i) **Char(n):** Char datatype is a fixed length character data of length n bytes. Default size is 1 byte and it can hold a maximum of 2000 bytes. Character datatypes pad blank spaces to the fixed length if the user enters a value lesser than the specified length.
    Syntax: Char(n)
    Example: X char(4) stores upto 4 characters of data in the column X.

    (ii) **Varchar2(size):** Varchar2 datatypes are variable length character strings. They can store alpha-numeric values and the size must be specified. The maximum length of varchar2 datatype is 4000 bytes. Unlike char datatype, blank spaces are not padded to the length of the string. So, this is more preferred than character datatypes since it does not store the maximum length.
    Syntax: Varchar2(Size)
    Example: X varchar2(10) stores upto 10 characters of data in the column X.

2. **Numeric datatypes:**

    (i) **Number:** The number datatypes can store numeric values where p stands for the precision and s stands for the scale. The precision can range between 1 to 38 and the scale ranges from –84 to 127.
    Syntax: Number (p, s)
    Example:

    Sal number   : Here the scale is 0 and the precision is 38.
    Sal number(7)   : Here the scale is 0 and the number is a fixed point number of 7 digits.
    Sal number(7, 2)   : Stores 5 digits followed by 2 decimal points.

3. **DATE datatype:**

    Date datatype is used to store data and time values. The default format is DD-MM-YY. The valid data for a date datatype ranges from January 1, 4712 BC to December 31, 4712 AD. Date datatype stores 7 bytes one each for century, year, month, day, hour, minute and second.

4. RAW Datatype:

RAW datatype stores binary date of length n bytes. The maximum size is 255 bytes. "Specifying the size is a must for this datatype".

Syntax: `Raw(n)`

5. LONG Datatype:

Stores character data of variable length upto 2 Gigabyte(GB) or $2^{s1} - 1$.

6. LOB Datatypes:

In addition to the above datatypes, Oracle 8 supports LOB datatypes. LOB is the acronym for LARGE OBJECTS. The LOB datatypes stores upto 4 GB of data. This datatype is used for storing video clippings, large images, history documents etc. LOB datatypes can be

(i) CLOB   :   Character Large Objects (Internal LOB)

(ii) BLOB   :   Binary Large Objects (Internal LOB)

(iii) BFILE :   Binary File (External LOB)

4.5.3 SQL Languages and their Commands

4.5.3.1 Data Definition Language (DDL)

- A DDL is a language used to define data structures within a database.
- It is typically considered to be a subset of SQL, the Structured Query Language, but can also refer to languages that define other types of data.
- A Data Definition Language has a pre-defined syntax for describing data. For example, to build a new table using SQL syntax, the CREATE command is used, followed by parameters for the table name and column definitions.
- The DDL can also define the name of each column and the associated data type.

DDL Commands:

1. Create table command:

The SQL CREATE TABLE statement is used to create a new table.

Syntax:

```
CREATE TABLE table_name(
    column1 datatype,
    column2 datatype,
    column3 datatype,
    .....
    columnN datatype,
    PRIMARY KEY( one or more columns )
);
```

Following is an example which creates a CUSTOMERS table with ID as primary key and NOT NULL are the constraints showing that these fileds can not be NULL while creating records in this table:

```
SQL> CREATE TABLE CUSTOMERS(
    ID      INT              NOT NULL,
    NAME    VARCHAR (20)     NOT NULL,
    AGE     INT              NOT NULL,
    ADDRESS CHAR (25) ,
    SALARY  DECIMAL (18, 2),
    PRIMARY KEY (ID)
);
```

2. DESC Command:

The table structure can be described by using Describe command.

Syntax: `DESC table_name;`

Example: `DESC CUSTOMERS;`

`SQL> DESC CUSTOMERS`

Field	Type	Null	Key	Default	Extra
ID	int(11)	NO	PRI		
NAME	varchar(20)	NO			
AGE	int(11)	NO			
ADDRESS	char(25)	YES		NULL	
SALARY	decimal(18,2)	YES		NULL	

`5 rows in set (0.00 sec)`

3. ALTER Command:

- The ALTER TABLE statement is used to add or drop columns in existing table.

   Syntax:

   `ALTER TABLE tabe_name ADD column_name datatype;`

   `ALTER TABLE tabe_name DROP COLUMN column_name;`

Person:

LastName	FirstName	Address
Johnson	Kari	RTO Road 20

Example: To add a column named "City" in the "Person" table:

`ALTER TABLE Person ADD City varchar2(10);`

Result:

LastName	FirstName	Address	City
Johnson	Kari	RTO Road 20	

Example: To drop the "Address" column in the "Person" table:

    ALTER TABLE Person DROP (address);

Result:

LastName	FirstName	City
Johnson	Kari	

To modify the "Address" column in the "Person" table:"

    ALTER TABLE Person modify (Address varchar2(10))'

4. **DROP TABLE Command:**
- A table and its rows can be deleted by issuing the command drop table.

    Syntax: Drop table table_name;

    Example: Drop table Person;

5. **Truncate Commands:**
- Truncate table command is used to delete the whole rows of the table. The structure of table remains as it is. You can add new data to the table again.

    Syntax: Truncate table table_name;

    Example: Truncate table Person;

4.5.3.2 Data Manipulation Language (DML)

- DML used to retrieve, store, modify, delete, insert and update data in database.

1. **INSERT INTO Command:**
- The SQL INSERT INTO Statement is used to add new rows of data to a table in the database.

    Syntax:

        INSERT INTO TABLE_NAME (column1, column2, column3,...columnN)]
        VALUES (value1, value2, value3,...valueN);

    Here column1, column2, ..., columnN are the names of the columns in the table into which you want to insert data.

- Following statements would create six records in CUSTOMERS table:

        INSERT INTO CUSTOMERS (ID,NAME,AGE,ADDRESS,SALARY)
        VALUES (1, 'Ramesh', 32, 'Ahmedabad', 2000.00);

        INSERT INTO CUSTOMERS (ID,NAME,AGE,ADDRESS,SALARY)
        VALUES (2, 'Amar', 25, 'Delhi', 1500.00);

```
INSERT INTO CUSTOMERS (ID,NAME,AGE,ADDRESS,SALARY)
VALUES (3, 'kaushik', 23, 'Kota', 2000.00 );

INSERT INTO CUSTOMERS (ID,NAME,AGE,ADDRESS,SALARY)
VALUES (4, 'Chaitali', 25, 'Mumbai', 6500.00 );

INSERT INTO CUSTOMERS (ID,NAME,AGE,ADDRESS,SALARY)
VALUES (5, 'Hardik', 27, 'Bhopal', 8500.00 );

INSERT INTO CUSTOMERS (ID,NAME,AGE,ADDRESS,SALARY)
VALUES (6, 'Komal', 22, 'MP', 4500.00 );
```
- You can create a record in CUSTOMERS table using second syntax as follows:
```
INSERT INTO CUSTOMERS
VALUES (7, 'Akbar', 24, 'Indore', 10000.00 );
```
- All the above statement would product following records in CUSTOMERS table:

ID	NAME	AGE	ADDRESS	SALARY
1	Ramesh	32	Ahmedabad	2000.00
2	Amar	25	Delhi	1500.00
3	Kaushik	23	Kota	2000.00
4	Chaitali	25	Mumbai	6500.00
5	Hardik	27	Bhopal	8500.0
6	Komal	22	MP	4500.0
7	Akbar	24	Indore	10000.00

2. Update Command:
- The SQL UPDATE query is used to modify the existing records in a table.
- You can use WHERE clause with UPDATE query to update selected rows otherwise all the rows would be effected.

    Syntax: `UPDATE table_name`
    `SET column1 = value1, column2 = value2...., columnN = valueN`
    `WHERE [condition];`

- Consider CUSTOMERS table is having following records:

ID	NAME	AGE	ADDRESS	SALARY
1	Ramesh	32	Ahmedabad	2000.00
2	Amar	25	Delhi	1500.00
3	Kaushik	23	Kota	2000.00
4	Chaitali	25	Mumbai	6500.00
5	Hardik	27	Bhopal	8500.0
6	Komal	22	MP	4500.0
7	Akbar	24	Indore	10000.00

- Following is an example which would update ADDRESS for a customer whose ID is 6:

    ```
    SQL> UPDATE CUSTOMERS
    SET ADDRESS = 'Pune'
    WHERE ID = 6;
    ```

- Now CUSTOMERS table would have following records:

ID	NAME	AGE	ADDRESS	SALARY
1	Ramesh	32	Ahmedabad	2000.00
2	Amar	25	Delhi	1500.00
3	Kaushik	23	Kota	2000.00
4	Chaitali	25	Mumbai	6500.00
5	Hardik	27	Bhopal	8500.0
6	Komal	22	Pune	4500.0
7	Akbar	24	Indore	10000.00

- If you want to modify all ADDRESS and SALARY column values in CUSTOMERS table, you do not need to use WHERE clause and UPDATE query would be as follows:

    ```
    SQL> UPDATE CUSTOMERS
    SET ADDRESS = 'Pune', SALARY = 1000.00;
    ```

- Now CUSTOMERS table would have following records:

ID	NAME	AGE	ADDRESS	SALARY
1	Ramesh	32	Pune	1000.00
2	Amar	25	Pune	1000.00
3	Kaushik	23	Pune	1000.00
4	Chaitali	25	Pune	1000.00
5	Hardik	27	Pune	1000.00
6	Komal	22	Pune	1000.00
7	Akbar	24	Pune	1000.00

3. **DELETE Command:**

- The SQL DELETE Query is used to delete the existing records from a table.
- You can use WHERE clause with DELETE query to delete selected rows, otherwise all the records would be deleted.

    Syntax:
    ```
    DELETE FROM table_name
    WHERE [condition];
    ```

- Consider CUSTOMERS table is having following records:

ID	NAME	AGE	ADDRESS	SALARY
1	Ramesh	32	Ahmedabad	2000.00
2	Amar	25	Delhi	1500.00
3	Kaushik	23	Kota	2000.00
4	Chaitali	25	Mumbai	6500.00
5	Hardik	27	Bhopal	8500.0
6	Komal	22	MP	4500.0
7	Akbar	24	Indore	10000.00

- Following is an example which would DELETE a customer whose ID is 6:

    SQL> DELETE FROM CUSTOMERS
    WHERE ID = 6;

- Now CUSTOMERS table would have following records:

ID	NAME	AGE	ADDRESS	SALARY
1	Ramesh	32	Ahmedabad	2000.00
2	Amar	25	Delhi	1500.00
3	Kaushik	23	Kota	2000.00
4	Chaitali	25	Mumbai	6500.00
5	Hardik	27	Bhopal	8500.0
7	Akbar	24	Indore	10000.00

- If you want to DELETE all the records from CUSTOMERS table, you do not need to use WHERE clause and DELETE query would be as follows:

    SQL> DELETE FROM CUSTOMERS;

    Now CUSTOMERS table would not have any record.

4.5.3.3 SQL Queries

SQL SELECT Statement:

- The SELECT statement is used to select data from a table. The tabular result is stored in a result table.
- SQL SELECT Statement is used to fetch the data from a database table which returns data in the form of result table. These result tables are called result-sets.
- The basic syntax of SELECT statement is as follows:

    SELECT column1, column2, columnN FROM table_name;

- Here column1, column2...are the fields of a table whose values you want to fetch. If you want to fetch all the fields available in the field then you can use following syntax:

    SELECT * FROM table_name;

- Consider CUSTOMERS table is having following records:

ID	NAME	AGE	ADDRESS	SALARY
1	Ramesh	32	Ahmedabad	2000.00
2	Amar	25	Delhi	1500.00
3	Kaushik	23	Kota	2000.00
4	Chaitali	25	Mumbai	6500.00
5	Hardik	27	Bhopal	8500.0
6	Komal	22	MP	4500.0
7	Akbar	24	Indore	10000.00

- Following is an example which would fetch ID, Name and Salary fields of the customers available in CUSTOMERS table:

    SQL> SELECT ID, NAME, SALARY FROM CUSTOMERS;

- This would produce following result:

ID	NAME	SALARY
1	Ramesh	2000.00
2	Amar	1500.00
3	Kaushik	2000.00
4	Chaitali	6500.00
5	Hardik	8500.0
6	Komal	4500.0
7	Akbar	10000.00

- If you want to fetch all the fields of CUSTOMERS table then use the following query:

    SQL> SELECT * FROM CUSTOMERS;

- This would produce following result:

ID	NAME	AGE	ADDRESS	SALARY
1	Ramesh	32	Ahmedabad	2000.00
2	Amar	25	Delhi	1500.00
3	Kaushik	23	Kota	2000.00
4	Chaitali	25	Mumbai	6500.00
5	Hardik	27	Bhopal	8500.0
6	Komal	22	MP	4500.0
7	Akbar	24	Indore	10000.00

WHERE Clause:

- The SQL WHERE clause is used to specify a condition while fetching the data from single table or joining with multiple table.
- If the given condition is satisfied then only it returns specific value from the table. You would use WHERE clause to filter the records and fetching only necessary records.

    Syntax: SELECT column1, column2, columnN

    FROM table_name

    WHERE [condition]

- Consider CUSTOMERS table is having following records:

ID	NAME	AGE	ADDRESS	SALARY
1	Ramesh	32	Ahmedabad	2000.00
2	Amar	25	Delhi	1500.00
3	Kaushik	23	Kota	2000.00
4	Chaitali	25	Mumbai	6500.00
5	Hardik	27	Bhopal	8500.0
6	Komal	22	MP	4500.0
7	Akbar	24	Indore	10000.00

- Following is an example which would fetch ID, Name and Salary fields from the CUSTOMERS table where salary is greater than 2000:

    SQL> SELECT ID, NAME, SALARY

    FROM CUSTOMERS

    WHERE SALARY > 2000;

    This would produce following result:

ID	NAME	SALARY
4	Chaitali	6500.00
5	Hardik	8500.0
6	Komal	4500.0
7	Akbar	10000.00

- Following is an example which would fetch ID, Name and Salary fields from the CUSTOMERS table for a customer with name Hardik. Here it is important to note that all the strings should be given inside single quotes ('') where as numeric values should be given without any quote as in above example:

    SQL> SELECT ID, NAME, SALARY

    FROM CUSTOMERS

    WHERE NAME = 'Hardik';

- This would produce following result:

ID	NAME	SALARY
5	Hardik	8500.00

Operators in SQL:

- An operator is a reserved word or a character used primarily in an SQL statement's WHERE clause to perform operation(s), such as comparisons and arithmetic operations.
- Operators are used to specify conditions in an SQL statement and to serve as conjunctions for multiple conditions in a statement.

   1. **SQL Arithmetic Operators:** Assume variable a holds 10 and variable b holds 20 then:

Operator	Description	Example
+ (Addition)	Adds values on either side of the operator	a + b will give 30
– (Subtraction)	Subtracts right hand operand from left hand operand	a - b will give -10
* (Multiplication)	Multiplies values on either side of the operator	a * b will give 200
/ (Division)	Divides left hand operand by right hand operand	b / a will give 2
% (Modulus)	Divides left hand operand by right hand operand and returns remainder	b % a will give 0

   2. **SQL Comparison Operators:** Assume variable a holds 10 and variable b holds 20 then:

Operator	Description	Example
=	Checks if the value of two operands are equal or not, if yes then condition becomes true.	(a = b) is not true.
!=	Checks if the value of two operands are equal or not, if values are not equal then condition becomes true.	(a != b) is true.
<>	Checks if the value of two operands are equal or not, if values are not equal then condition becomes true.	(a <> b) is true.
>	Checks if the value of left operand is greater than the value of right operand, if yes then condition becomes true.	(a > b) is not true.

contd. ...

<	Checks if the value of left operand is less than the value of right operand, if yes then condition becomes true.	(a < b) is true.
>=	Checks if the value of left operand is greater than or equal to the value of right operand, if yes then condition becomes true.	(a >= b) is not true.
<=	Checks if the value of left operand is less than or equal to the value of right operand, if yes then condition becomes true.	(a <= b) is true.
!<	Checks if the value of left operand is not less than the value of right operand, if yes then condition becomes true.	(a !< b) is false.
!>	Checks if the value of left operand is not greater than the value of right operand, if yes then condition becomes true.	(a !> b) is true.

3. **SQL Logical Operators:** Here is a list of all the logical operators available in SQL.

Operator	Description
ALL	The ALL operator is used to compare a value to all values in another value set.
AND	The AND operator allows the existence of multiple conditions in an SQL statement's WHERE clause.
ANY	The ANY operator is used to compare a value to any applicable value in the list according to the condition.
BETWEEN	The BETWEEN operator is used to search for values that are within a set of values, given the minimum value and the maximum value.
EXISTS	The EXISTS operator is used to search for the presence of a row in a specified table that meets certain criteria.
IN	The IN operator is used to compare a value to a list of literal values that have been specified.
LIKE	The LIKE operator is used to compare a value to similar values using wildcard operators.
NOT	The NOT operator reverses the meaning of the logical operator with which it is used. Eg. NOT EXISTS, NOT BETWEEN, NOT IN etc. **This is negate operator.**
OR	The OR operator is used to combine multiple conditions in an SQL statement's WHERE clause.
IS NULL	The NULL operator is used to compare a value with a NULL value.
UNIQUE	The UNIQUE operator searches every row of a specified table for uniqueness (no duplicates).

Order By Clause:
- The SQL ORDER BY clause is used to sort the data in ascending or descending order, based on one or more columns. Some database sorts query results in ascending order by default.

    Syntax: SELECT column-list

    FROM table_name

    [WHERE condition]

    [ORDER BY column1, column2, .. columnN] [ASC | DESC];

- Consider CUSTOMERS table is having following records:

ID	NAME	AGE	ADDRESS	SALARY
1	Ramesh	32	Ahmedabad	2000.00
2	Khilan	25	Delhi	1500.00
3	Kaushik	23	Kota	2000.00
4	Chaitali	25	Mumbai	6500.00
5	Hardik	27	Bhopal	8500.0
6	Komal	22	MP	4500.0
7	Muffy	24	Indore	10000.00

- Following is an example which would sort the result in ascending order by NAME and SALARY:

    SQL> SELECT * FROM CUSTOMERS

    ORDER BY NAME, SALARY;

- This would produce following result:

ID	NAME	AGE	ADDRESS	SALARY
4	Chaitali	25	Mumbai	6500.00
5	Hardik	27	Bhopal	8500.00
3	Kaushik	23	Kota	2000.00
2	Khilan	25	Delhi	1500.00
6	Komal	22	MP	4500.00
7	Muffy	24	Indore	10000.00
1	Ramesh	32	Ahmedabad	2000.00

- Following is an example which would sort the result in descending order by NAME:

    SQL> SELECT * FROM CUSTOMERS

    ORDER BY NAME DESC;

- This would produce following result:

ID	NAME	AGE	ADDRESS	SALARY
1	Ramesh	32	Ahmedabad	2000.00
7	Muffy	24	Indore	10000.00
6	Komal	22	MP	4500.00
2	Khilan	25	Delhi	1500.00
3	Kaushik	23	Kota	2000.00
5	Hardik	27	Bhopal	8500.00
4	Chaitali	25	Mumbai	6500.00

Group By Clause:

- The SQL GROUP BY clause is used in collaboration with the SELECT statement to arrange identical data into groups.
- The GROUP BY clause follows the WHERE clause in a SELECT statement and precedes the ORDER BY clause.

   Syntax: SELECT column1, column2

   FROM table_name

   WHERE [conditions]

   GROUP BY column1, column2

   ORDER BY column1, column2

- Consider CUSTOMERS table is having following records:

ID	NAME	AGE	ADDRESS	SALARY
1	Ramesh	32	Ahmedabad	2000.00
2	Khilan	25	Delhi	1500.00
3	Kaushik	23	Kota	2000.00
4	Chaitali	25	Mumbai	6500.00
5	Hardik	27	Bhopal	8500.00
6	Komal	22	MP	4500.00
7	Muffy	24	Indore	10000.00

- If you want to know the total amount of salary on each customer, then GROUP BY query would be as follows:

   SQL> SELECT NAME, SUM(SALARY) FROM CUSTOMERS

   GROUP BY NAME;

- This would produce following result:

NAME	SALARY
Chaitali	6500.00
Hardik	8500.00
Kaushik	2000.00
Khilan	1500.00
Komal	4500.00
Muffy	10000.00
Ramesh	2000.00

- Now let us has following table where CUSTOMERS table has following records with duplicate names:

ID	NAME	AGE	ADDRESS	SALARY
1	Ramesh	32	Ahmedabad	2000.00
2	Ramesh	25	Delhi	1500.00
3	Kaushik	23	Kota	2000.00
4	Kaushik	25	Mumbai	6500.00
5	Hardik	27	Bhopal	8500.00
6	Komal	22	MP	4500.00
7	Muffy	24	Indore	10000.00

- Now again, if you want to know the total amount of salary on each customer, then GROUP BY query would be as follows:

    ```
    SQL> SELECT NAME, SUM(SALARY) FROM CUSTOMERS
    GROUP BY NAME;
    ```

- This would produce following result:

NAME	SALARY
Hardik	8500.00
Kaushik	8500.00
Komal	4500.00
Muffy	10000.00
Ramesh	3500.00

SQL Aggregate Functions:

- SQL has a lot of built-in functions for counting and calculations. The syntax for built-in SQL functions is:

    ```
    SELECT function(column) FROM table;
    ```

Aggregate functions operate against a collection of values, but return a single value.

Function	Description
1. AVG(column)	Returns the average value of a column.
2. COUNT(column)	Returns the number of rows (without a NULL value) of a column.
3. COUNT(*)	Returns the number of selected rows.
4. MAX(column)	Returns the highest value of a column.
5. MIN(column)	Returns the lowest value of a column.
6. SUM(column)	Returns the total sum of a column.

SQL Having Clause:

- The HAVING clause enables you to specify conditions that filter which group results appear in the final results.
- The WHERE clause places conditions on the selected columns, whereas the HAVING clause places conditions on groups created by the GROUP BY clause.
- The following is the position of the HAVING clause in a query:

    SELECT

    FROM

    WHERE

    GROUP BY

    HAVING

    ORDER BY

- The HAVING clause must follow the GROUP BY clause in a query and must also precede the ORDER BY clause if used.
- The following is the syntax of the SELECT statement, including the HAVING clause:

    SELECT column1, column2

    FROM table1, table2

    WHERE [conditions]

    GROUP BY column1, column2

    HAVING [conditions]

    ORDER BY column1, column2

- Consider CUSTOMERS table is having following records:

ID	NAME	AGE	ADDRESS	SALARY
1	Ramesh	32	Ahmedabad	2000.00
2	Khilan	25	Delhi	1500.00
3	Kaushik	23	Kota	2000.00
4	Chaitali	25	Mumbai	6500.00
5	Hardik	27	Bhopal	8500.00
6	Komal	22	MP	4500.00
7	Muffy	24	Indore	10000.00

- Following is the example which would display record for which similar age count would be more than or equal to 2:

```
SQL > SELECT *
FROM CUSTOMERS
GROUP BY age
HAVING COUNT(age) >= 2;
```

- This would produce following result:

ID	NAME	AGE	ADDRESS	SALARY
2	Khilan	25	Delhi	1500.00

String Functions:

- SQL string functions are used primarily for string manipulation. The following table details the important string functions:

Name	Description
ASCII()	Return numeric value of left-most character
BIN()	Return a string representation of the argument
BIT_LENGTH()	Return length of argument in bits
CHAR_LENGTH()	Return number of characters in argument
CHAR()	Return the character for each integer passed
CHARACTER_LENGTH()	A synonym for CHAR_LENGTH()
CONCAT_WS()	Return concatenate with separator
CONCAT()	Return concatenated string
CONV()	Convert numbers between different number bases
ELT()	Return string at index number

contd. ...

EXPORT_SET()	Return a string such that for every bit set in the value bits, you get an on string and for every unset bit, you get an off string
FIELD()	Return the index (position) of the first argument in the subsequent arguments
FIND_IN_SET()	Return the index position of the first argument within the second argument
FORMAT()	Return a number formatted to specified number of decimal places
HEX()	Return a string representation of a hex value
INSERT()	Insert a substring at the specified position up to the specified number of characters
INSTR()	Return the index of the first occurrence of substring
LCASE()	Synonym for LOWER()
LEFT()	Return the leftmost number of characters as specified
LENGTH()	Return the length of a string in bytes
LOAD_FILE()	Load the named file
LOCATE()	Return the position of the first occurrence of substring
LOWER()	Return the argument in lowercase
LPAD()	Return the string argument, left-padded with the specified string
LTRIM()	Remove leading spaces
MAKE_SET()	Return a set of comma-separated strings that have the corresponding bit in bits set
MID()	Return a substring starting from the specified position
OCT()	Return a string representation of the octal argument
OCTET_LENGTH()	A synonym for LENGTH()
ORD()	If the leftmost character of the argument is a multi-byte character, returns the code for that character
POSITION()	A synonym for LOCATE()
QUOTE()	Escape the argument for use in an SQL statement
REGEXP	Pattern matching using regular expressions

contd. ...

REPEAT()	Repeat a string the specified number of times
REPLACE()	Replace occurrences of a specified string
REVERSE()	Reverse the characters in a string
RIGHT()	Return the specified rightmost number of characters
RPAD()	Append string the specified number of times
RTRIM()	Remove trailing spaces
SOUNDEX()	Return a soundex string
SOUNDS LIKE	Compare sounds
SPACE()	Return a string of the specified number of spaces
STRCMP()	Compare two strings
SUBSTRING_INDEX()	Return a substring from a string before the specified number of occurrences of the delimiter
SUBSTRING(), SUBSTR()	Return the substring as specified
TRIM()	Remove leading and trailing spaces
UCASE()	Synonym for UPPER()
UNHEX()	Convert each pair of hexadecimal digits to a character
UPPER()	Convert to uppercase

SQL Joins:
- The SQL Joins clause is used to combine records from two or more tables in a database.
- A JOIN is a means for combining fields from two tables by using values common to each.
- Consider following two tables, (a) CUSTOMERS table is as follows:

ID	NAME	AGE	ADDRESS	SALARY
1	Ramesh	32	Ahmedabad	2000.00
2	Amar	25	Delhi	1500.00
3	Kaushik	23	Kota	2000.00
4	Chaitali	25	Mumbai	6500.00
5	Hardik	27	Bhopal	8500.00
6	Komal	22	MP	4500.00
7	Akbar	24	Indore	10000.00

- (b) Another table is ORDERS as follows:

OID	DATE	CUSTOMER_ID	AMOUNT
102	2009-10-08 00:00:00	3	3000
100	2009-10-08 00:00:00	3	1500
101	2009-11-2 00:00:00	2	1560
103	2008-05-28 00:00:00	4	2060

- Now let us join these two tables in our SELECT statement as follows:

    ```
    SQL> SELECT ID, NAME, AGE, AMOUNT
    FROM CUSTOMERS, ORDERS
    WHERE  CUSTOMERS.ID = ORDERS.CUSTOMER_ID;
    ```

- This would produce following result:

ID	NAME	AGE	AMOUNT
3	Kaushik	23	3000
3	Kaushik	23	1500
2	Amar	25	1560
4	Chaitali	25	2060

- Here it is noteable that the join is performed in the WHERE clause. Several operators can be used to join tables, such as =, <, >, <>, <=, >=, !=, BETWEEN, LIKE, and NOT; they can all be used to join tables. However, the most common operator is the equal symbol.
- There are different type of joins available in SQL these are listed below:

1. Inner Join:

- Returns rows when there is a match in both tables. The most frequently used and important of the joins is the INNER JOIN. They are also referred to as an EQUIJOIN.
- The INNER JOIN creates a new result table by combining column values of two tables (table1 and table2) based upon the join-predicate. The query compares each row of table1 with each row of table2 to find all pairs of rows which satisfy the join-predicate. When the join-predicate is satisfied, column values for each matched pair of rows of A and B are combined into a result row.

Syntax:

```
SELECT table1.column1, table2.column2...
FROM table1
INNER JOIN table2
ON table1.common_filed = table2.common_field;
```

- Consider following two tables, (a) CUSTOMERS table is as follows:

ID	NAME	AGE	ADDRESS	SALARY
1	Ramesh	32	Ahmedabad	2000.00
2	Amar	25	Delhi	1500.00
3	Kaushik	23	Kota	2000.00
4	Chaitali	25	Mumbai	6500.00
5	Hardik	27	Bhopal	8500.00
6	Komal	22	MP	4500.00
7	Akbar	24	Indore	10000.00

- (b) Another table is ORDERS as follows:

OID	DATE	CUSTOMER_ID	AMOUNT
102	2009-10-08 00:00:00	3	3000
100	2009-10-08 00:00:00	3	1500
101	2009-11-20 00:00:00	2	1560
103	2008-05-20 00:00:00	4	2060

- Now let us join these two tables using INNER JOIN as follows:

    SQL> SELECT ID, NAME, AMOUNT, DATE
        FROM CUSTOMERS
        INNER JOIN ORDERS
        ON CUSTOMERS.ID = ORDERS.CUSTOMER_ID;

- This would produce following result:

ID	NAME	AMOUNT	DATE
3	Kaushik	3000	2009-10-08 00:00:00
3	Kaushik	1500	2009-10-08 00:00:00
2	Amar	1560	2009-11-20 00:00:00
4	Chaitali	2060	2008-05-20 00:00:00

2. **Left Join:**

- Returns all rows from the left table, even if there are no matches in the right table. The SQL LEFT JOIN returns all rows from the left table, even if there are no matches in the right table. This means that if the ON clause matches 0 (zero) records in right table, the join will still return a row in the result,but with NULL in each column from right table.
- This means that a left join returns all the values from the left table, plus matched values from the right table or NULL in case of no matching join predicate.

Syntax:
```
SELECT table1.column1, table2.column2...
FROM table1
LEFT JOIN table2
ON table1.common_filed = table2.common_field;
```
Here given condition could be any given expression based on your requirement.

- Consider following two tables, (a) CUSTOMERS table is as follows:

ID	NAME	AGE	ADDRESS	SALARY
1	Ramesh	32	Ahmedabad	2000.00
2	Amar	25	Delhi	1500.00
3	Kaushik	23	Kota	2000.00
4	Chaitali	25	Mumbai	6500.00
5	Hardik	27	Bhopal	8500.00
6	Komal	22	MP	4500.00
7	Akbar	24	Indore	10000.00

- (b) Another table is ORDERS as follows:

OID	DATE	CUSTOMER_ID	AMOUNT
102	2009-10-08 00:00:00	3	3000
100	2009-10-08 00:00:00	3	1500
101	2009-11-20 00:00:00	2	1560
103	2008-05-20 00:00:00	4	2060

- Now let us join these two tables using LEFT JOIN as follows:
```
SQL> SELECT ID, NAME, AMOUNT, DATE
     FROM CUSTOMERS
     LEFT JOIN ORDERS
     ON CUSTOMERS.ID = ORDERS.CUSTOMER_ID;
```
- This would produce following result:

ID	NAME	AMOUNT	DATE
1	Ramesh	NULL	NULL
2	Amar	1560	2009-11-20 00:00:00
3	Kaushik	3000	2009-10-08 00:00:00
3	Kaushik	1500	2009-10-20 00:00:00
4	Chaitali	2060	2008-05-20 00:00:00
5	Hardik	NULL	NULL
6	Komal	NULL	NULL
7	Akbar	NULL	NULL

3. Right join:

- This join returns all rows from the right table, even if there are no matches in the left table.
- The SQL RIGHT JOIN returns all rows from the right table, even if there are no matches in the left table. This means that if the ON clause matches 0 (zero) records in left table, the join will still return a row in the result.but with NULL in each column from left table.
- This means that a right join returns all the values from the right table, plus matched values from the left table or NULL in case of no matching join predicate.

    Syntax: SELECT table1.column1, table2.column2...

    FROM table1

    RIGHT JOIN table2

    ON table1.common_filed = table2.common_field;

- Consider following two tables, (a) CUSTOMERS table is as follows:

ID	NAME	AGE	ADDRESS	SALARY
1	Ramesh	32	Ahmedabad	2000.00
2	Amar	25	Delhi	1500.00
3	Kaushik	23	Kota	2000.00
4	Chaitali	25	Mumbai	6500.00
5	Hardik	27	Bhopal	8500.00
6	Komal	22	MP	4500.00
7	Akbar	24	Indore	10000.00

- (b) Another table is ORDERS as follows:

OID	DATE	CUSTOMER_ID	AMOUNT
102	2009-10-08 00:00:00	3	3000
100	2009-10-08 00:00:00	3	1500
101	2009-11-20 00:00:00	2	1560
103	2008-05-20 00:00:00	4	2060

- Now let us join these two tables using RIGHT JOIN as follows:

    SQL> SELECT ID, NAME, AMOUNT, DATE

    FROM CUSTOMERS

    RIGHT JOIN ORDERS

    ON CUSTOMERS.ID = ORDERS.CUSTOMER_ID;

- This would produce following result:

ID	NAME	AMOUNT	DATE
3	Kaushik	3000	2009-10-08 00:00:00
3	Kaushik	1500	2009-10-08 00:00:00
2	Amar	1560	2009-11-20 00:00:00
4	Chaitali	2060	2008-05-20 00:00:00

4. **Full Join:**
- This join returns rows when there is a match in one of the tables.
- The SQL FULL JOIN combines the results of both left and right outer joins. The joined table will contain all records from both tables, and fill in NULLs for missing matches on either side.

    Syntax:
    ```
    SELECT table1.column1, table2.column2...
    FROM table1
    FULL JOIN table2
    ON table1.common_filed = table2.common_field;
    ```

- Consider following two tables, (a) CUSTOMERS table is as follows:

ID	NAME	AGE	ADDRESS	SALARY
1	Ramesh	32	Ahmedabad	2000.00
2	Amar	25	Delhi	1500.00
3	Kaushik	23	Kota	2000.00
4	Chaitali	25	Mumbai	6500.00
5	Hardik	27	Bhopal	8500.00
6	Komal	22	MP	4500.00
7	Akbar	24	Indore	10000.00

- (b) Another table is ORDERS as follows:

OID	DATE	CUSTOMER_ID	AMOUNT
102	2009-10-08 00:00:00	3	3000
100	2009-10-08 00:00:00	3	1500
101	2009-11-20 00:00:00	2	1560
103	2008-05-20 00:00:00	4	2060

- Now let us join these two tables using FULL JOIN as follows:

    ```
    SQL> SELECT ID, NAME, AMOUNT, DATE
         FROM CUSTOMERS
         FULL JOIN ORDERS
         ON CUSTOMERS.ID = ORDERS.CUSTOMER_ID;
    ```

- This would produce following result:

ID	NAME	AMOUNT	DATE
1	Ramesh	NULL	NULL
2	Amar	1560	2009-11-20 00:00:00
3	Kaushik	3000	2009-10-08 00:00:00
3	Kaushik	1500	2009-10-20 00:00:00
4	Chaitali	2060	2008-05-20 00:00:00
5	Hardik	NULL	NULL
6	Komal	NULL	NULL
7	Akbar	NULL	NULL
3	Kaushik	3000	2009-10-08 00:00:00
3	Kaushik	1500	2009-10-08 00:00:00
2	Amar	1560	2009-11-20 00:00:00
4	Chaitali	2060	2008-05-20 00:00:00

- If your Database does not support FULL JOIN like MySQL does not support FULL JOIN, then you can use **UNION ALL** clause to combile two JOINS as follows:

```
SQL> SELECT  ID, NAME, AMOUNT, DATE
     FROM CUSTOMERS
     LEFT JOIN ORDERS
     ON CUSTOMERS.ID = ORDERS.CUSTOMER_ID
UNION ALL
     SELECT  ID, NAME, AMOUNT, DATE
     FROM CUSTOMERS
     RIGHT JOIN ORDERS
     ON CUSTOMERS.ID = ORDERS.CUSTOMER_ID
```

5. Self join:

- It is used to join a table to itself, as if the table were two tables, temporarily renaming at least one table in the SQL statement.
- The SQL SELF JOIN is used to join a table to itself, as if the table were two tables, temporarily renaming at least one table in the SQL statement.

  Syntax:
  ```
  SELECT a.column_name, b.column_name...
  FROM table1 a, table1 b
  WHERE a.common_filed = b.common_field;
  ```

  Here WHERE clause could be any given expression based on your requirement.

- Consider following two tables, (a) CUSTOMERS table is as follows:

ID	NAME	AGE	ADDRESS	SALARY
1	Ramesh	32	Ahmedabad	2000.00
2	Amar	25	Delhi	1500.00
3	Kaushik	23	Kota	2000.00
4	Chaitali	25	Mumbai	6500.00
5	Hardik	27	Bhopal	8500.00
6	Komal	22	MP	4500.00
7	Akbar	24	Indore	10000.00

- Now let us join this table using SELF JOIN as follows:

```
SQL> SELECT a.ID, b.NAME, a.SALARY
     FROM CUSTOMERS a, CUSTOMERS b
     WHERE a.SALARY < b.SALARY;
```

- This would produce following result:

ID	NAME	SALARY
2	Ramesh	1500.00
2	Kaushik	1500.00
1	Chaitali	2000.00
2	Chaitali	1500.00
3	Chaitali	2000.00
6	Chaitali	4500.00
1	Hardik	2000.00
2	Hardik	1500.00
3	Hardik	2000.00
4	Hardik	6500.00
6	Hardik	4500.00
1	Komal	2000.00
2	Komal	1500.00
3	Komal	2000.00
1	Akbar	2000.00
2	Akbar	1500.00
3	Akbar	2000.00
4	Akbar	6500.00
5	Akbar	8500.00
6	Akbar	4500.00

6. Cartesian join:

- This join returns the cartesian product of the sets of records from the two or more joined tables.

- The CARTESIAN JOIN or CROSS JOIN returns the cartesian product of the sets of records from the two or more joined tables. Thus, it equates to an inner join where the join-condition always evaluates to True or where the join-condition is absent from the statement.

    Syntax: `SELECT table1.column1, table2.column2...`

    `FROM  table1, table2 [, table3 ]`

- Consider following two tables, (a) CUSTOMERS table is as follows:

ID	NAME	AGE	ADDRESS	SALARY
1	Ramesh	32	Ahmedabad	2000.00
2	Amar	25	Delhi	1500.00
3	Kaushik	23	Kota	2000.00
4	Chaitali	25	Mumbai	6500.00
5	Hardik	27	Bhopal	8500.00
6	Komal	22	MP	4500.00
7	Akbar	24	Indore	10000.00

- (b) Another table is ORDERS as follows:

OID	DATE	CUSTOMER_ID	AMOUNT
102	2009-10-08 00:00:00	3	3000
100	2009-10-08 00:00:00	3	1500
101	2009-11-20 00:00:00	2	1560
103	2008-05-20 00:00:00	4	2060

- Now let us join these two tables using INNER JOIN as follows:

    `SQL> SELECT ID, NAME, AMOUNT, DATE`

    `FROM CUSTOMERS, ORDERS;`

- This would produce following result:

ID	NAME	AMOUNT	DATE
1	Ramesh	3000	2009-10-08 00:00:00
1	Ramesh	1500	2009-10-08 00:00:00
1	Ramesh	1560	2009-11-20 00:00:00
1	Ramesh	2060	2008-05-20 00:00:00
2	Amar	3000	2009-10-08 00:00:00
2	Amar	1500	2009-10-08 00:00:00
2	Amar	1560	2009-11-20 00:00:00
2	Amar	2060	2008-05-20 00:00:00
3	Kaushik	3000	2009-10-08 00:00:00
3	Kaushik	1500	2009-10-08 00:00:00
3	Kaushik	1560	2009-11-20 00:00:00
3	Kaushik	2060	2008-05-20 00:00:00
4	Chaitali	3000	2009-10-08 00:00:00
4	Chaitali	1500	2009-10-08 00:00:00
4	Chaitali	1560	2009-11-20 00:00:00
4	Chaitali	2060	2008-05-20 00:00:00
5	Hardik	3000	2009-10-08 00:00:00
5	Hardik	1500	2009-10-08 00:00:00
5	Hardik	1560	2009-11-20 00:00:00
5	Hardik	2060	2008-05-20 00:00:00
6	Komal	3000	2009-10-08 00:00:00
6	Komal	1500	2009-10-08 00:00:00
6	Komal	1560	2009-11-20 00:00:00
6	Komal	2060	2008-05-20 00:00:00
7	Akbar	3000	2009-10-08 00:00:00
7	Akbar	1500	2009-10-08 00:00:00
7	Akbar	1560	2009-11-20 00:00:00
7	Akbar	2060	2008-05-20 00:00:00

Questions

1. Define database.
2. What is meant by D.B.M.S. and R.D.B.M.S.
3. Listout various feature of R.D.B.M.S.
4. Define R.D.B.M.S. Enlist characteristics of R.D.B.M.S.
5. With the neat diagram explain components of R.D.B.M.S.
6. Enlist properties of R.D.B.M.S. with suitable diagram.
7. State advantages of R.D.B.M.S.
8. Give limitations of R.D.B.M.S.
9. What are the different types of keys used in R.D.B.M.S.?
10. Discuss integrity Rule of R.D.B.M.S.
11. Explain the term primary key.
12. Explain the term referential integrity rule.
13. Explain the term candidate key.
14. Write short note on: Foreign key.
15. Describe database normalization.

16. Why we required normalization.
17. Define 1NF with suitable example.
18. Define 2NF with suitable example.
19. Define 3NF with suitable example.
20. Explain entity relationships using its symbols.
21. Define the following terms:
    (a) Entities, (b) Relationship, and (c) Attribute.
22. Write short note on: mapping cardianality.
23. Explain SQL with its different languages.
24. Describe following terms:
    (a) Joins, (b) DML, (c) SQL operators, and (d) DDL.
25. Draw an E-R for hospital which includes various entities, attributes and relationship such as Doctors, (Doc_id, Doc_add, Doc_name), Hospital (Hos_name, Hos_address, Hos_id), Patient (Pat_id, Pat_name, Pat_gender, Pat_add); Hos_workers (HosW_id, HosW_name, HosW_add) etc.
26. Draw a E-R diagram for university which includes courses, branches, student, colleges information etc.
27. An insurance agent sells insurance policies to clients. Policies can be of different types such as vehicle insurance, life insurance, accident insurance etc. The agent collects monthly premiums on the policies in the form of cheques of local banks. Appropriate attributes must be assumed for various entities such as agents, vehicles, policy.
    Draw an E-R model for above system. Your E-R model should take advantage of extended E-R notation where relevant.
28. Following information is maintained manually in a library.
    Books (Accession_number, name, authors, price, book_type, publisher)
    Borrowers (membership_no., name, address,
        category, max_no of books that can be issued,
        Accession_number of books borrowed)
    The following constraints are observed:
    1. Each book has unique accession-number.
    2. A book may have more than one author.
    3. There may be more than one copy of a book.
    4. The category of borrower determines the max. Number of books that may be issued to borrower.
       Draw E-R diagram for above statement.
29. Explain strong and weak entity with example.
30. What is relationship? Explain relationship set in detail.
31. Write short note on:
    (i) Group by clause,
    (ii) Having clause, and
    (iii) Order by clause.

Chapter 5...

Management Information System (MIS)

Contents ...

5.1 Introduction to MIS
    5.1.1 Definition
    5.1.2 Objectives of MIS
    5.1.3 Characteristics of MIS
    5.1.4 Advantages
    5.1.5 Disadvantages
5.2 Cryptography
    5.2.1 Purpose of Cryptography
    5.2.2 Encryption and Decryption
5.3 Digital Signature
    5.3.1 Definition
    5.3.2 How Digital Signature Works?
    5.3.3 Advantages and Disadvantages
5.4 IT Act
5.5 Security Threats to Information
    5.5.1 Viruses
    5.5.2 Hacking
    5.5.3 Natural Calamities
    5.5.4 Failure of System
5.6 Preventive Measures and Data Recovery
    5.6.1 Antivirus
    5.6.2 Firewall
    5.6.3 Data Recovery Methods
- Questions

5.1 Introduction to MIS

- A Management Information System (MIS) provides information that organisations require to manage themselves efficiently and effectively.
- Management information systems are typically computer systems used for managing five primary components:
  - Hardware,
  - Software,
  - Data (information for decision making),
  - Procedures (design, development and documentation), and
  - People (individuals, groups, or organisations).

- Management Information Systems (MIS) referred to as Information Management and Systems, is the discipline covering the application of people, technologies and procedures collectively information systems, to solving business problems.
- MIS is planned system of collecting, storing and disseminating data in the form of information needed to carry out the functions of management.
- There are four types of MIS that will be introduced in ascending order of sophistication:
    1. **Transaction Processing Systems:** These systems are designed to handle a large volume of routine, recurring transactions. Supermarkets use them to record sales and track inventory. Most managers use these systems to deal with tasks such as payroll, customer billing and payments to suppliers.
    2. **Operations Information Systems:** These systems were introduced after transaction processing systems. An operations information system gathers comprehensive data, organizes it and summarizes it in a form that is useful for managers. Managers use operations information systems to obtain sales, inventory, accounting and other performance-related information.
    3. **Decision Support Systems (DSS):** A DSS is an interactive computer system that can be used by managers without help from computer specialists. A DSS provides managers with the necessary information to make intelligent decisions. A DSS has three fundamental components:
        (i) **Database Management System (DBMS):** Stores large amounts of data relevant to problems the DSS has been designed to tackle.
        (ii) **Model-based Management System (MBMS):** Transforms data from the DBMS into information that is useful in decision making.
        (iii) **Dialog Generation and Management System (DGMS):** Provides a user-friendly interface between the system and the managers who do not have extensive computer training.
    4. **Expert Systems and Artificial Intelligence:** These systems use human knowledge captured in a computer to solve problems that ordinarily need human expertise. Mimicking human expertise and intelligence requires that the computer (1) recognize, formulate and solve a problem; (2) explain solutions and (3) learn from experience. These systems explain the logic of their advice to the user; hence, in addition to solving problems they can also serve as a teacher.

5.1.1 Definition

- The Management Information System (MIS) is a concept of the last decade or two. It has been understood and described in a number of ways. It is also known as the Information System, the Information and Decision System, the Computer-based Information System.
- The MIS has more than one definition, some of which are given below:
    o The MIS is defined as "a system provides information support for decision making in the organisation".

OR
- The MIS is defined as "an integrated system of man and machine for providing the information to support the operations, the management and decision making function in the organisation".

OR
- The MIS is defined as a system based on the database of the organisation evolved for the purpose of providing information to the people in the organisation.

OR
- A Management Information System is an integrated user-machine system, for providing information to the support the operations, management, analysis and decision-making functions in an organisation.

5.1.2 Objectives of MIS

- Following are the objectives provided by the MIS:
  1. **Data Capturing:** MIS capture data from various internal and external sources of organsiation. Data capturing may, be manual or through computer terminals.
  2. **Processing of Data:** The captured data is processed to convert into required information. Processing of data is done by. such activities as calculating, sorting, classifying, and summarizing.
  3. **Storage of Information:** MIS stores the processed or unprocessed data for future use. If any information is not immediately required, it is saved as an organisation record, for later use.
  4. **Retrieval of Information:** MIS retrieves information from its stores as and when required by various users.
  5. **Dissemination of Information:** Information, which is a finished product of MIS is disseminated to the users in the organisation. It is periodic or online through Computer terminal.
- Fig. 5.1 shows objectives of MIS.

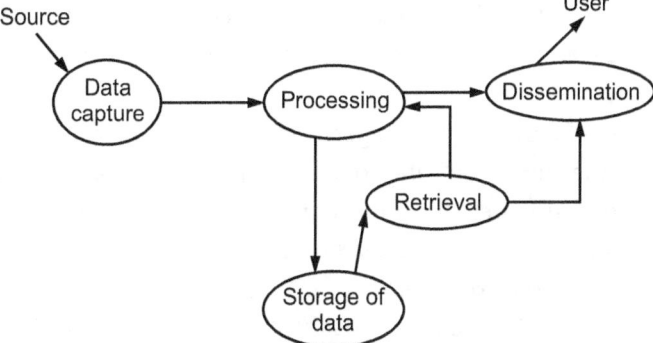

Fig. 5.1: Objectives of MIS

5.1.3 Characteristics of MIS
- MIS provides following characteristics:
    1. **Systems Approach:** The information system follows a systems approach. Systems approach means taking a comprehensive view or a complete look at the interlocking sub-systems that operate within in organisation.
    2. **Management Oriented:** Management oriented characteristic of MIS implies that the management actively directs the system development effort. For planning of MIS, top-down approach should be followed. Top down approach suggests that the system development starts from the determination of management's needs and overall business objective. To ensure that the implementation of system's polices meet the specification of the system, continued review and participation of the manager is necessary.
    3. **Need Based:** MIS design should be as per the information needs of managers at different levels,
    4. **Exception Based:** MIS shooed be developed on the exception based also, which means that in an abnormal situation, there should be immediate reporting about the exceptional situation to the decision-makers at the required level.
    5. **Future Oriented:** MIS should not merely provide past of historical information; rather it should provide information, on the basis of future projections on the actions to be initiated.
    6. **Integrated:** Integration is significant because of its ability to reduce more meaningful information. Integration means taking a comprehensive view or looking at the complete picture if the interlocking subsystems that operate within the company.
    7. **Common Data Flow:** Common data flow includes avoiding duplication, combining similar functions and simplifying operations wherever possible. The development of common data flow is an economically sound and logical concept, but it must be viewed from a practical angle.
    8. **Long Term Planning:** MIS is developed over relatively long periods. A heavy dement of planning, should be involved.
    9. **Sub System Concept:** The MIS should be viewed as a single entity; but it must be broken down into digestible sub-systems which are more meaningful.
    10. **Central database:** In the MIS there should be common data base for whole system.

5.1.4 Advantages
- An MIS provides the following advantages:
    1. **It facilitates planning:** MIS improves the quality of plants by providing relevant information for sound decision - making . Due to increase in the size and complexity of organisations, managers have lost personal contact with the scene of operations.
    2. **In minimizes information overload:** MIS change the larger amount of data in to summarized form and there by avoids the confusion which may arise when managers are flooded with detailed facts.

3. **MIS encourages decentralization:** Decentralization of authority is possibly when there is a system for monitoring operations at lower levels. MIS is successfully used for measuring performance and making necessary change in the organisational plans and procedures.
4. **It brings coordination:** MIS facilities integration of specialized activities by keeping each department aware of the problem and requirements of other departments. It connects all decision centers in the organisation.
5. **It makes control easier:** MIS serves as a link between managerial planning and control. It improves the ability of management to evaluate and improve performance. The used computers has increased the data processing and storage capabilities and reduced the cost.
6. MIS assembles, process, stores, Retrieves, evaluates and Disseminates the information.

5.1.5 Disadvantages

- Disadvantages of MIS are listed below:
    1. Highly sensitive requires constant monitoring.
    2. Budgeting of MIS extremely difficult.
    3. Quality of outputs governed by quality of inputs.
    4. Lack of flexibility to update itself.
    5. Effectiveness decreases due to frequent changes in top management
    6. Takes into account only qualitative factors and ignores non-qualitative factors like morale of worker, attitude of worker etc.

5.2 Cryptography

- Cryptography is the study of secret (crypto) writing (graphy).
- Cryptography is an algorithmic process of converting a plain text or clear text message to a cipher text or cipher message based on an algorithm that both the sender and receiver know, so that the cipher text message can be returned to its original, plain text form.
- Concerned with developing algorithms which may be used to:
    1. Conceal the context of some message from all except the sender and recipient (privacy or secrecy), and/or
    2. Verify the correctness of a message to the recipient (authentication).
- Form the basis of many technological solutions to computer and communications security problems.
- Cryptography is the study of mathematical techniques for all aspects of information security. Cryptanalysis is the complementary science concerned with the methods to defeat these techniques.
- Modern cryptography concerns itself with the following four objectives:
    1. **Confidentiality:** The information cannot be understood by anyone for whom it was unintended.

2. **Integrity:** The information cannot be altered in storage or transit between sender and intended receiver without the alteration being detected.
3. **Non-repudiation:** The creator/sender of the information cannot deny at a later stage his or her intentions in the creation or transmission of the information.
4. **Authentication:** The sender and receiver can confirm each other's identity and the origin/destination of the information.

5.2.1 Purpose of Cryptography

- Cryptography is the science of writing in secret code and is an ancient art; the first documented use of cryptography in writing dates back to circa 1900 B.C. when an Egyptian scribe used non-standard hieroglyphs in an inscription.
- In computer field cryptography is necessary when communicating over any untrusted medium, which includes just about any network, particularly the Internet.
- Within the context of any application-to-application communication, there are some specific security requirements, including:
    1. **Authentication:** The process of proving one's identity. (The primary forms of host-to-host authentication on the Internet today are name-based or address-based, both of which are notoriously weak.)
    2. **Privacy/Confidentiality:** Ensuring that no one can read the message except the intended receiver.
    3. **Integrity:** Assuring the receiver that the received message has not been altered in any way from the original.
    4. **Non-repudiation:** A mechanism to prove that the sender really sent this message.
- Cryptography, then, not only protects data from theft or alteration, but can also be used for user authentication.
- There are, in general, three types of cryptographic schemes typically used to accomplish these goals: secret key (or symmetric) cryptography, public-key (or asymmetric) cryptography, and hash functions, each of which is described below.
- In all cases, the initial unencrypted data is referred to as plaintext. It is encrypted into ciphertext, which will in turn (usually) be decrypted into usable plaintext.

5.2.2 Encryption and Decryption

1. **Encryption:**

Definition of Encryption:

- Encryption is a process of coding information which could either be a file or mail message in into cipher text a form unreadable without a decoding key in order to prevent anyone except the intended recipient from reading that data.

OR

- Encryption is the process of encoding messages (or information) in such a way that eavesdroppers or hackers cannot read it, but that authorized parties can.

- Data that can be read and understood without any special measures is called plaintext or cleartext. The method of disguising plaintext in such a way as to hide its substance is called encryption.
- Encrypting plaintext results in unreadable gibberish called cipher text. You use encryption to ensure that information is hidden from anywhere for whom it is not intended, even those who can see the encrypted data.

2. Decription:

Definition:

- The process of reverting cipher text to its original plaintext is called decryption.

OR

- Decription is the reverse process of converting encoded data to its original un-encoded form, plaintext.

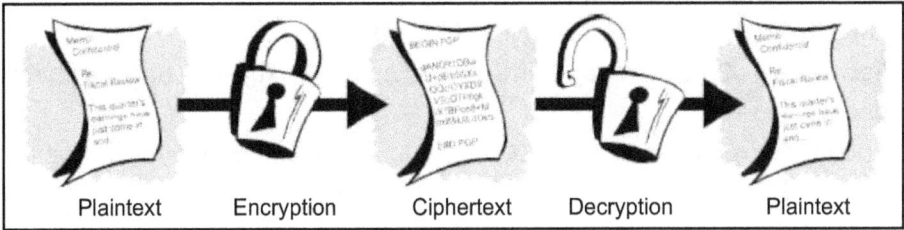

Fig. 5.2: Encryption and Decryption

Encryption Model:

- Fig. 5.3 show basic encryption model.

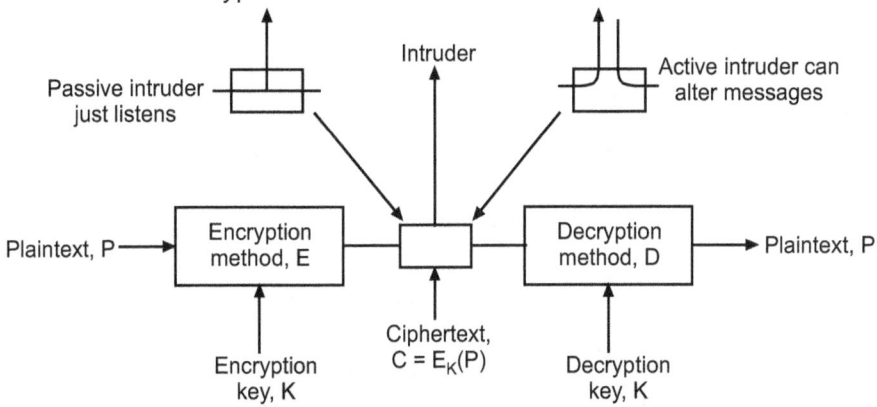

Fig. 5.3: The basic encryption model

- The messages to be encrypted, known as the 'plaintext', are transformed by a function that is parameterized by a 'key'.
- The output of the encryption process, known as the 'ciphertext', is then transmitted, often by messenger or radio.
- We assume that the enemy, or 'intruder', hears and accurately copies down the complete ciphertext.

- However, unlike the intended recipient, he does not know what the decryption key is and so cannot decrypt the ciphertext easily.
- Sometimes the intruder can not only listen to the communication channel (passive intruder) but can also record messages and play them back later, inject his own messages, or modify messages before they get to the receiver (active intruder).
- The art of breaking ciphers, called cryptanalysis, and the art devising them (cryptography) is collectively known as cryptology.
- Encryption methods have historically been divided into two categories: substitution ciphers and transposition ciphers.

Types of Cryptographic Algorithms:
- There are several ways of classifying cryptographic algorithms. They will be categorized based on the number of keys that are employed for encryption and decryption, and further defined by their application and use.
- The three types of algorithms that will be discussed in Fig. 5.4.
    1. **Secret Key Cryptography (SKC):** Uses a single key for both encryption and decryption.
    2. **Public Key Cryptography (PKC):** Uses one key for encryption and another for decryption.
    3. **Hash Functions:** Uses a mathematical transformation to irreversibly "encrypt" information.

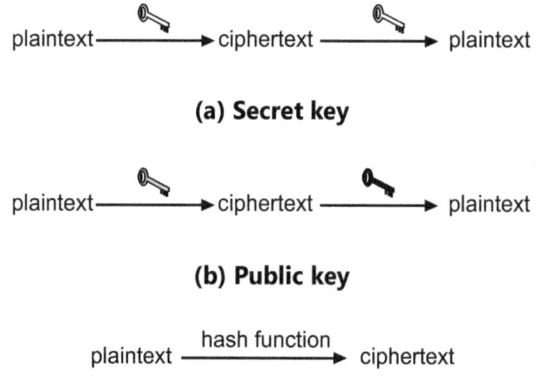

(a) Secret key

(b) Public key

(c) Hash function

Fig. 5.4: Three types of cryptography

1. Symmetric Key Encryption:
- Symmetric encryption is the oldest and best-known technique. A secret key, which can be a number, a word, or just a string of random letters, is applied to the text of a message to change the content in a particular way.
- This might be as simple as shifting each letter by a number of places in the alphabet. As long as both sender and recipient know the secret key, they can encrypt and decrypt all messages that use this key.

- Symmetric key encryption is also known as shared-key, single-key, secret-key, private-key or one-key encryption.
- In this type of message encryption, both sender and receiver share the same key which is used to both encrypt and decrypt messages. Sender and receiver only have to specify the shared key in the beginning and then they can begin to encrypt and decrypt messages between them using that key.
- Examples include AES (Advanced Encryption Standard) and TripleDES (Data Encryption Standard).
- In symmetric cryptography (or symmetric-key encryption), the same key is used for both encryption and decryption as shown in Fig. 5.5.

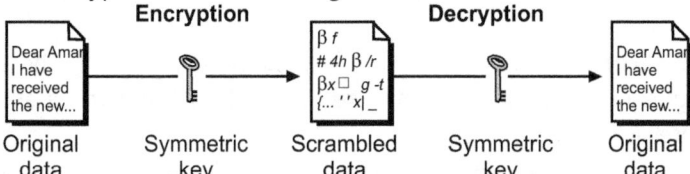

Fig. 5.5: Symmetric key encryption

- Symmetric key ciphers are valuable because:
  1. It is relatively inexpensive to produce a strong key for these ciphers.
  2. The keys tend to be much smaller for the level of protection they afford.
  3. The algorithms are relatively inexpensive to process.
- Therefore, implementing symmetric cryptography (particularly with hardware) can be highly effective because you do not experience any significant time delay as a result of the encryption and decryption.
- Symmetric cryptography also provides a degree of authentication because data encrypted with one symmetric key cannot be decrypted with any other symmetric key.
- Therefore, as long as the symmetric key is kept secret by the two parties using it to encrypt communications, each party can be sure that it is communicating with the other as long as the decrypted messages continue to make sense.
- Typically, with a symmetric key, you can exchange the key with another trusted participant; usually you produce a unique key for each pair of participants. You can be assured that any messages that you exchange, which are encrypted in a specific key, between the participants can only be deciphered by the other participant that has that key. In this way, the key must be kept secret to each participant.
- Consequently, these keys are also referred to as secret-key ciphers. If anyone else finds the key, it affects both confidentiality and authentication. A person with an unauthorized symmetric key not only can decrypt messages sent with that key, but can encrypt new messages and send them as if they came from one of the two parties who were originally using the key.

Advantages:
1. **Simple:** This type of encryption is easy to carry out. All users have to do is specify and share the secret key and then begin to encrypt and decrypt messages.

2. **Encrypt and decrypt your own files:** If you use encryption for messages or files which you alone intend to access, there is no need to create different keys. Single-key encryption is best for this.
3. **Fast:** Symmetric key encryption is much faster than asymmetric key encryption.
4. **Uses less computer resources:** Single-key encryption does not require a lot of computer resources when compared to public key encryption.
5. **Prevents widespread message security compromise:** A different secret key is used for communication with every different party. If a key is compromised, only the messages between a particular pair of sender and receiver are affected. Communications with other people are still secure.

Disadvantages:
1. **Need for secure channel for secret key exchange:** Sharing the secret key in the beginning is a problem in symmetric key encryption. It has to be exchanged in a way that ensures it remains secret.
2. **Too many keys:** A new shared key has to be generated for communication with every different party. This creates a problem with managing and ensuring the security of all these keys.
3. **Origin and authenticity of message cannot be guaranteed:** Since both sender and receiver use the same key, messages cannot be verified to have come from a particular user. This may be a problem if there is a dispute.

2. **Asymmetric Key Encryption:**
- The most commonly used implementations of public key cryptography (also known as public-key encryption and asymmetric encryption) are based on algorithms presented by Rivest-Shamir-Adelman (RSA) for data security.
- Public key cryptography involves a pair of keys known as a public key and a private key (a public key pair), which are associated with an entity that needs to authenticate its identity electronically or to sign or encrypt data.
- Each public key is published and the corresponding private key is kept secret. Data that is encrypted with the public key can be decrypted only with the corresponding private key.
- RSA public key can be of any size. Typical sizes today are 1024 and 2048 bits.
- Public key cryptography enables the following:
  1. Encryption and decryption, which allow two communicating parties to disguise data that they send to each other. The sender encrypts, or scrambles, the data before sending it. The receiver decrypts, or unscrambles, the data after receiving it. While in transit, the encrypted data is not understood by an intruder.
  2. Non-repudiation, which prevents:
     (i) The sender of the data from claiming, at a later date, that the data was never sent.
     (ii) The data from being altered.

- Fig. 5.6 shows you a simplified view of how public key cryptography works.

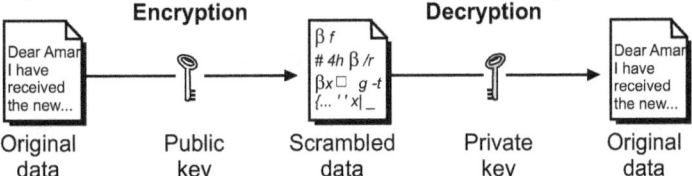

Fig. 5.6: Asymmetric cryptography

- Fig. 5.8 shows how you can freely distribute the public key so that only you (the owner of the private key) can read data that was encrypted with the public key.
- In general, to send encrypted data to someone, you must encrypt the data with that person's public key, and the person receiving the data decrypts it with the corresponding private key.
- If you compare symmetric-key encryption with public-key encryption, you will find that public-key encryption requires more calculations. Therefore, public-key encryption is not always appropriate for large amounts of data. However, it is possible to use public-key encryption to send a symmetric key, which you can then use to encrypt additional data.
- The reverse of what is shown in the previous figure also works. That is, data encrypted with your private key can be decrypted only with your public key.
- However, this is not a desirable way to encrypt sensitive data because it means that anyone with your public key, which is by definition published, could decrypt the sensitive data. Despite this, private-key encryption is useful because it enables you to use your private key to sign data with your digital signature; anyone with your public key can be assured that only you sent the data. This is an important requirement for electronic commerce and other commercial applications of cryptography.

Advantages:
1. **Convenience:** It solves the problem of distributing the key for encryption. Everyone publishes their public keys and private keys are kept secret.
2. **Provides for message authentication:** Public key encryption allows the use of digital signatures which enables the recipient of a message to verify that the message is truly from a particular sender.
3. **Detection of tampering:** The use of digital signatures in public key encryption allows the receiver to detect if the message was altered in transit. A digitally signed message cannot be modified without invalidating the signature.
4. **Provide for non-repudiation:** Digitally signing a message is akin to physically signing a document. It is an acknowledgement of the message and thus, the sender cannot deny it.

Disadvantages:
1. **Public keys should/must be authenticated:** No one can be absolutely sure that a public key belongs to the person it specifies and so everyone must verify that their public keys belong to them.

2. **Slow:** Public key encryption is slow compared to symmetric encryption. Not feasible for use in decrypting bulk messages.
3. **Uses more computer resources:** It requires a lot more computer supplies compared to single-key encryption.
4. **Widespread security compromise is possible:** If an attacker determines a person's private key, his or her entire messages can be read.
5. **Loss of private key may be irreparable:** The loss of a private key means that all received messages cannot be decrypted.

5.3 Digital Signature

- Signatures are commonly used to authenticate documents. When one signs a physical document, he/she is authenticating its contents.
- Similarly, digital signatures are used to authenticate the contents of electronic documents. They can be used with PDF, e-mail messages, and word processing documents.
- A digital signature is a unique, mathematically computed signature that ensures accountability.
- A digital signature (not to be confused with a digital certificate) is an electronic signature that can be used to authenticate the identity of the sender of a message or the signer of a document, and possibly to ensure that the original content of the message or document that has been sent is unchanged.
- A digital signature is a small block of data attached with document which are signed.
- Digital signatures are easily transportable, cannot be imitated by someone else, and can be automatically time-stamped. The ability to ensure that the original signed message arrived means that the sender cannot easily repudiate it later.
- A digital signature can be used with any kind of message, whether it is encrypted or not, simply so that the receiver can be sure of the sender's identity and that the message arrived intact.
- A digital certificate contains the digital signature of the certificate-issuing authority so that anyone can verify that the certificate is real.
- A digital certificate serves two purposes: it establishes the owner's identity, and it makes the owner's public key available.
- A digital certificate is issued by a certification authority (CA), for example VeriSign, or Thawte. It is issued only for a limited time period and when its expiry date has passed, it must be replaced.
- A digital signature or digital signature scheme is a mathematical scheme for demonstrating the authenticity of a digital message or document.
- A valid digital signature gives a recipient reason to believe that the message was created by a known sender such that they cannot deny sending it (authentication and non-repudiation) and that the message was not altered in transit (integrity).
- Digital signatures are commonly used for software distribution, financial transactions, and in other cases where it is important to detect forgery or tampering.

Fig. 5.7: Signing digital signature

5.3.1 Definition

- A digital signature is an electronic signature that can be used to authenticate the identity of the sender of a message or the signer of a document, and possibly to ensure that the original content of the message or document that has been sent is unchanged.

OR

- Digital signature is a block of data that can be attached to documents like e-mail messages, word files etc.

OR

- Digital signature is a digital code that can be attached to an electronically transmitted messages that uniquely identifies the sender.
- A digital certificate establishes the credentials when doing business or other transactions on the Web.
- In simple words Digital Certificate is the attachment to an electronic message used for security purposes.

5.3.2 How Digital Signature Works?

- Fig. 5.8 shows working of digital signature.

1. User views document:
User views document, fills in form fields, chooses credential, and clicks signature field to approve.

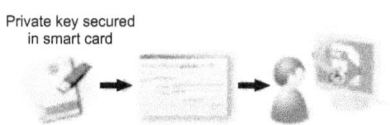

2. Signing process:
User initiates signing process, is prompted for smart card pin to authenticate to credentials stored on the hardware token or smartcard

---

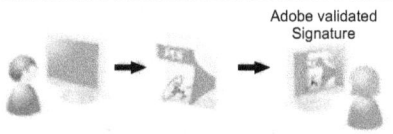

3. Document received:
Adobe validates signature from trusted CA. Recipient view signed document

---

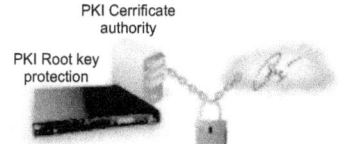

Digital ID Protection
Secure certificate issuance and key management provided by HSMs

Fig. 5.8: Working mechanism of digital signature

5.3.3 Advantages and Disadvantages

- Advantages of digital signature are:
    1. **Imposter prevention:** By using digital signatures you are actually eliminating the possibility of committing fraud by an imposter signing the document. Since the digital signature cannot be altered, this makes forging the signature impossible.
    2. **Message integrity:** By having a digital signature you are in fact showing and simply proving the document to be valid. You are assuring the recipient that the document is free from forgery or false information.
    3. **Legal requirements:** Using a digital signature satisfies some type of legal requirement for the document in question. A digital signature takes care of any formal legal aspect of executing the document.
- The **disadvantages** of using digital signatures involve the primary avenue for any business money. This is because the business may have to spend more money than usual to work with digital signatures including buying certificates from Certification Authorities (CA) and getting the verification software.

5.4 IT ACT

1. **IT Act 2000:**
- The Information Technology Act 2000 (also known as ITA-2000, or the IT Act) is an Act of the Indian Parliament (No 21 of 2000) notified on October 17, 2000. This act is being opposed by Save Your Voicecampaign and other civil society organisations in India.
- Information technology Act 2000 consisted of 94 sections segregated into 13 chapters. Four schedules form part of the Act. In the 2008 version of the Act, there are 124 sections (excluding 5 sections that have been omitted from the earlier version) and 14 chapters. Schedule I and II have been replaced. Schedules III and IV are deleted.
- Information Technology Act 2000 addressed the following issues:
    (i) Legal Recognition of Electronic Documents
    (ii) Legal Recognition of Digital Signatures
    (iii) Offenses and Contraventions
    (iv) Justice Dispensation Systems for Cybercrimes

2. **The Information Technology Act, 2008:**
- The Government of India has brought major amendments to ITA-2000 in form of the Information Technology Amendment Act, 2008. ITAA 2008 (Information Technology Amendment Act 2008) as the new version of Information Technology Act 2000 is often referred has provided additional focus on Information Security.
- It has added several new sections on offences including Cyber Terrorism and Data Protection. A set of Rules relating to Sensitive Personal Information and Reasonable Security Practices (mentioned in section 43A of the ITAA, 2008) was release.

3. **Cyber law:**
   - Cyberlaw or Internet law is a term that encapsulates the legal issues related to use of the Internet. It is less a distinct field of law than intellectual property or contract law, as it is a domain covering many areas of law and regulation. Some leading topics include internet access and usage, privacy, freedom of expression, and jurisdiction.
   - "Computer law" is a third term which tends to relate to issues including both Internet law and the patent and copyright aspects of computer technology and software.
   - There is intellectual property in general, including copyright, rules on fair use, and special rules on copy protection for digital media, and circumvention of such schemes. The area of software patents is controversial, and still evolving in Europe and elsewhere.
   - The related topics of software licenses, end user license agreements, free software licenses and open-source licenses can involve discussion of product liability, professional liability of individual developers, warranties, contract law, trade secrets and intellectual property.
   - In various countries, areas of the computing and communication industries are regulated – often strictly – by government bodies.
   - There are rules on the uses to which computers and computer networks may be put, in particular there are rules on unauthorized access, data privacy and spamming. There are also limits on the use of encryption and of equipment which may be used to defeat copy protection schemes. The export of Hardware and Software between certain states is also controlled.
   - There are laws governing trade on the Internet, taxation, consumer protection, and advertising.
   - There are laws on censorship versus freedom of expression, rules on public access to government information, and individual access to information held on them by private bodies. There are laws on what data must be retained for law enforcement, and what may not be gathered or retained, for privacy reasons.
   - In certain circumstances and jurisdictions, computer communications may be used in evidence, and to establish contracts. New methods of tapping and surveillance made possible by computers have wildly differing rules on how they may be used by law enforcement bodies and as evidence in court.
   - Computerized voting technology, from polling machines to internet and mobile-phone voting, raise a host of legal issues.
   - Some states limit access to the Internet, by law as well as by technical means.
4. **Jurisdiction:**
   - Issues of jurisdiction and sovereignty have quickly come to the fore in the era of the Internet. Jurisdiction is an aspect of state sovereignty and it refers to judicial, legislative and administrative competence.
   - Although jurisdiction is an aspect of sovereignty, it is not coextensive with it. The laws of a nation may have extraterritorial impact extending the jurisdiction beyond the sovereign and territorial limits of that nation.

- This is particularly problematic as the medium of the Internet does not explicitly recognize sovereignty and territorial limitations. There is no uniform, international jurisdictional law of universal application, and such questions are generally a matter of conflict of laws, particularly private international law.
- An example would be where the contents of a web site are legal in one country and illegal in another. In the absence of a uniform jurisdictional code, legal practitioners are generally left with a conflict of law issue.

5.5 Security Threats to Information

- In computer security a threat is a possible danger that might exploit a vulnerability to breach security and thus cause possible harm.
- A threat, refers to anything that has the potential to cause serious harm to a computer system.
- A threat is something that may or may not happen, but has the potential to cause serious damage. Threats can lead to attacks on computer systems, networks and more.
- Threats are potentials for vulnerabilities to turn into attacks on computer systems, networks, and more. They can put individual's computer systems and business computers at risk, so vulnerabilities have to be fixed so that attackers cannot infiltrate the system and cause damage.
- Threats can include everything from viruses, trojans, back doors to outright attacks from hackers. Often, the term blended threat is more accurate, as the majority of threats involve multiple exploits. For example, a hacker might use a phishing attack to gain information about a network and break into a network.

Definition of threat:

- Threat is the potential for the occurrence of a harmful event such as an attack.

OR

- In computer security a threat is a possible danger that might exploit a vulnerability to breach security and thus cause possible harm.
- A security policy defines what user can and cannot do with network components and resources.
- Fig. 5.9 shows network security threats.

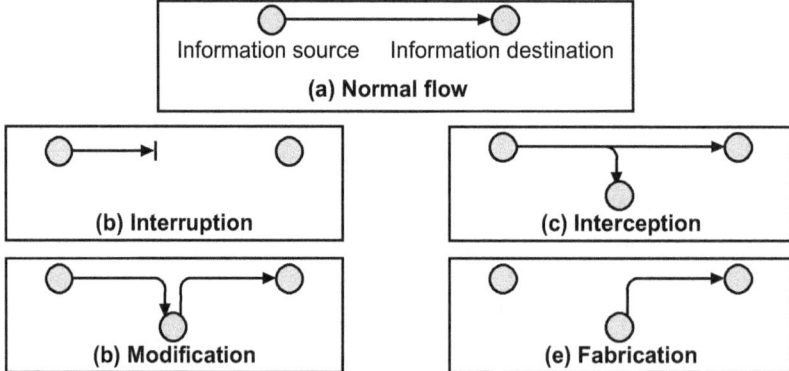

Fig. 5.9: Network security threats

1. **Interruption:** An asset of the system is destroyed or becomes unavailable or unusable. This is an attack on availability.
   Examples:
   (i) Destroying some hardware, (disk or wire).
   (ii) Disabling file system.
   (iii) Swamping a computer with jobs or communication link with packets.
2. **Interception:** An unauthorized party gains access to an asset. This is an attack on confidentiality.
   Examples:
   (i) Wiretapping to capture data in a network.
   (ii) Illicitly copying data or programs.
3. **Modification:** An unauthorized party gains access and tampers an asset. This is an attack on integrity.
   Examples:
   (i) Changing data files.
   (ii) Altering a program.
   (iii) Altering the contents of a message.
4. **Fabrication:** An unauthorized party inserts a counterfeit object into the system. This is an attack on authenticity.
   Examples:
   (i) Insertion of records in data files.
   (ii) Insertion of spurious messages in a network, (message replay).
- Fig. 5.10 shows various types of threats.

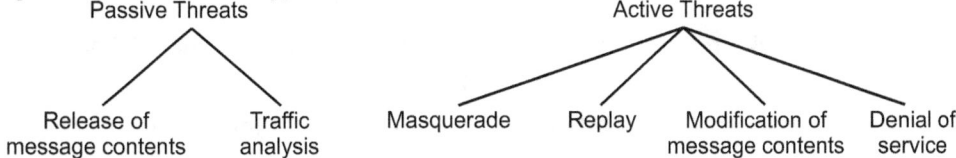

Fig. 5.10: Active and Passive security threats

1. **Active Attack:**
- In an active attack, the attacker tries to bypass or break into secured systems. This can be done through stealth, viruses, worms, or trojan horses.
- Active attacks include attempts to circumvent or break protection features, to introduce malicious code, and to steal or modify information.
2. **Passive Attack:**
- A passive attack monitors unencrypted traffic and looks for clear-text passwords and sensitive information that can be used in other types of attacks.
- Passive attacks include traffic analysis, monitoring of unprotected communications, decrypting weakly encrypted traffic, and capturing authentication information such as passwords.
- Passive interception of network operations enables adversaries to see upcoming actions.
- Passive attacks result in the disclosure of information or data files to an attacker without the consent or knowledge of the user.

5.5.1 Viruses
- A computer virus is an executable program. Depending on the nature of a virus, it may cause damage of your hard disk contents, and/or interfere normal operation of your computer.
- A computer virus is a special kind of computer program which:
    - Spreads across disks and networks by making copies of itself, usually surreptitiously.
    - Can produce undesired side-effects in computers in which it is active.

What is Computer Virus?
- A virus is a small piece of software that piggybacks on real programs. For example, a virus might attach itself to a program such as a spreadsheet program. Each time the spreadsheet program runs, the virus runs, too, and it has the chance to reproduce (by attaching to other programs).
- A virus program contains instructions to initiate some sort of event that affects the infected computer. Each virus has an unique event associated with it.
- These events and their effects can range from harmless to devastating.
- For examples:
    1. An annoying message appearing on the computer screen.
    2. Reduced memory or disk space.
    3. Hard drive erased.
    4. Files overwritten or damaged.
    5. Modification of data.

Definition of Virus:
- A virus is a computer program that executes when an infected program is executed.

OR

- Computer viruses are small programs or scripts that can negatively affect the health of your computer.

OR

- A computer virus is a program that spreads between computers by hiding itself within a - seemingly innocent - document or application.

Types of Viruses:
- Computer viruses can be classified in many different ways based on a number of factors, such as their entry point, infection strategy, objectives, etc.
- Every virus contains at least two modules, a search module and a copy module. The search module looks for infection targets, while the copy module copies the virus into identified targets.

1. **Trojan Horse:**
- A trojan horse program has the appearance of having a useful and desired function. While it advertises its activity after launching, this information is not apparent to the user beforehand. Secretly the program performs other, undesired functions.

- A Trojan Horse neither replicates nor copies itself, but causes damage or compromises the security of the computer.
- A Trojan Horse must be sent by someone or carried by another program and may arrive in the form of a joke program or software of some sort.
- The malicious functionality of a Trojan Horse may be anything undesirable for a computer user, including data destruction or compromising a system by providing a means for another computer to gain access, thus bypassing normal access controls.

2. **Worms:**
- A worm is a program that makes and facilitates the distribution of copies of itself; for example, from one disk drive to another, or by copying itself using email or another transport mechanism.
- The worm may damage and compromise the security of the computer. It may arrive via exploitation of a system vulnerability or by clicking on an infected e-mail.
- **Examples:** Mapson, Lovgate.F, Trile.C etc.

3. **Bootsector Virus:**
- A virus which attaches itself to the first part of the hard disk that is read by the computer upon bootup. These viruses are normally spread by floppy disks and hard disk.
   Examples: Polyboot.B, AntiExe. etc.

4. **Macro Virus:**
- Macro viruses are viruses that use another application's macro programming language to distribute themselves.
- They infect documents such as MS Word or MS Excel and are typically spread to other similar documents.
   Examples: Relax, Bablas, Melissa etc.

5. **Memory Resident Viruses:**
- Memory Resident Viruses reside in a computer's volatile memory (RAM).
- They are initiated from a virus which runs on the computer and they stay in memory after it's initiating program closes.
   Examples: CMJ Meve, Randex Mrklunky etc.

6. **Rootkit Virus:**
- A rootkit virus is an undetectable virus which attempts to allow someone to gain control of a computer system.
- The term rootkit comes from the linux administrator root user. These viruses are usually installed by trojans and are normally disguised as operating system files.

7. **Polymorphic Viruses:**
- A polymorphic virus not only replicates itself by creating multiple files of itself, but it also changes it's digital signature every time it replicates.
- This makes it difficult for less sophisticated antivirus software to detect.
   Examples: Elekern, Tuareg, Satan Bug, Marburg etc.

8. Logic Bombs/Time Bombs:
- These are viruses which are programmed to initiate at a specific date or when a specific event occurs.

  Some examples are a virus which deletes your photos on Halloween, or a virus which deletes a database table if a certain employee gets fired.

9. Direct Action Viruses:
- The main purpose of this virus is to replicate and take action when it is executed. When a specific condition is met, the virus will go into action and infect files in the directory or folder that it is in and in directories that are specified in the AUTOEXEC.BAT file PATH.
- This batch file is always located in the root directory of the hard disk and carries out certain operations when the computer is booted.

10. Overwrite Viruses:
- Virus of this kind is characterized by the fact that it deletes the information contained in the files that it infects, rendering them partially or totally useless once they have been infected. The only way to clean a file infected by an overwrite virus is to delete the file completely, thus losing the original content.

  Examples of this virus include: Way, Trj.Reboot, Trivial.88.D.

11. Directory Virus:
- Directory viruses change the paths that indicate the location of a file.
- By executing a program (file with the extension .EXE or .COM) which has been infected by a virus, you are unknowingly running the virus program, while the original file and program have been previously moved by the virus. Once infected it becomes impossible to locate the original files.

12. Metamorphic Virus:
- Metamorphic Viruses can reprogram itself. Often, it does this by translating its own code into a temporary representation, edit the temporary representation of itself, and then write itself back to normal code again.

13. File Infectors:
- This type of virus infects programs or executable files (files with an .EXE or .COM extension).
- When one of these programs is run, directly or indirectly, the virus is activated, producing the damaging effects it is programmed to carry out.
- The majority of existing viruses belong to this category, and can be classified depending on the actions that they carry out.

14. Companion Viruses:
- Companion viruses can be considered file infector viruses like resident or direct action types.
- They are known as companion viruses because once they get into the system they accompany the other files that already exist.

- In other words, in order to carry out their infection routines, companion viruses can wait in memory until a program is run (resident viruses) or act immediately by making copies of themselves (direct action viruses).
  Examples, Stator, Asimov.1539, and Terrax.1069

15. Script Viruses:
- A subset of file viruses these are written in a variety of script languages like Javascript, VBS, BAT, PHP etc.
- They are also able to infect other file formats such as HTML (if the file format allows script execution)

16. Email Viruses:
- Email viruses are different types of viruses, which uses email messages to transport, and can automatically send itself to hundreds, and thousands of people depending on whose email address they victimize.

5.5.2 Hacking
- Computer hacking is when someone modifies computer hardware or software in a way that alters the creator's original intent.
- People who hack computers are known as hackers.
- Hackers are usually real technology buffs who enjoy learning all they can about computers and how they work.
- Hackers think that what they do is like an art form.
- They usually have expert-level skills in one specific program. For most hackers, hacking gives them the opportunity to use their problem-solving skills and a chance to show off their abilities. Most of them do not wish to harm others.
- A hacker is basically someone who breaks into computer networks or standalone personal computer systems for the challenge of it or because they want to profit from their innate hacking capabilities.
- The hacker subculture that has developed among these new-age outlaws is often defined as the computer underground, although as of late it has evolved into a more open society of sorts. At any rate, here are the different types of hackers.
    1. **White Hat:** A white hat hacker is someone who has non-malicious intent whenever he breaks into security systems and whatnot. In fact, a large number of white hat hackers are security experts themselves who want to push the boundaries of their own IT security ciphers and shields or even penetration testers specifically hired to test out how vulnerable or impenetrable (at the time) a present protective setup currently is. A white hat that does vulnerability assessments and penetration tests is also known as an ethical hacker.
    2. **Black Hat:** A black hat hacker, also known as a cracker, is the type of hacker that has malicious intent whenever he goes about breaking into computer security systems with the use of technology such as a network, phone system, or computer and without authorization. His malevolent purposes can range from all sorts cybercrimes

such as piracy, identity theft, credit card fraud, vandalism, and so forth. He may or may not utilize questionable tactics such as deploying worms and malicious sites to meet his ends.

3. **Grey Hat:** A grey hat hacker is someone who exhibits traits from both white hats and black hats. More to the point, this is the kind of hacker that is not a penetration tester but will go ahead and surf the Internet for vulnerable systems he could exploit. Like a white hat, he will inform the administrator of the website of the vulnerabilities he found after hacking through the site. Like a black hat and unlike a pen tester, he will hack any site freely and without any prompting or authorization from owners whatsoever. He will even offer to repair the vulnerable site he exposed in the first place for a small fee.

4. **Elite Hacker:** As with any society, better than average people are rewarded for their talent and treated as special. This social status among the hacker underground, the elite are the hackers among hackers in this subculture of sorts. They are the masters of deception that have a solid reputation among their peers as the cream of the hacker crop.

5. **Script Kiddie:** A script kiddie is basically an amateur or non-expert hacker wannabe who breaks into people's computer systems not through his knowledge in IT security and the ins and outs of a given website, but through the prepackaged automated scripts (hence the name), tools, and software written by people who are real hackers, unlike him. He usually has little to know knowledge of the underlying concept behind how those scripts he has on hand works.

5.5.3 Natural Calamities

- Natural disasters (calamities) occur when forces of nature damage the environment and manmade structures. If people live in the area, natural disasters can cause a great deal of human suffering. As a result of disasters, people may be injured or killed, or may lose their homes and possessions.
- A natural calamity is anything that occurs in nature that results in a disaster or damage to something or someone. It is a result of natural forces rather than a direct result of man made forces. .
- There are different types of natural calamities:
    1. **Earthquake:** An earthquake is the result of a sudden release of energy in the Earth's crust that creates seismic waves. Earthquakes are recorded with a seismometer, also known as a seismograph. The magnitude of an earthquake is conventionally reported on the Richter scale, with magnitude 3 or lower earthquakes being mostly imperceptible and magnitude 7 causing serious damage over large areas. Intensity of shaking is measured on the modified Mercalli scale. At the Earth's surface, earthquakes manifest themselves by shaking and sometimes displacement of the ground.

2. **Volcanic eruption:** A volcanic eruption is the point in which a volcano is active and releases lava and poisonous gasses in to the air. They range from daily small eruptions to extremely infrequent supervolcano eruptions (where the volcano expels at least 1,000 cubic kilometers of material.) Some eruptions form pyroclastic flows, which are high-temperature clouds of ash and steam that can travel down mountainsides at speeds exceeding that of an airliner.
3. **Flood:** A flood is an overflow of an expanse of water that submerges land, a deluge. It is usually due to the volume of water within a body of water, such as a river or lake, exceeding the total capacity of the body, and as a result some of the water flows or sits outside of the normal perimeter of the body. It can also occur in rivers, when the strength of the river is so high it flows right out of the river channel, usually at corners or meanders.
4. **Landslide:** A landslide is a disaster involving elements of the ground, including rocks, trees, parts of houses, and anything else which may happen to be swept up. Landslides can be caused by an earthquake, volcanic eruptions, or general instability in the surrounding land. Mudslides or mudflows, are a special case of landslides, in which heavy rainfall causes loose soil on steep terrain to collapse and slide downwards.
5. **Tsunami:** A tsunami is a series of waves created when a body of water, such as an ocean, is rapidly displaced. Earthquakes, mass movements above or below water, volcanic eruptions and other underwater explosions, landslides, large meteorite impacts comet impacts and testing with nuclear weapons at sea all have the potential to generate a tsunami. A tsunami is not the same thing as a tidal wave, which will generally have a far less damaging effect than a Tsunami.
6. **Tornado:** Tornadoes are violent, rotating columns of air which can blow at speeds between 50 and 300 mph, and possibly higher. Tornadoes can occur one at a time, or can occur in large tornado outbreaks along squall lines or in other large areas of thunderstorm development. Waterspouts are tornadoes occurring over water in light rain conditions.

5.5.4 Failure of System
- A system failure can occur because of a hardware failure or a severe software issue. Commonly, a system failure will cause the system tofreeze, reboot, or stop functioning altogether.
- There are two types of failures:
  1. **Logical Failures:** A logical failure is when the media has not been physically damaged. A file may have been deleted, reformatted or contaminated with a virus. Generally, in these situations, data is easier to recover as long as the data has not been overwritten by subsequent usage.
  2. **Physical Failures:** A physical failure is when the media has been damaged or experienced a mechanical failure. Fire or water damage can result in a physical failure or, in the case of a disk drive, part of the mechanism such as a spindle or head may

have failed. In these cases, the media, such as a disk drive, must first be rebuilt before data recovery can be attempted. Often, by utilizing technology and specialized techniques, data can be recovered but, in some cases where the drive or device is too damaged, data recovery is impossible.

5.6 Preventive Measures and Data Recovery

5.6.1 Antivirus

- Antivirus software is software used to prevent, detect and remove malware (of all descriptions), such as computer viruses, malicious BHOs, hijackers, ransomware, keyloggers, backdoors, rootkits, trojan horses, worms, and so on.
- Antivirus software is a computer program that detects, prevents, and takes action to disarm or remove malicious software programs, such as viruses and worms.

What is the purpose of an anti-virus?

- An anti-virus program protects a computer from getting malicious viruses from the internet, through websites, email, and instant messenger.
- Usually, it consists of a firewall, a virus scanner and remover, and sometimes other tools as well.
- Anti-virus software offers computers and the network they are connected with protection against a type of malware called viruses.
- Antivirus software can be used to prevent an infection or by finding and removing an infection. To prevent an infection software usually uses a firewall.
- The best firewall is a 2 way firewall. A two way firewall grants or denies internet access to programs already installed on your computer. It also denies or grants access to other computers trying to access your computer. Removing infections is important because it stops pop ups, irregular behavior, system faliure and more.

Definition of Antivirus:

- Antivirus" is protective software designed to defend your computer against malicious software.

OR

- Antivirus software is a type of utility used for scanning and removing viruses from your computer.

OR

- Antivirus software is a class of program that searches your hard drive and floppy disks for any known or potential viruses.

OR

- Computer antivirus refers to a software program that can protect your computer from unwanted viruses and remove any that penetrate your computer's defenses.

Antivirus measures:
- The fight against computer viruses involves five kinds of counter-measure:
    1. **Preparation** includes making backups of all software (including operating systems) and making a contingency plan.
    2. **Prevention** includes creating user awareness, implementing hygiene rules, using disk authorisation software, or providing isolated quarantine PCs.
    3. **Detection** involves the use of anti-virus software to detect, report and (sometimes) disinfect viruses.
    4. **Containment** involves identifying and isolating the infected items.
    5. **Recovery** involves disinfecting or removing infected items, and recovering or replacing corrupted data.

Examples of Computer Antivirus Softwares:
1. **Norton AntiVirus:** Norton is one of the most well-known antivirus software. One of its key features is that it updates every 5 to 15 minutes to make sure you system is up to date.
2. **McAfee Virus Scan Plus:** McAfee Virus Scan Plus is another software that shields your PC from viruses and spyware, and includes a firewall that can help prevent hacker attacks to your system.
3. **AVG Anti-Virus:** AVG is unique in that it provides consumers a completely free version, as well as a version that costs $34.99 for a one-year subscription. The free version works extremely well if you are just looking for simple antivirus protection without all the bells and whistles.
4. **Trend Micro ("PC-Cillin") Internet Security:** Trend Micro provides an award-winning antivirus engine that protects from viruses, spam, spyware, trojans and other online security threats. The cost for a one-year subscription is $49.95.
5. **Bit Defender:** Bit Defender offers protection from viruses, spyware, rootkits, provides anti-phishing help, and offers a gamer and laptop mode. This software is only $29.99 annually and can be used on up to three computers.

5.6.2 Firewalls
- A firewall is a set of related programs, located at a network gateway server, that protects the resources of a private network from users from other networks.
- A firewall can either be software-based or hardware-based and is used to help keep a network secure.
- Firewall's primary objective is to control the incoming and outgoing network traffic by analyzing the data packets and determining whether it should be allowed through or not, based on a predetermined rule set.
- A network's firewall builds a bridge between an internal network that is assumed to be secure and trusted, and another network, usually an external network, such as the Internet, that is not assumed to be secure and trusted.

- A firewall's basic task is to regulate some of the flow of traffic between computer networks of different trust levels.
- A firewall is a part of a computer system or network that is designed to block unauthorized access while permitting authorized communications.
- Firewall is a device or set of devices configured to permit, deny, encrypt, decrypt or proxy all (in and out) computer traffic between different security domains based on upon a set of rules and other criteria.

Characteristics of Firewall:

1. All traffic from inside to outside, and vice versa, must pass through the firewall. This is achieved by physically blocking all access to the local network except via the firewall. Various configurations are possible in firewalls.
2. Only authorized traffic, as defined by the local security policy, will be allowed to pass. Various types of firewalls are used, which implement various types of security policies.

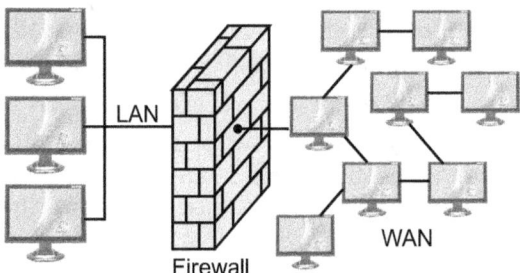

Fig. 5.11: Typical firewall structure

3. The firewall itself is immune to penetration. This implies that use of a trusted system with a secure operating system.

What is a firewall?

- A firewall protects networked computers from intentional hostile intrusion that could compromise confidentiality or result in data corruption or denial of service.
- It may be a hardware device (See Fig. 5.12) or a software program (See Fig. 5.13) running on a secured host computer.
- In either case, it must have at least two network interfaces, one for the network it is intended to protect, and one for the network it is exposed to.
- A firewall sits at the junction point or gateway between the two networks, usually a private network and a public network such as the Internet.
- The earliest firewalls were simply routers. The term firewall comes from the fact that by segmenting a network into different physical subnetworks, they limit the damage that could spread from one subnet to another just like firedoors or firewalls.
- Hardware firewall provides protection to a Local Network.

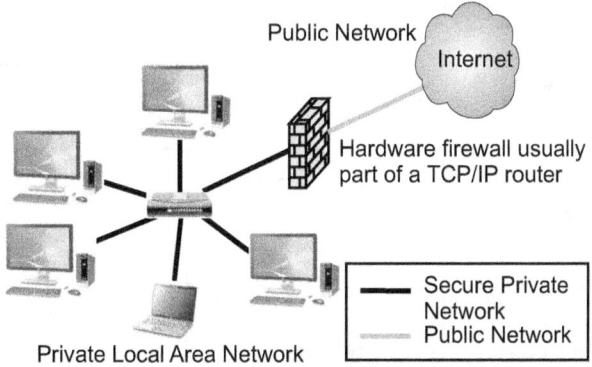

Fig. 5.12: Hardware firewall

- Computer running firewall software to provide protection.

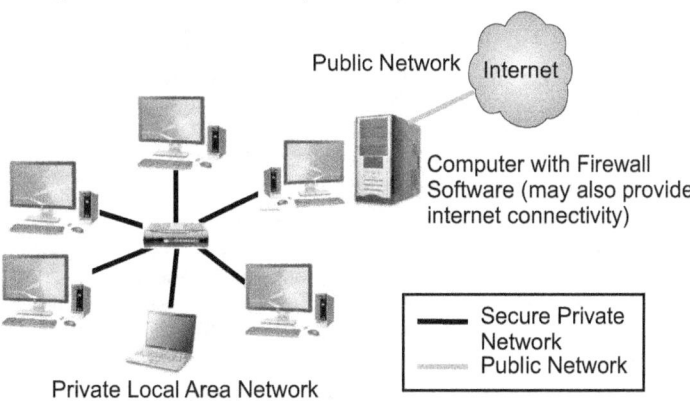

Fig. 5.13: Software firewall

How does a firewall work?

- There are two access denial methodologies used by firewalls. A firewall may allow all traffic through unless it meets certain criteria, or it may deny all traffic unless it meets certain criteria, (See Fig. 5.14).

- The type of criteria used to determine whether traffic should be allowed through, varies from one type of firewall to another.

- Firewalls may be concerned with the type of traffic, or with source or destination addresses and ports. They may also use complex rule bases that analyse the application data to determine if the traffic should be allowed through.

- How a firewall determines what traffic to let through depends on which network layer it operates at.

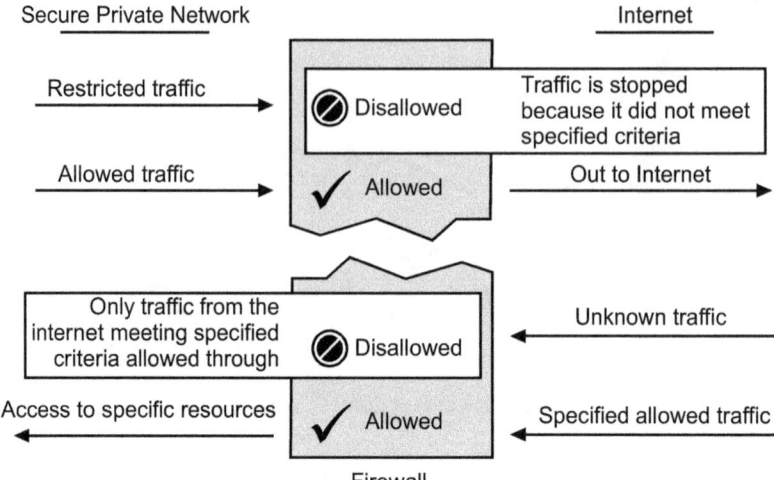

Fig. 5.14: Basic firewall operations

- Based on the criteria used for filtering traffic, firewalls are generally classified into two types of as shown in Fig. 5.15.

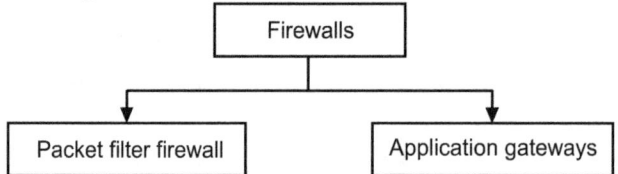

Fig. 5.15: Types of firewalls

1. Packet Filter Firewall:
- Packet filter applies a set of rules to each packet and based on the outcome decides to either forward or discard the packet.
- It is also called as screening router or screening filter.
- Such a firewall implementation involves a router, which is configured to filter packets going in either direction.
- The filtering rules are based on a number of fields in the IP and TCP/UDP headers, such as source and destination IP addresses, IP protocol field, TCP/UDP port numbers.

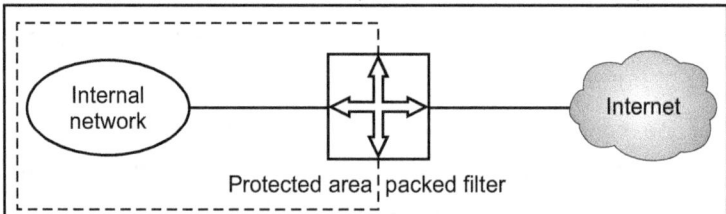

Fig. 5.16: Packet filter firewall

- Packet filter looks at each packet entering or leaving the network and accepts or rejects it based on user-defined rules.
- Packet filtering is fairly effective and transparent to users, but it is difficult to configure. In addition, it is susceptible to IP spoofing.

2. Application Gateways:
- Application gateway applies security mechanisms to specific applications, such as FTP and Telnet servers etc.
- This is very effective, but can impose a performance degradation.
- Application gateways are generally more secure than packet filters.
- The disadvantages of application gateways is the overhead in terms of connections.

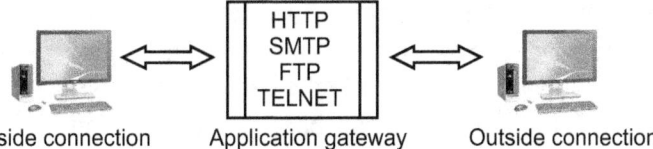

Fig. 5.17: Application gateways

- Application gateway is also called as a proxy server.

Advantages of firewalls:
1. A feeling of increased security that your PC and contents are being protected.
2. Relatively inexpensive or free for personal use.
3. New releases are becoming user friendly.
4. You can monitor incoming and outgoing security alerts and the firewall company will record and track down an intrusion attempt depending on the severity.
5. Some firewalls but not all can detect viruses, worms, trojan horses, or data collectors.
6. All firewalls can be tested for effectiveness by using products that test for leaks or probe for open ports.

Disadvantages of firewalls:
1. Firewalls evolve due to cracker's ability to circumvent their increases.
2. Always on connections created by Cable and DSL connections create major problems for firewalls. This can be compared to leaving you car running with the keys in it and the doors unlocked which a thief may interpret as an invitation to Please steal me.
3. Firewalls cannot protect you from internal sabotage within a network or from allowing other users access to your PC.
4. Firewalls cannot edit indecent material like pornography, violence, drugs and bad language. This would require you to adjust your browser security options or purchase special software to monitor your children's Internet activity.
5. Firewalls offer weak defense from viruses so antiviral software and an IDS (Intrusion Detection System) which protects against trojans and port scans should also complement your firewall in the layering defense.

5.6.3 Data Recovery Methods
- Data recovery is the process of salvaging data from damaged, failed, corrupted, or inaccessible secondary storage media when it cannot be accessed normally.
- Often the data are being salvaged from storage media such as internal or external hard disk drives, solid-state drives (SSD), USB flash drive, storage tapes, CDs, DVDs, RAID, and other electronics.

- Recovery may be required due to physical damage to the storage device or logical damage to the file system that prevents it from being mounted by the host operating system.
- Data recovery is the process of restoring data that has been lost, accidentally deleted, corrupted or made inaccessible for any reason.
- In enterprise Information Technology (IT), data recovery typically refers to the restoration of data to a desktop, laptop, server, or external storage system from a backup.
- The data recovery process may vary, depending on the circumstances of the data loss, the data recovery software used to create the backup, and the backup target media.
- For example, many desktop and laptop backup software platforms allow end users to restore lost files themselves, while restoration of a corrupted database from a tape backup is a more complicated process that requires IT intervention.
- Data recovery can also be provided as service. Such services are typically used to retrieve important files that were not backed up and accidentally deleted from a computer's file system but still remain on disk in fragments.
- The majority of data loss situations are recoverable.
- Computer storage systems may fail, but the data stored on; them is not always completely lost.
- There are occasions when damage to data is permanent and complete data recovery is not possible. However, some data is usually always recoverable.
- Data recovery professionals can recover data from crashed hard drives, operating systems, storage devices, servers, desktops, and laptops using various proprietary data recovery tools and techniques.

Methods of Data Recovery:

1. **Scanning Probe Microscopy (SPM):**
   - Use a sharp magnetic tip attached to a flexible cantilever placed close to the surface to be analyzed, where it interacts with the stray field emanating from the sample to produce a topographic view of the surface.
   - Reasonable capable SPM can be built for about US $ 1400, using a PC a controller.
   - Thousands in use today.

2. **Magnetic Force Microscopy (MFM):**
   - Recent technique for imaging magnetization patterns with high resolution and minimal sample preparation.
   - Derived from scanning probe microscopy (SPM).
   - Uses a sharp magnetic tip attached to a flexible cantilever placed close to the surface to be analyzed where it interacts with the stray magnetic field.
   - An image of the field at the surface is formed by moving the tip across the surface and measuring the force (or force gradient) as a function of position. The strength of the interaction is measured by monitoring the position of the cantilever using an optical interferometer.

3. Scanning Tunneling Microscopy (STM):

- STM (Scanning Tunneling Microscopy) is a more recent variation of MFM which uses a probe tip typically made by plating nickel onto a pre-patterned surface.
- The probe is scanned across the surface that is to be analyzed. STM measures a weak electrical current flowing between the tip and the sample. The image is then generatd in the same way as MFM.

4. Backup:

- A backup, or the process of backing up, refers to the copying and archiving of computer data so it may be used to restorethe original after a data loss event. The verb form is to back up in two words, whereas the noun is backup.
- Backup is the activity of copying files or databases so that they will be preserved in case of equipment failure or other catastrophe.
- Backup is usually a routine part of the operation of large businesses with mainframes as well as the administrators of smaller business computers. For personal computer users, backup is also necessary but often neglected.
- The retrieval of files you backed up is called restoring them.

Data Recovery Tips:

DO's	DON'ts
• Backup you data frequently. • If you believer there is something wrong with your computer shut it down, do not continue to power up because you may do more damage. • If you here a clunk, clunk sound when you power up the drive, shut down ! Do not panic nor turn the power button on and off. • Package the drive properly when you send it into a data recovery specialist. You can cause additional damage to the hard drive if it is poorly packed.	• Do not ever assume that data recovery is impossible; even in the worst cases, such as natural disasters data recovery specialists have been able to retrieve valuable data. • Never remove the cover from the hard drive, this will only cause further damage. • Do not rest your computer on a moveable object or piece of furniture. Shock and vibration can result in serious damage to the hard drive. • Do not subject the drive to extreme temperatures changes both hot and cold. • In the case where a drive has been exposed to water, fire or even smoke do not try to power up.

Questions

1. What is MIS? Explain its characteristics in detail.
2. What are the objectives of MIS?
3. Define the following terms:
   (i) MIS,
   (ii) Virus, and
   (iii) Antivirus.
4. State advantages and disadvantages of MIS.
5. What is cryptography?
6. What is meant by encryption and decryption?
7. With the help of diagram describe encryption model.
8. Write short note on:
   (i) Symmetric key encryption, and
   (ii) Asymmetric key encryption.
9. What is digital signature?
10. Write short note on: IT Act.
11. What is meant by threat? What are its types? Explain in detail.
12. Define the following terms:
    (i) Cyber law,
    (ii) Digital signature, and
    (iii) Cryptography.
13. What are the types of viruses?
14. State advantages and disadvantages of digital signature.
15. What is hacking and hackers.
16. Write short note on failure of system.
17. Define antivirus? List any four examples of antivirus softwares.
18. What is firewall? How it works?
19. Define data recovery also explain its different methods.
20. Give advantages and disadvantages of firewalls.
21. Write short note on: Natural calamities.
22. Compare encryption and decryption.

■■■

Chapter 6...

MS-Office

Contents ...

6.1 Introduction
6.2 MS-Word
6.3 MS-Excel
6.4 MS PowerPoint
- Questions

6.1 Introduction

- Microsoft Office 2007 is a version of Microsoft Office, a family of office suites and productivity software for Windows, developed and published by Microsoft.

Features of MS-Office 2007:

1. **User interface:** The new user interface (UI), officially known as Fluent User Interface, has been implemented in the core Microsoft Office applications: Word, Excel, PowerPoint, Access, and in the item inspector used to create or edit individual items in Outlook. These applications have been selected for the UI overhaul because they center around document authoring.

2. **Office button:** The Office 2007 button, located on the top-left of the window, replaces the File menu and provides access to functionality common across all Office applications, including opening, saving, printing, and sharing a file. It can also close the application. Users can also choose color schemes for the interface.

3. **Ribbon:** The ribbon, a panel that houses a fixed arrangement of command buttons and icons, organizes commands as a set of tabs, each grouping relevant commands. The ribbon is present in Microsoft Word 2007, Excel 2007, PowerPoint 2007, Access 2007 and some Outlook 2007 windows. The ribbon is not user customizable in Office 2007. Each application has a different set of tabs which expose the functionality that application offers.

4. **Contextual Tabs:** Some tabs, called Contextual Tabs, appear only when certain objects are selected. Contextual Tabs expose functionality specific only to the object with focus. For example, selecting a picture brings up the Pictures tab, which presents options for dealing with the picture. Similarly, focusing on a table exposes table-related options in a specific tab. Contextual Tabs remain hidden except when an applicable object is selected.

5. **Mini Toolbar:** The new "Mini Toolbar" is a type of context menu that is automatically shown (by default) when text is selected. The purpose of this feature is to provide easy access to the most-used formatting commands without requiring a right-mouse-button click, as was necessary in older versions of the software.
6. **Quick Access Toolbar:** The Quick Access toolbar, which sits in the title bar, serves as a repository of most used functions, regardless of which application is being used, such as save, undo/redo and print. The Quick Access toolbar is customizable, although this feature is limited compared to toolbars in previous Office versions. Any command available in the entire Office application can be added to the Quick Access toolbar, including commands not available in the ribbon and macros.
7. **Super-tooltips or Screentips:** That can house formatted text and even images, are used to provide detailed descriptions of what most buttons do.
8. **Zoom slider:** It is present in the bottom-right corner, allowing for dynamic and rapid magnification of documents.
9. **Status bar:** It is fully customizable. Users can right click the status bar and add or remove what they want the status bar to display.
10. **SmartArt:** It is found under the Insert tab in the ribbon in PowerPoint, Word, Excel, and Outlook, is a new group of editable and formatted diagrams.
11. **File formats:** Microsoft Office 2007 introduced a new file format, called Office Open XML, as the default file format. Such files are saved using an extra X letter in their extension (.docx/xlsx/pptx/etc.).

    Initially, Microsoft promised to support exporting to Portable Document Format (PDF) in Office 2007.

    Office 2007 documents can also be exported as XPS documents. This is part of service pack 2 and prior to that, was available as a free plug-in in a separate download.

    Microsoft backs an open-source effort to support OpenDocument in Office 2007, as well as earlier versions (up to Office 2000), through a converter add-in for Word, Excel and PowerPoint, and also a command-line utility.
12. **Themes and Quick Styles:** Microsoft Office 2007 places more emphasis on Document Themes and Quick Styles. The Document Theme defines the colors, fonts and graphic effects for a document.

    Quick Styles are galleries with a range of styles based on the current theme. There are quick styles galleries for text, tables, charts, SmartArt, WordArt and more. The style range goes from simple/light to more graphical/darker.

Components of MS-Office 2007:
- Microsoft Office 2007 Professional Software contains five programs:
    1. **Word** is the word processing software that has replaced the typewriter. It is commonly used to create letters, mass mailings, resumes, newsletters and so on.

2. **Excel** is a program used to create spread sheets. Spread sheets are commonly used to create payroll, balance a check book or track an organization's finances.
3. **PowerPoint** is used to create a slideshow that helps address the topics being covered. It is commonly used to help discuss a topic or provide training.
4. **Access** is a database management program. It allows large quantity of information to be easily searched, referenced, compared, changed or otherwise manipulated without a lot of work.
5. **Outlook** is an e-mail software program that allows users to send and receive e-mail. It also allows you to keep a personal calendar and/or group schedule, personal contacts, personal tasks and has the ability to collaborate and schedule with other users.

- Table 6.1 shows file extensions of MS-Office 2007.

Table 6.1: File extensions in MS-Office

Program/Application	2003 Version	2007 Version
Word	.doc	.docx
Excel	.xls	.xlsx
PowerPoint	.ppt	.pptx
Access	.mdb	.accdb

6.2 MS-Word

- Microsoft Word is an example of a program called a "word processor."
- Word processors are used to create and print text documents in much the same way that you would use a typewriter.
- Microsoft Word can be used for the following purposes:
  1. To create business documents having various graphics including pictures, charts, and diagrams.
  2. To store and reuse ready-made content and formatted elements such as cover pages and sidebars.
  3. To create letters and letterheads for personal and business purpose.
  4. To design different documents such as resumes or invitation cards etc.
  5. To create a range of correspondence from a simple office memo to legal copies and reference documents.

Screen components of MS-Word:
- Fig. 6.1 shows various components of MS-Word screen.

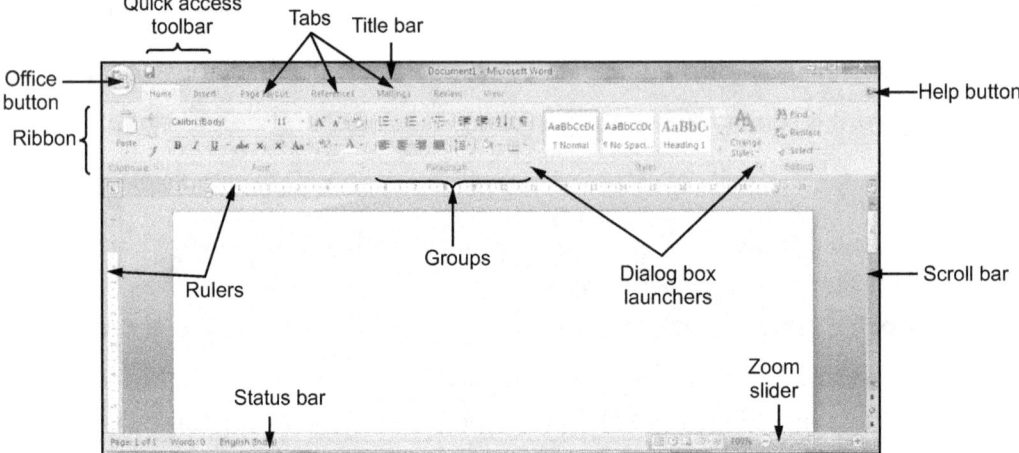

Fig. 6.1: Screen components

1. **Microsoft Office Button:** The Microsoft Office button performs many of the functions that were located in the File menu of older versions of Word. This button allows you to create a new document, open an existing document, save or save as, print, send (through email or fax), publish or close.
2. **Ribbon:** The Ribbon is the panel at the top portion of the document. It has seven tabs: Home, Insert, Page Layout, References, Mailings, Review, and View that contain many new and existing features of Word. Each tab is divided into groups. The groups are logical collections of features designed to perform functions that you will utilize in developing or editing your Word document. Commonly used features are displayed on the Ribbon, to view additional features within each group, click on the arrow at the bottom right of each group.

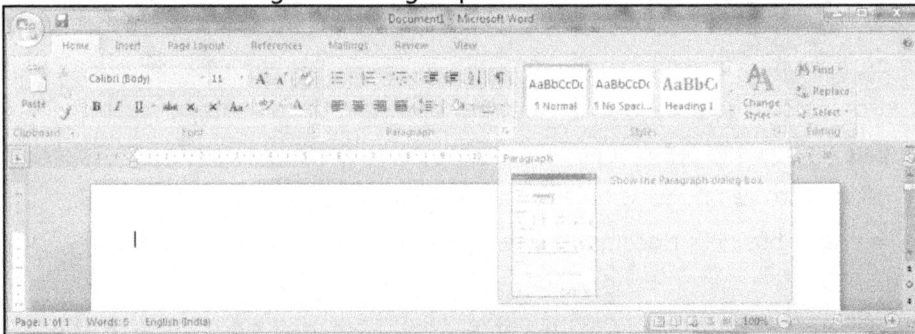

Fig. 6.2: Ribbon

3. **Quick Access Toolbar:** The quick access toolbar is a customizable toolbar that contains commands that you may want to use. You can place the quick access toolbar above or below the ribbon. To change the location of the quick access toolbar, click on the arrow at the end of the toolbar and click on Show Below the Ribbon.

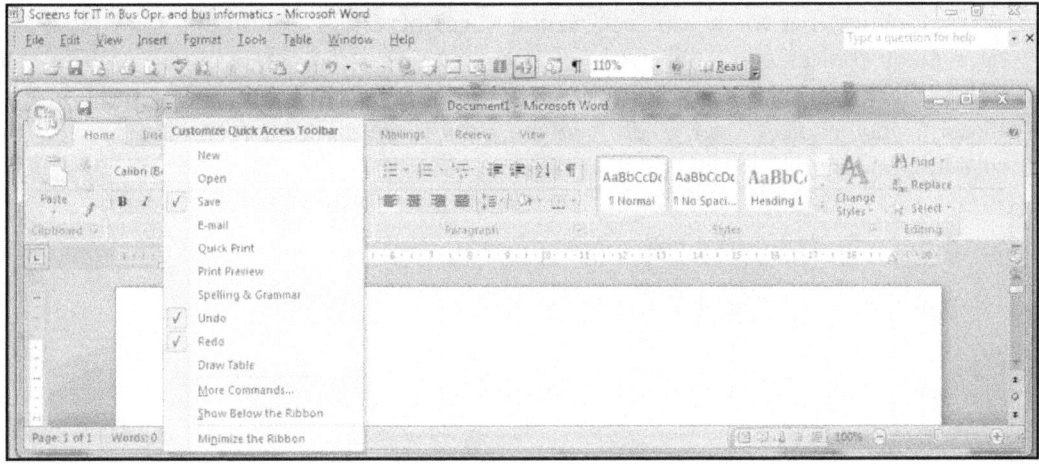

Fig. 6.3: Quick Access Toolbar (QAT)

4. **Title Bar:** The Title bar is located at the top of the screen. The Title bar displays the word Microsoft Word and the name of the document on which you are currently working.

5. **Menu Bar:** Located directly below the Title bar, the Menu bar displays the menu such as File and continues with Edit, View, Insert, Format, Tools, Table, Window, and Help. These menus are used to give instructions to the software.

6. **Toolbars:** Toolbars have buttons or shortcuts to menu commands. Toolbars are generally located just below the Menu bar but these toolbars can be move or customize if you want.

7. **The Vertical and Horizontal Ruler:** The ruler is located below the main toolbars. The ruler is used to change the format of your document quickly especially the margins.

8. **Scroll bars and Scroll buttons:** These elements are use to navigate your document quickly and easily. Scroll bars are use by dragging while scroll buttons is by clicking.

9. **Status bar:** This element is located at the bottom of horizontal scroll bar or the drawing toolbar. This indicates the current page, current section, total number of pages, inches from the top of the page, current line number, and current column number. The Status bar also provides options that enable you to track changes or turn on the Record mode, the Extension mode, the Overtype mode, and the Spelling and Grammar check.

Working with Documents:
1. **Create a New Document:** There are several ways to create new documents, open existing documents, and save documents in Word.

   Follow the following steps for creating new word document:
   (i) Click the Microsoft Office Button and Click New or
   (ii) Press CTRL+N (Depress the CTRL key while pressing the "N") on the keyboard

- You will notice that when you click on the Microsoft Office Button and Click **New**, you have many choices about the types of documents you can create. If you wish to start from a blank document, click **Blank**. If you wish to start from a template, you can browse through your choices on the left, see the choices on center screen, and preview the selection on the right screen.

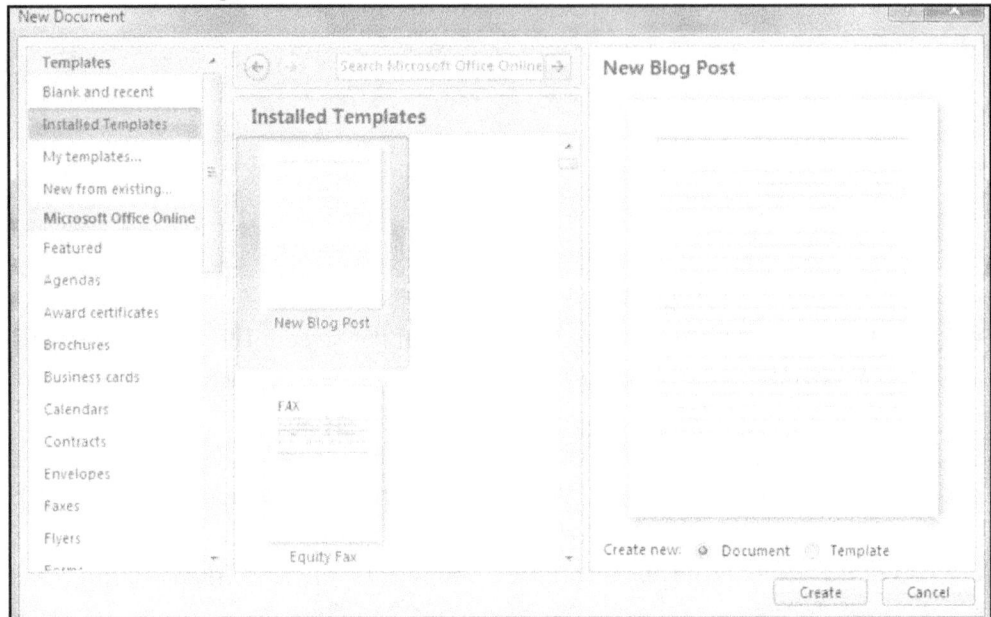

Fig. 6.4: Creating new document

Opening an Existing Document

1. Click the Microsoft Office Button  and Click **Open**, or
2. Press CTRL+O (Depress the CTRL key while pressing the "O") on the keyboard, or
3. If you have recently used the document you can click the **Microsoft Office Button** and click the name of the document in the **Recent Documents** section of the window Insert picture of recent docs (documents).

Saving a Document:

1. Click the **Microsoft Office Button**  and Click **Save** or **Save As** (remember, if you're sending the document to someone who does not have Office 2007, you will need to click the **Office Button**, click **Save As**, and ClickWord 97-2003 Document), or
2. Press CTRL+S (Depress the CTRL key while pressing the "S") on the keyboard, or
3. Click the File icon on the Quick Access Toolbar.

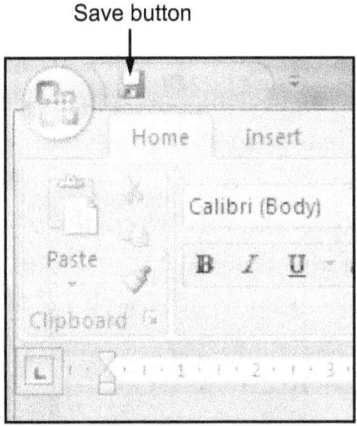

Fig. 6.5: Saving document

Close a Document:
To close a document:
1. Click the Office Button
2. Click Close

Working with Text in MS-Word 2007:
1. **Inserting Text:** Text can be inserted in a document at any point using any of the following methods:
2. **Type Text:** Put your cursor where you want to add the text and begin typing.
3. **Copy and Paste Text:** Highlight the text you wish to copy and right click and click **Copy**, put your cursor where you want the text in the document and right click and click **Paste**.
4. **Cut and Paste Text:** Highlight the text you wish to copy, right click, and click **Cut**, put your cursor where you want the text in the document, right click, and click **Paste**.
5. **Drag Text:** Highlight the text you wish to move, click on it and drag it to the place where you want the text in the document.
- You will notice that you can also use the Clipboard group on the Ribbon

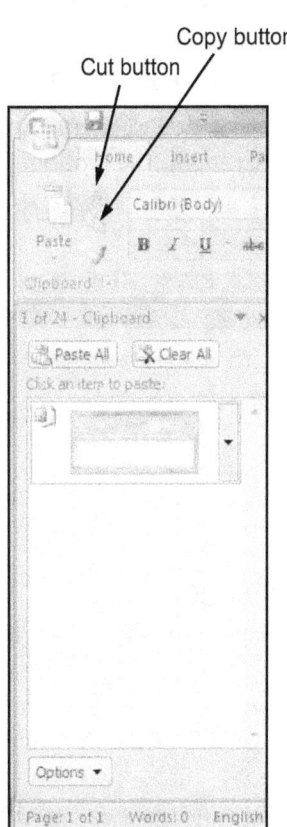

Fig. 6.6: Clipboard group

Rearranging Blocks of Text:
- To rearrange text within a document, you can utilize the Clipboard Group on the Home Tab of the Ribbon. Insert picture of clipboard group labeled,
    1. **Move text:** Cut and Paste or Drag as shown above
    2. **Copy Text:** Copy and Paste as above or use the Clipboard group on the Ribbon
    3. **Paste Text:** Ctrl + V (hold down the CTRL and the "V" key at the same time) or use the Clipboard group to Paste, Paste Special, or Paste as Hyperlink.

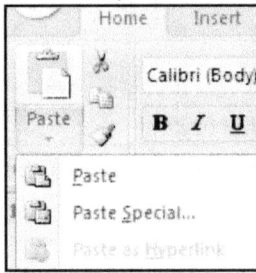

Fig. 6.7: Paste option

Search and Replace Text:
- To find a particular word or phrase in a document:
    1. Click **Find** on the **Editing Group** on the Ribbon.
    2. To find and replace a word or phrase in the document, click **Replace** on the Editing Group of the Ribbon.

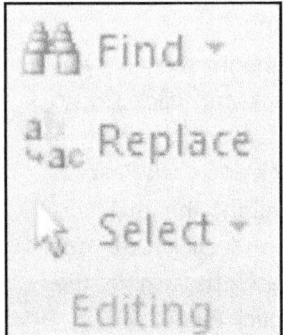

Fig. 6.8: Find and replace

Undo Changes:
- To undo changes; Click the **Undo Button** on the Quick Access Toolbar.

Undo button

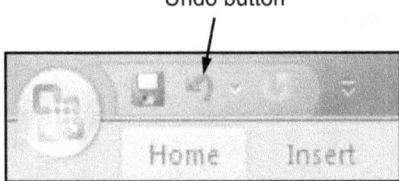

Fig. 6.9: Undo

Formatting Text in MS-Word 2007:

Styles:
- A style is a format-enhancing tool that includes font typefaces, font size, effects (bold, italics, underline, etc.), colors and more. You will notice that on the Home Tab of the Ribbon, that you have several areas that will control the style of your document: Font, Paragraph, and Styles.

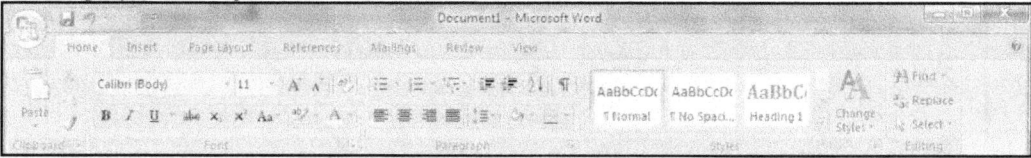

Fig. 6.10: Home tabs of Ribbon

- Fig. 6.11 shows font dialog box.

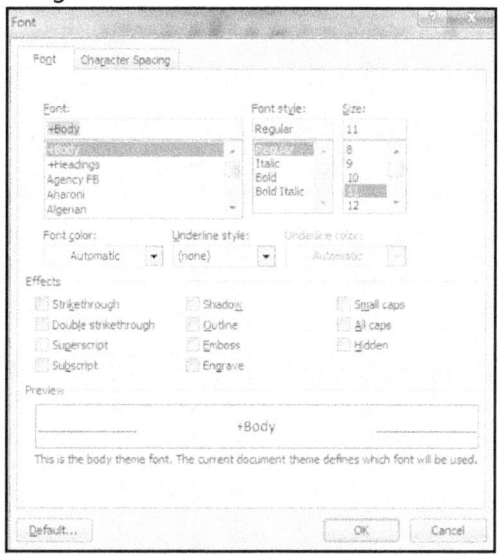

Fig. 6.11: Font dialog

Change Font Typeface and Size:
- **To change the font typeface:** Click the **arrow** next to the font name and choose a font.

Font typeface button

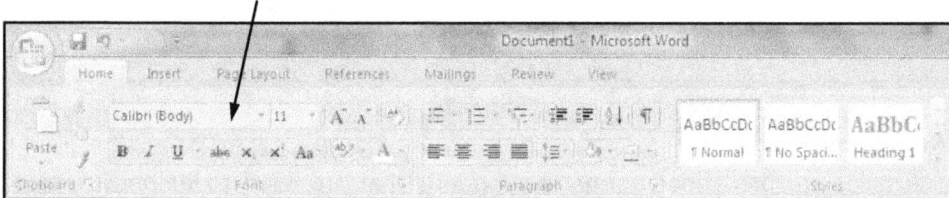

Fig. 6.12

- Remember that you can preview how the new font will look by highlighting the text, and hovering over the new font typeface.

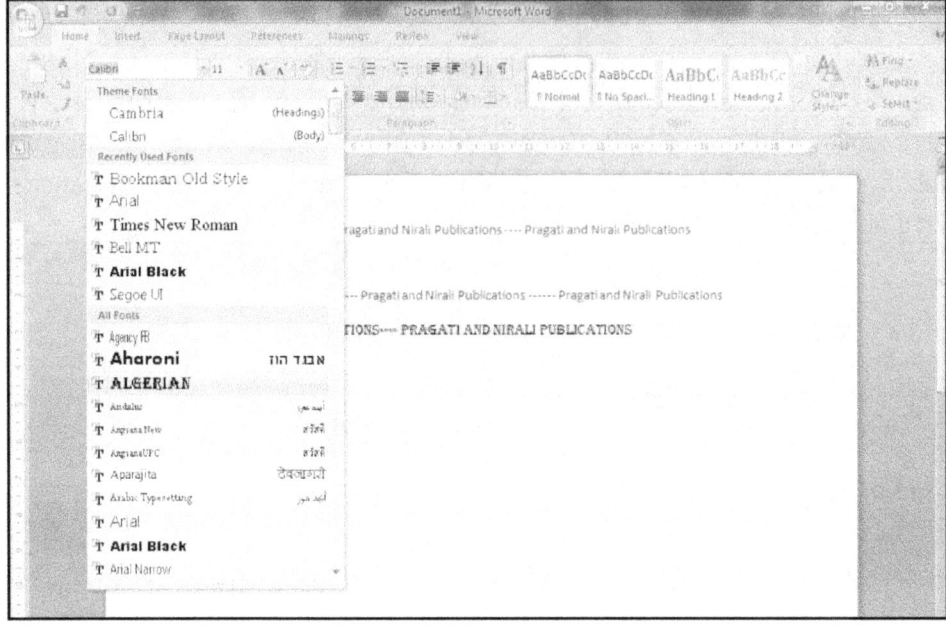

Fig. 6.13: Font list

To change the font size:
- Click the arrow next to the font size and choose the appropriate size, or
- Click the increase or decrease font size buttons.

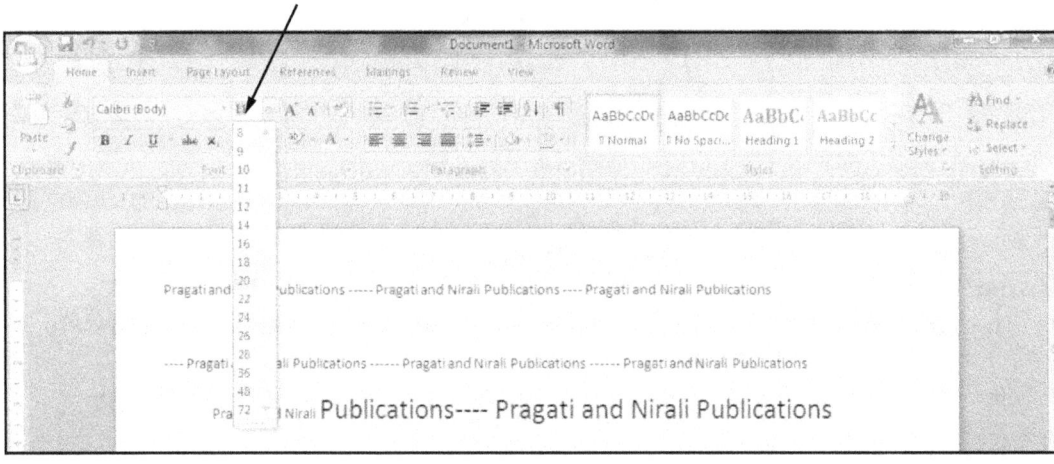

Fig. 6.14

Font Styles and Effects:
- Font styles are predefined formatting options that are used to emphasize text. They include: Bold, Italic, and Underline. To add these to text:
    1. Select the text and click the **Font Styles** included on the Font Group of the Ribbon, or
    2. Select the text and right click to display the font tools

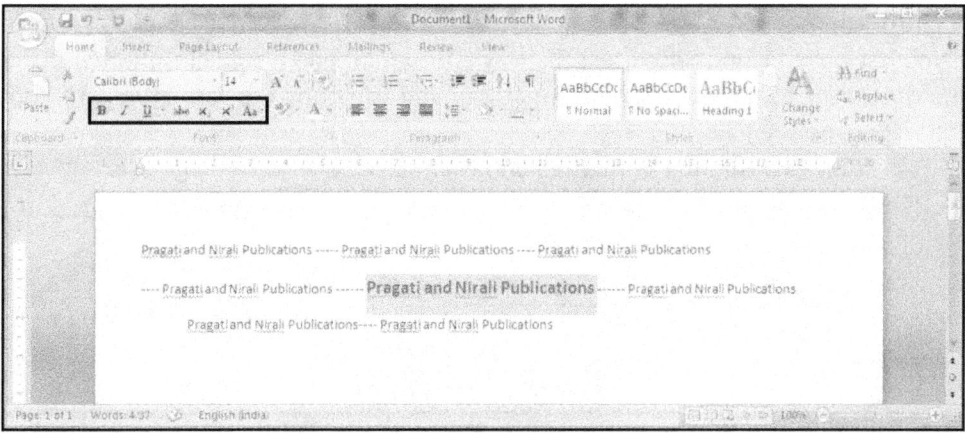

Fig. 6.15: Font tools

Change text color: To change the text color follow the following steps:
1. Select the text and click the **Colors** button included on the Font Group of the Ribbon, or
2. Highlight the text, right click, and choose the colors tool.
3. Select the color by clicking the down arrow next to the font color button.

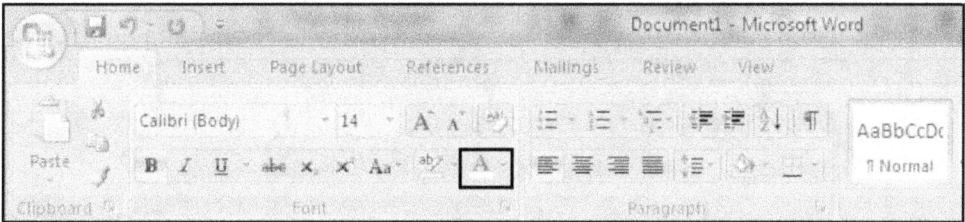

Fig. 6.16

Highlight Text:
- Highlighting text allows you to use emphasize text as you would if you had a marker. To highlight text:
    1. Select the text,
    2. Click the **Highlight Button** on the Font Group of the Ribbon, or
    3. Select the text and right click and select the highlight tool.
    4. To change the color of the highlighter click on down arrow next to the highlight button.

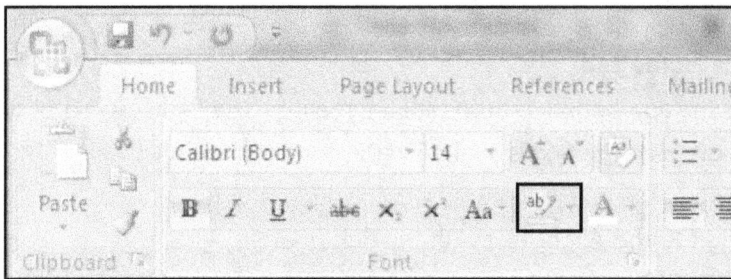

Fig. 6.17

Copy Formatting:
- If you have already formatted text the way you want it and would like another portion of the document to have the same formatting, you can copy the formatting. To copy the formatting, do the following:
    1. Select the text with the formatting you want to copy.
    2. Copy the format of the text selected by clicking the **Format Painter** button on the Clipboard Group of the Home Tab
    3. Apply the copied format by selecting the text and clicking on it.

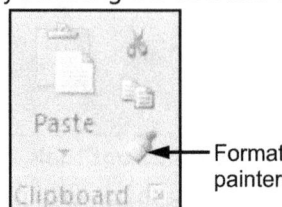

Fig. 6.18

Formatting Paragraphs:
- Formatting paragraphs allows you to change the look of the overall document.
- You can access many of the tools of paragraph formatting by clicking the **Page Layout** Tab of the Ribbon or the **Paragraph** Group on the Home Tab of the Ribbon.

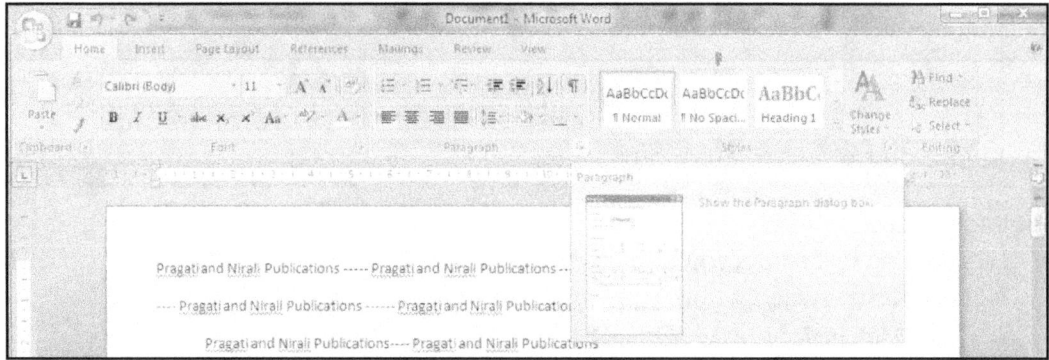

Fig. 6.19: Paragraph options of Ribbon

Change Paragraph Alignment:
- The paragraph alignment allows you to set how you want text to appear. To change the alignment:
    1. Click the **Home Tab**.
    2. Choose the appropriate button for alignment on the Paragraph Group.
        - (i) **Align Left:** The text is aligned with your left margin
        - (ii) **Center:** The text is centered within your margins
        - (iii) **Align Right:** Aligns text with the right margin
        - (iv) **Justify:** Aligns text to both the left and right margins.

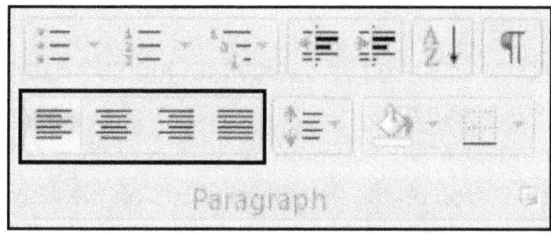

Fig. 6.20: Alignment options

Indent Paragraphs:
- Indenting paragraphs allows you set text within a paragraph at different margins. There are several options for indenting:
    - **(i) First Line:** Controls the left boundary for the first line of a paragraph
    - **(ii) Hanging:** Controls the left boundary of every line in a paragraph except the first one
    - **(iii) Left:** Controls the left boundary for every line in a paragraph
    - **(iv) Right:** Controls the right boundary for every line in a paragraph
- To indent paragraphs, you can do the following:
    - **(i)** Click the Indent buttons to control the indent.
    - **(ii)** Click the Indent button repeated times to increase the size of the indent.

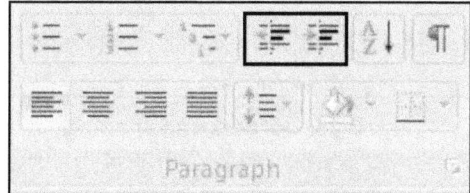

Fig. 6.21: Indenting options

- **(iii)** Click the dialog box of the Paragraph Group.
- **(iv)** Click the Indents and Spacing Tab.
- **(v)** Select your indents.

Fig. 6.22: Paragraph dialog

Add Borders and Shading:

- You can add borders and shading to paragraphs and entire pages. To create a border around a paragraph or paragraphs:
    (i) Select the area of text where you want the border or shading.
    (ii) Click the Borders Button on the Paragraph Group on the Home Tab.
    (iii) Choose the Border and Shading.
    (iv) Choose the appropriate options.

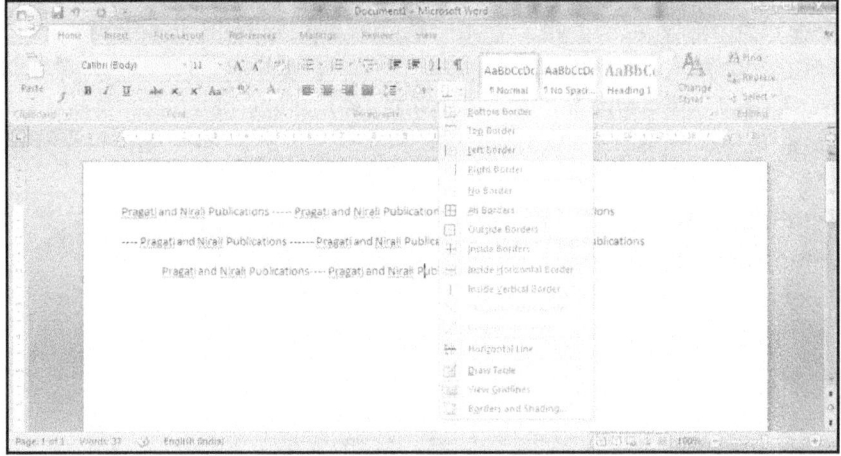

Fig. 6.23: Borders and shading

Apply Styles:

- Styles are a present collection of formatting that you can apply to text. To utilize Quick Styles:
    (i) Select the text you wish to format.
    (ii) Click the dialog box next to the **Styles Group** on the Home Tab.
    (iii) Click the style you wish to apply.

Fig. 6.24

Change Spacing Between Paragraphs and Lines:

- You can change the space between lines and paragraphs by doing the following:
    (i) Select the paragraph or paragraphs you wish to change.
    (ii) On the Home Tab, Click the **Paragraph** Dialog Box.
    (iii) Click the **Indents and Spacing** Tab.
    (iv) In the **Spacing** section, adjust your spacing accordingly.

Fig. 6.25

Adding Tables:
- Tables are used to display data in a table format.
- To create a table:
  (i) Place the cursor on the page where you want the new table.
  (ii) Click the **Insert** Tab of the Ribbon.
  (iii) Click the **Tables** Button on the Tables Group. You can create a table one of four ways:
  1. Highlight the number of row and columns.
  2. Click **Insert Table** and enter the number of rows and columns.
  3. Click the **Draw Table**, create your table by clicking and entering the rows and columns.
  4. Click **Quick Tables** and choose a table.

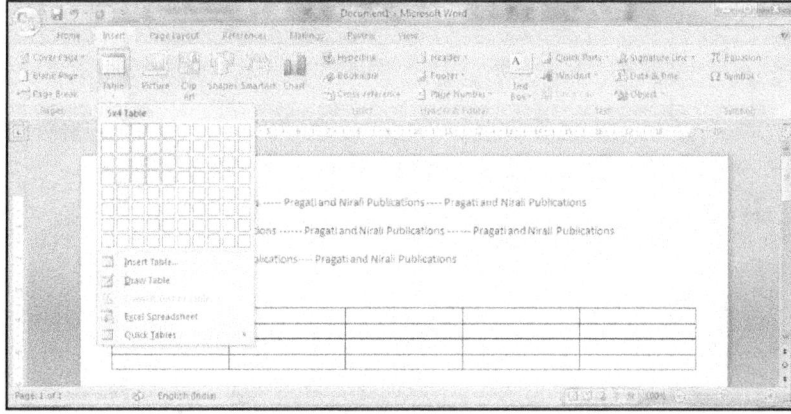

Fig. 6.26: Create a table

Symbols and Special Characters:
- Special characters are punctuation, spacing, or typographical characters that are not generally available on the standard keyboard.
- To insert symbols and special characters:
    (i) Place your cursor in the document where you want the symbol.
    (ii) Click the **Insert** Tab on the Ribbon.
    (iii) Click the **Symbol** button on the Symbols Group.
    (iv) Choose the appropriate symbol.

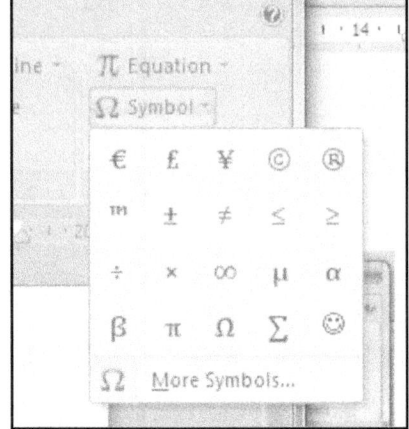

Fig. 6.27: Special character and symbols

Equations:
- Word 2007 also allows you to insert mathematical equations.
- To access the mathematical equations tool:
    (i) Place your cursor in the document where you want the symbol.
    (ii) Click the **Insert** Tab on the Ribbon.
    (iii) Click the **Equation** Button on the Symbols Group.
    (iv) Choose the appropriate equation and structure or click Insert New Equation.

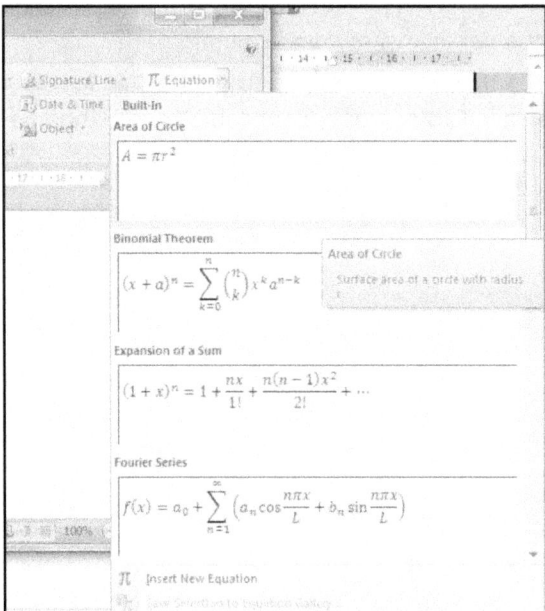

Fig. 6.28: Equations or mathematical symbols

- To edit the equation click the equation and the Design Tab will be available in the Ribbon

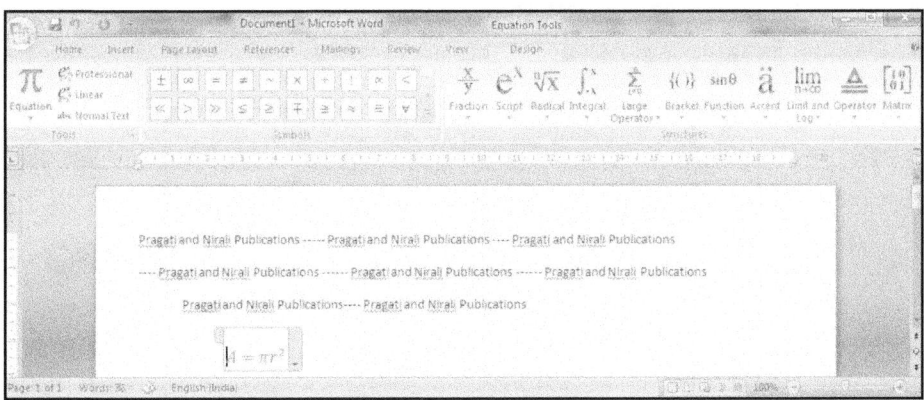

Fig. 6.29: Design tab

Pictures and Smart Art:
- Word 2007 allows you to insert illustrations and pictures into a document.

Inserting ClipArt:
- To insert illustrations:
    (i) Place your cursor in the document where you want the illustration/picture.
    (ii) Click the Insert Tab on the Ribbon.
    (iii) Click the Clip Art Button.
    (iv) The dialog box will open on the screen and you can search for clip art.
    (v) Choose the illustration you wish to include.

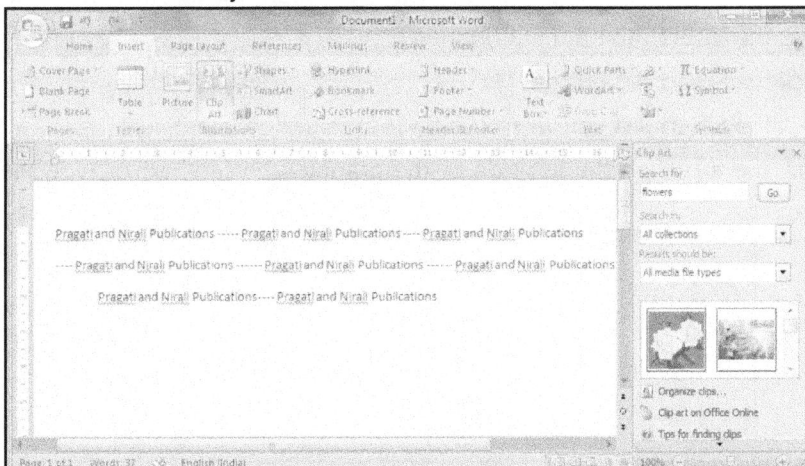

Fig. 6.30: Clip art option

Inserting Pictures:
- To insert a picture:
    (i) Place your cursor in the document where you want the illustration/picture.
    (ii) Click the **Insert** Tab on the Ribbon.

(iii) Click the **Picture** Button.
(iv) Browse to the picture you wish to include.
(v) Click the **Picture**.
(vi) Click **Insert**.

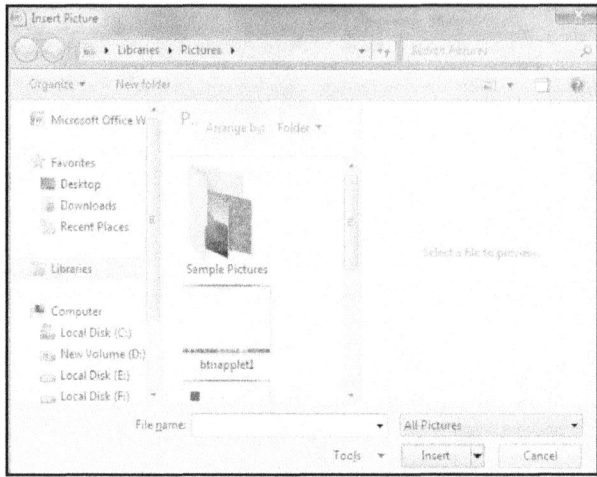

Fig. 6.31: Insert pictures dialog

- **Smart Art** is a collection of graphics you can utilize to organize information within your document. It includes timelines, processes, or workflow.
- To insert Smart Art:
    (i) Place your cursor in the document where you want the illustration/picture.
    (ii) Click the **Insert** Tab on the Ribbon.
    (iii) Click the **Smart A**rt button.
    (iv) Click the **Smart Art** you wish to include in your document.
    (v) Click the arrow on the left side of the graphic to insert text or type the text in the graphic.

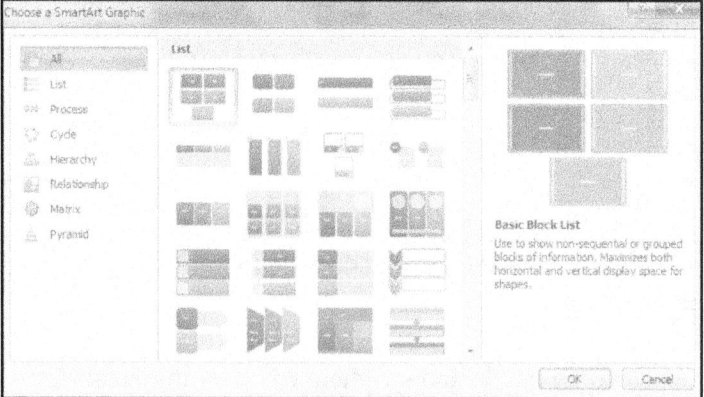

Fig. 6.32: Smart art option

Proofing a Document:
- There are many features to help you proofread your document. These include: Spelling and Grammar, Thesaurus, AutoCorrect, Default Dictionary, and Word Count.

Spelling and Grammar:
- To check the spelling and grammar of a document:
    (i) Place the cursor at the beginning of the document or the beginning of the section that you want to check
    (ii) Click the **Review** Tab on the Ribbon
    (iii) Click **Spelling & Grammar** on the Proofing Group.

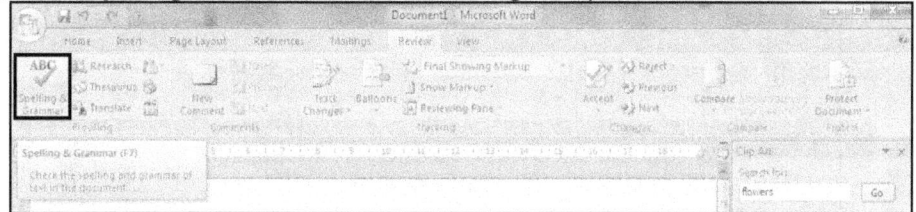

Fig. 6.33: Spelling and Grammar option

- Any errors will display a dialog box that allows you to choose a more appropriate spelling or phrasing.

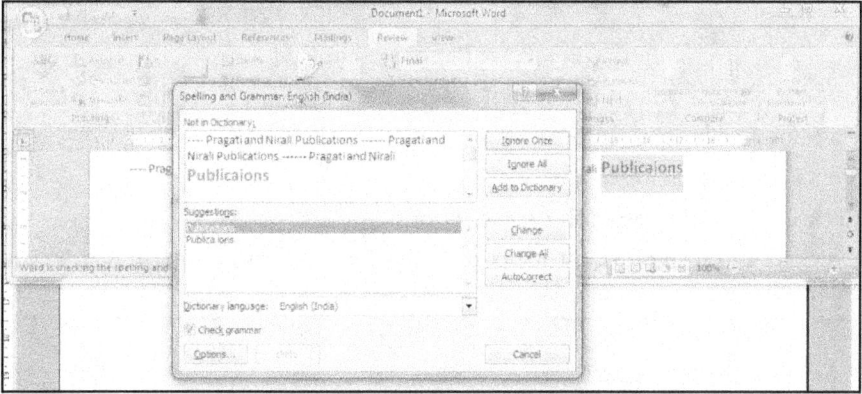

Fig. 6.34: Spelling and Grammar dialog

Page Formatting:
To Change Page Orientation:
(i) Select the Page Layout tab.
(ii) Click the Orientation command in the Page Setup group.

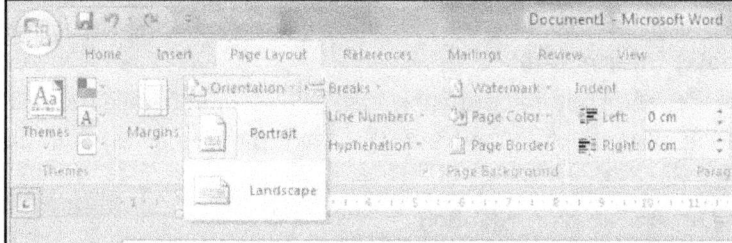

Fig. 6.35: Orientation option

(iii) Left-click either Portrait or Landscape to change the page orientation.

Change the Paper Size:
  (i) Select the Page Layout tab.
  (ii) Left-click the Size command and a drop-down menu will appear. The current paper size is highlighted.

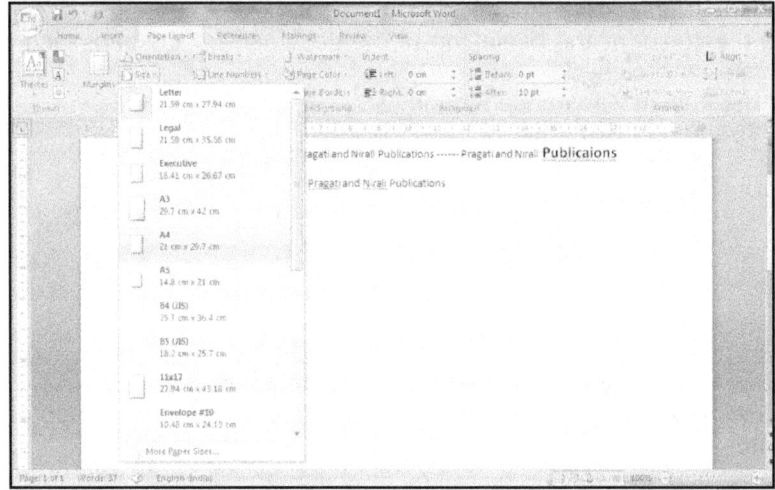

Fig. 6.36: Paper size option

  (iii) Left-click a size option to select it. The page size of the document changes.
- Apply a Page Border and Color.
- To apply a page border or color:
  (i) Click the **Page Layout** Tab on the Ribbon
  (ii) On the Page Background Group, click the **Page Colors** or **Page Borders** drop down menus

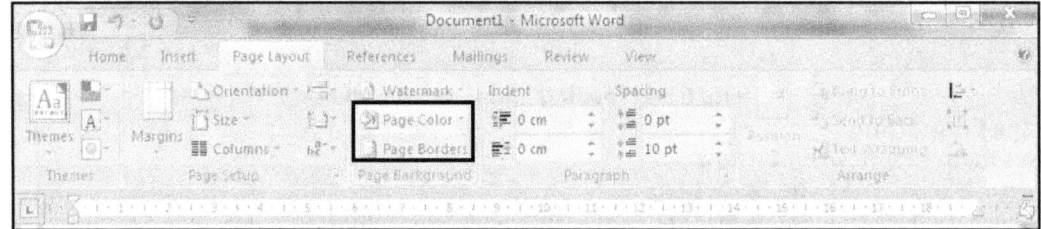

Fig. 6.37: Page border and Color option

Header and Footer Information:
- To insert Header and Footer information such as page numbers, date, or title, first, decide if you want the information in the header (at the top of the page) or in the Footer (at the bottom of the page), then:
  (i) Click the **Insert** Tab on the Ribbon
  (ii) Click **Header or Footer**
  (iii) Choose a **style**

Fig. 6.38: Header and Footer option

Create a Page Break:
- To insert a page break:
    (i) Click the **Page Layout** Tab on the Ribbon
    (ii) On the Page Setup Group, click the **Breaks Drop Down Menu**
    (iii) Click **Page Break**

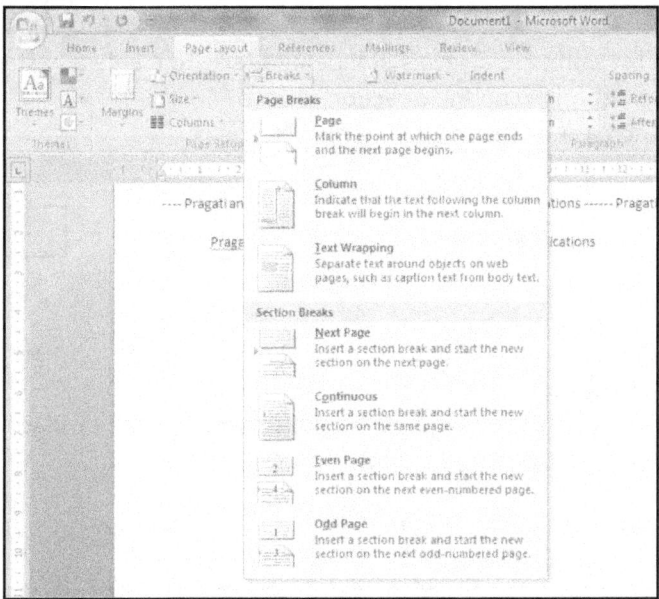

Fig. 6.39: Breaks options

Lists:
- Lists allow you to format and organize text with numbers, bullets, or in an outline.
- **Bulleted and Numbered Lists** Bulleted lists have bullet points, numbered lists have numbers, and outline lists combine numbers and letters depending on the organization of the list.
- To add a list to existing text:
    (i) Select the text you wish to make a list
    (ii) From the Paragraph Group on the Home Tab, Click the **Bulleted or Numbered Lists** button

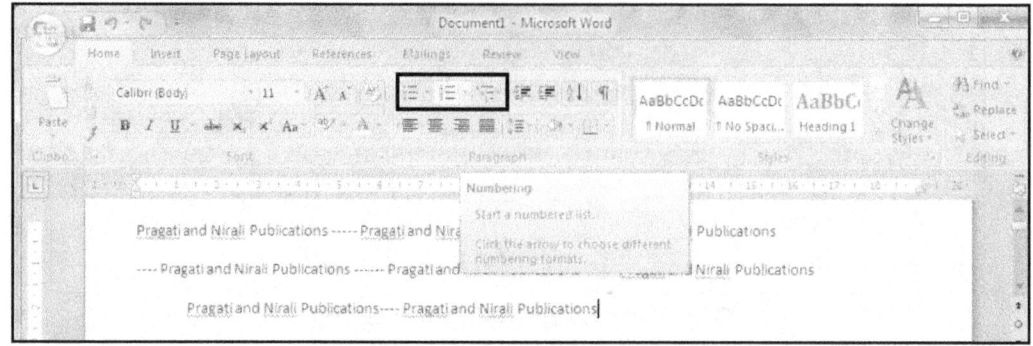

Fig. 6.40

- To create a new list:
    (i) Place your cursor where you want the list in the document.
    (ii) Click the **Bulleted or Numbered** Lists button.
    (iii) Begin typing

Nested Lists:
- A nested list is list with several levels of indented text. To create a nested list:
    (i) Create your list following the directions above
    (ii) Click the **Increase or Decrease** Indent button

Fig. 6.41

Formatting Lists:
- The bullet image and numbering format can be changed by using the Bullets or Numbering dialog box.
    (i) Select the entire list to change all the bullets or numbers, or Place the cursor on one line within the list to change a single bullet.
    (ii) Right click.
    (iii) Click the **arrow** next to the bulleted or numbered list and choose a bullet or numbering style.

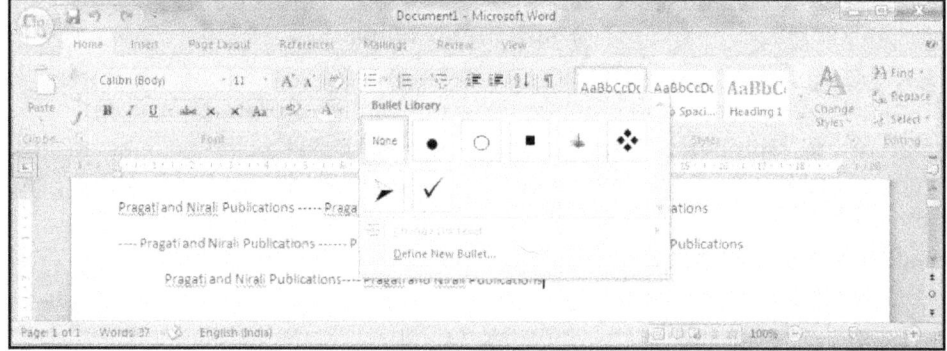

Fig. 6.42: Bullets are numbering option

Working with Shapes:
- You can add a variety of shapes to your document including arrows, callouts, squares, stars, flowchart symbols and more.

To Insert a Shape:
  (i)   Select the Insert tab.
  (ii) Click the Shape command.
  (iii) Left-click a shape from the menu. Your cursor is now a cross shape.
  (iv) Left-click your mouse and while holding it down, drag your mouse until the shape is the desired size.
  (v)   Release the mouse button.

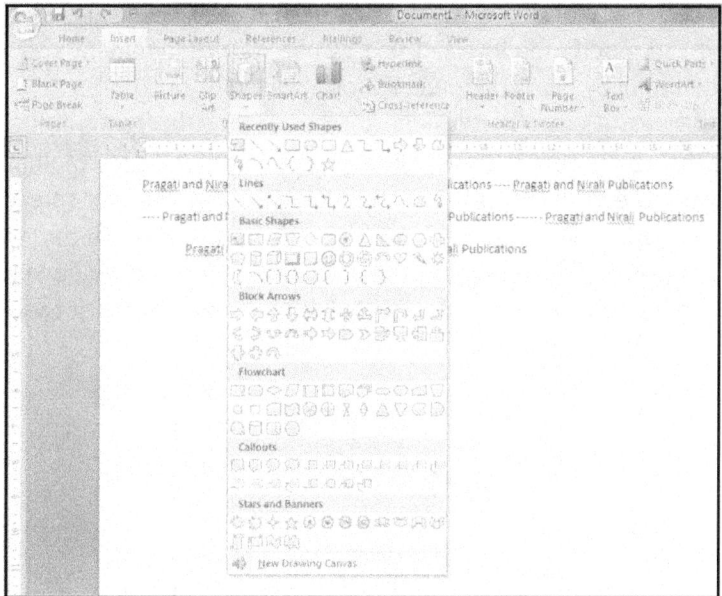

Fig. 6.43: Shapes options

- WordArt allows you to use special effects such as bending, twisting and rotating text in your documents.
- Microsoft Word provides the WordArt feature. WordArt is a way of converting normal text into graphics. WordArt adds special effects to the text. You can insert WordArt, while inserting a particular word in a document.

Adding WordArt in Document:
- Word Art provides a way to add fancy words in your word document. You can document your text in a variety of ways.
- Following are the simple steps to add a WordArt in your document.
  (i) Click in your document where you want to add a WordArt.
  (ii) Click the **Insert tab** and then click **WordArt** option available in Text group, which will display a gallery of WordArt.

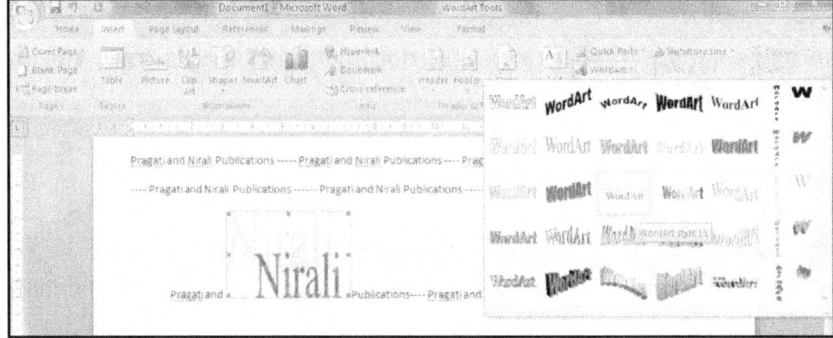

Fig. 6.44: WordArt options

(iii) You can select any of the WordArt style from the displayed gallery by clicking on it. Now you can modify the inserted text as per your requirement and you can make it further beautiful by using different options available.

Mail Merge:
- Mail merge is a useful tool that will allow you to easily produce multiple letters, labels, envelopes and more using information stored in a list, database, or spreadsheet.
- In this lesson, you will learn how to use the mail merge wizard to create a data source and a form letter, and explore other wizard features. Additionally, you will learn how to use the Ribbon commands to access the mail merge tools outside of the wizard.

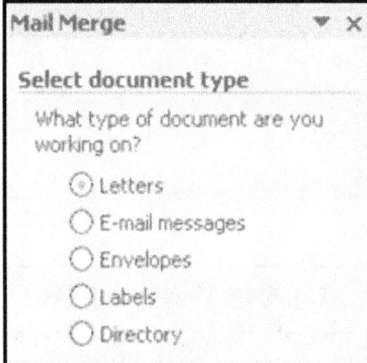

Fig. 6.45: Mail merge tool

To Use Mail Merge:
  (i) Select the Mailings on the Ribbon.
  (ii) Select the Start Mail Merge command.

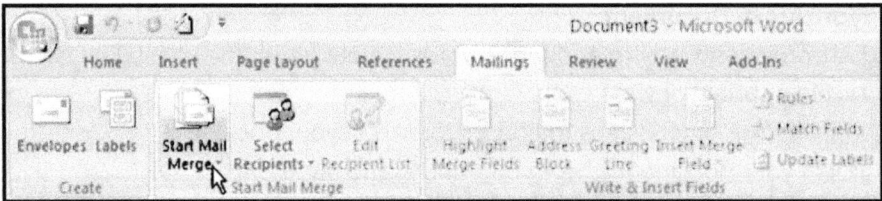

Fig. 6.46: Mail merge option

- Select Step by Step Mail Merge Wizard.
- The Mail Merge task pane appears and will guide you through the six main steps to complete a mail merge. You will have many decisions to make during the process. The following is an example of how to create a form letter and merge the letter with a data list.

Steps 1-3:
- Choose the type of document you wish to create. In this example, select Letters.
- Click Next:Starting document to move to Step 2.
- Select Use the current document.
- Click Next:Select recipients to move to Step 3.
- Select the Type a new list button.
- Click Create to create a data source. The New Address List dialog box appears.
    - Click Customize in the dialog box. The Customize Address List dialog box appears.
    - Select any field you do not need and click Delete.
    - Click Yes to confirm that you wish to delete the field.
    - Continue to delete any unnecessary fields.
    - Click Add. The Add Field dialog box appears.
    - Enter the new field name.
    - Click OK.
    - Continue to add any fields necessary.
    - Click OK to close the Customize Address List dialog box.

To Customize the New Address List:

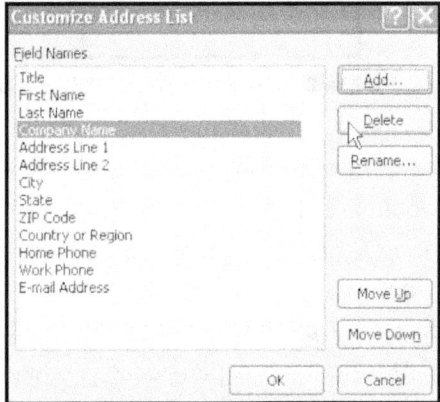

Fig. 6.47: Customize address list dialog box

- Enter the necessary data in the New Address List dialog box.
    - Click New Entry to enter another record.
    - Click Close when you have entered all your data records.
    - Enter the file name you wish to save the data list as.
    - Choose the location you wish to save the file.

- o Click Save. The Mail Merge Recipients dialog box appears and displays all the data records in the list.
- o Confirm the data list is correct and click OK.
- o Click Next:Write your letter to move to Step 4.

Steps 4-6:
- Write a letter in the current Word document, or use an open, existing document.

To Insert Recipient Data from the List:
- o Place the insertion point in the document where you wish the information to appear.
- o Select Address block, Greeting line, or Electronic postage from the task pane. A dialog box with options will appear based on your selection.

Fig. 6.48: Mail Merge Recipients Dialog Box

OR

- Select More Items. The Insert Merge Field dialog box will appear.
    - o Select the field you would like to insert in the document.
    - o Click Insert. Notice that a placeholder appears where information from the data record will eventually appear.
    - o Repeat these steps each time you need to enter information from your data record.
- Click Next: Preview your letters in the task pane once you have completed your letter.
- Preview the letters to make sure the information from the data record appears correctly in the letter.
    - o Click Next: Complete the merge.
    - o Click Print to print the letters.
    - o Click All.
    - o Click OK in the Merge to Printer dialog box.
    - o Click OK to send the letters to the printer.

6.3 MS-Excel

- Microsoft Excel is an example of a program called a "spreadsheet." Spreadsheets are used to organize real world data, such as a check register or a rolodex. Data can be numerical or alphanumeric (involving letters or numbers).
- The key benefit to using a spreadsheet program is that you can make changes easily, including correcting spelling or values, adding, deleting, formatting, and relocating data.

Spreadsheets:
- A spreadsheet is an electronic document that stores various types of data. There are vertical columns and horizontal rows.
- A cell is where the column and row intersect. A cell can contain data and can be used in calculations of data within the spreadsheet.
- An Excel spreadsheet can contain workbooks and worksheets. The workbook is the holder for related worksheets.

Working with Excel:
- The Excel 2007 program window is easy to navigate and simple to use (See Fig. 6.49 and Table 6.2 for the main elements of the program window). It is designed to help you quickly find the commands that you need to complete a task.

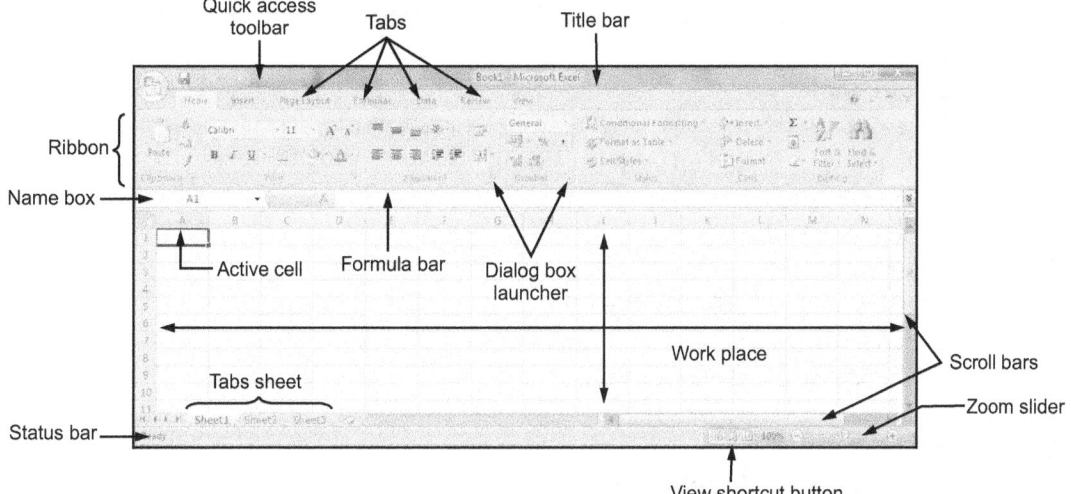

Fig. 6.49: Excel 2007 program window

Table 6.2: Excel 2007 program window elements

Element of Excel Window	Description
Title bar	Displays the name of the workbook and the program.
Minimize, Restore Down/ Maximize and Close buttons	Used to control the program window. Use the Minimize button to hide the window. Use the Restore Down/Maximize button to adjust he size of the window. Use the Close button to exit Excel.

contd. ...

Quick Access toolbar	Contains frequently used commands that are independent of the tab displayed on the Ribbon.
Ribbon	Contains all the commands related to managing workbooks and working with workbook content.
Formula bar	Displays the data or formula stored in the active cell. It can also be used to enter or edit a formula, a function, or data in a cell.
Name box	Displays the active cell address or the name of the selected cell, range or object.
Workbook window	Displays a portion of the worksheet.
Sheet tabs	Each tap represents a different worksheet in the workbook. A workbook can have any number of sheets and each sheet has its name displayed on its sheet tab.
Scroll bars	Used to scroll through the worksheet.
Status bar	Displays various messages as well as the status of the Num Lock, Caps Lock and Scroll Lock keys on the keyboard.
View Shortcuts toolbar	Used to display the worksheet in a variety of views, each suited to a specific purpose.
Zoom Level button and Zoom slider	Used to change the magnification of the worksheet.

Creating a Workbook:
- To create a new Workbook:
    - (i) Click the Microsoft Office **Toolbar**.
    - (ii) Click **New**.
    - (iii) Choose **Blank Document**.

Save a Workbook:
- When you save a workbook, you have two choices: Save or Save As.
- To save a document:
    - (i) Click the **Microsoft Office Button**.
    - (ii) Click **Save**.

Open a Workbook:
- To open an existing workbook:
    - (i) Click the **Microsoft Office Button**.
    - (ii) Click **Open**.
    - (iii) Browse to the workbook.
    - (iv) Click the title of the workbook.
    - (v) Click **Open**.

Entering Data:
- There are different ways to enter data in Excel: in an active cell or in the formula bar.
- To enter data in an active cell:
    - (i) Click in the **cell** where you want the data.
    - (ii) Begin typing.

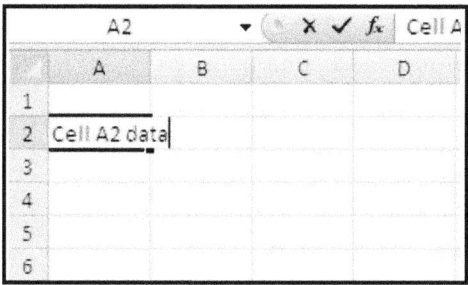

Fig. 6.50: Entering data in Excel

Insert Cells, Rows, and Columns:
- To insert cells, rows, and columns in Excel:
  - (i) Place the cursor in the row below where you want the new row, or in the column to the left of where you want the new column.
  - (ii) Click the **Insert** button on the **Cells** group of the **Home** tab.
  - (iii) Click the appropriate choice: **Cell**, **Row**, or **Column**.

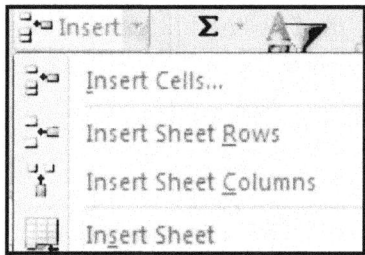

Fig. 6.51: Insert options

Delete Cells, Rows and Columns:
- To delete cells, rows, and columns:
  - (i) Place the cursor in the cell, row, or column that you want to delete.
  - (ii) Click the **Delete** button on the **Cells** group of the **Home** tab.
  - (iii) Click the appropriate choice: **Cell, Row**, or **Column**.

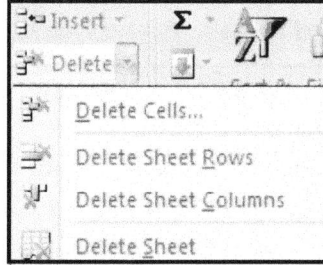

Fig. 6.52: Delete options

Find and Replace:
- To find data or find and replace data:
  - (i) Click the **Find & Select** button on the Editing group of the Home tab.
  - (ii) Choose **Find** or **Replace**.

(iii) Complete the **Find What** text box.
(iv) Click on **Options** for more search options.

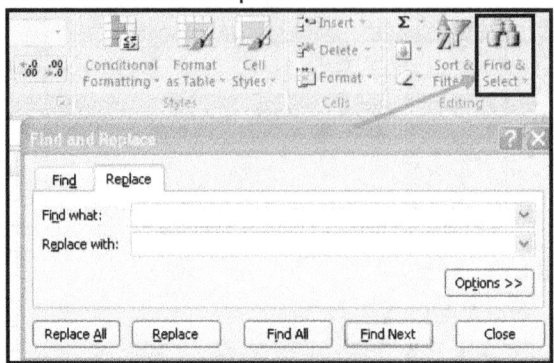

Fig. 6.53: Find and Replace Dialog box

Spell Check:
- To check the spelling:
    (i) On the **Review** tab click the **Spelling** button.

Fig. 6.54: Review options

Excel Formulas:
- A formula is a set of mathematical instructions that can be used in Excel to perform calculations. Formals are started in the formula box with an = sign.

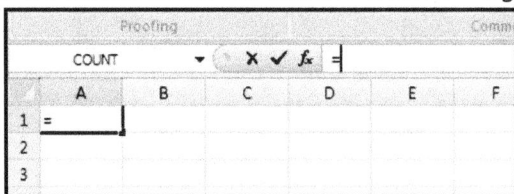

Fig. 6.55: Formula box

- There are many elements to and excel formula.
    - **References:** The cell or range of cells that you want to use in your calculation.
    - **Operators:** Symbols (+, -, *, /, etc.) that specify the calculation to be performed.
    - **Constants:** Numbers or text values that do not change.
    - **Functions:** Predefined formulas in Excel.
- To create a basic formula in Excel:
    (i) Select the cell for the formula.
    (ii) Type = (the equal sign) and the formula.
    (iii) Click Enter.

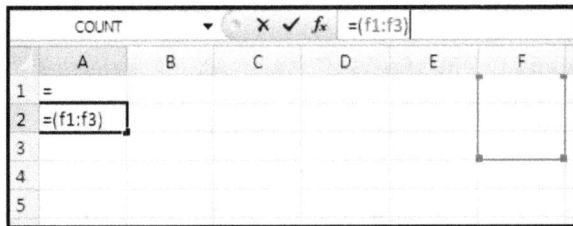

Fig. 6.56: Apply formula on cell

Functions in Excel:
- A function is a built in formula in Excel. A function has a name and arguments (the mathematical function) in parentheses.
- Common functions in Excel:
  - **Sum:** Adds all cells in the argument.
  - **Average:** Calculates the average of the cells in the argument.
  - **Min:** Finds the minimum value.
  - **Max:** Finds the maximum value.
  - **Count:** Finds the number of cells that contain a numerical value within a range of the argument.
- To calculate a function:
  - (i) Click the **cell** where you want the function applied.
  - (ii) Click the **Insert Function** button.
  - (iii) Choose the function.
  - (iv) Click **OK**.

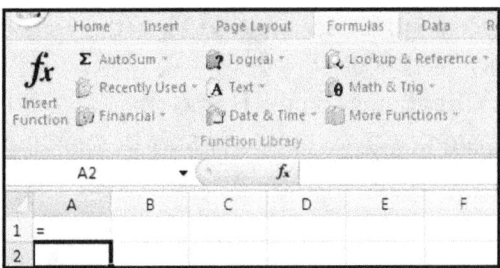

Fig. 6.57: Insert function option

- (v) Complete the Number 1 box with the first cell in the range that you want calculated
- (vi) Complete the Number 2 box with the last cell in the range that you want calculated

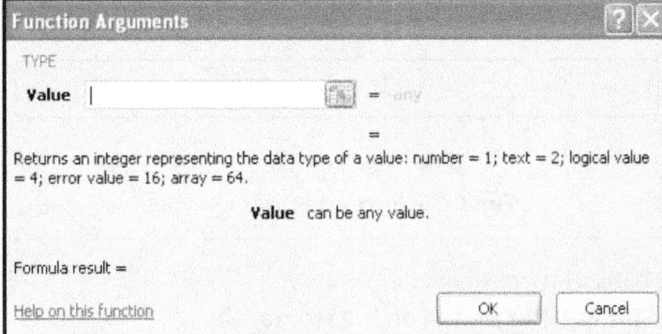

Fig. 6.58: Function arguments dialog

Function Library:
- The function library is a large group of functions on the Formula Tab of the Ribbon. These functions include:
  1. **AutoSum**: Easily calculates the sum of a range.
  2. **Recently Used**: All recently used functions.
  3. **Financial**: Accrued interest, cash flow return rates and additional financial functions.
  4. **Logical**: And, If, True, False, etc.
  5. **Text**: Text based functions.
  6. **Date & Time**: Functions calculated on date and time.
  7. **Math & Trig**: Mathematical Functions.

Fig. 6.59: Function library

- Sorting and Filtering allow you to manipulate data in a worksheet based on given set of criteria.

Basic Sorts:
- To execute a basic descending or ascending sort based on one column:
  (i) Highlight the cells that will be sorted.
  (ii) Click the **Sort & Filter** button on the **Home** tab.
  (iii) Click the **Sort Ascending** (A-Z) button or **Sort Descending** (Z-A) button.

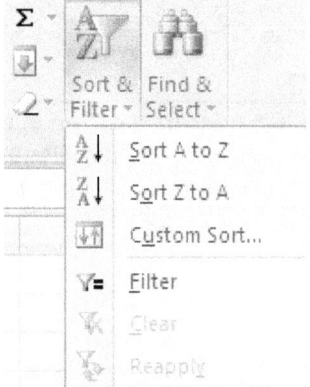

Fig. 6.60: Sort and filter options

Custom Sorts:
- To sort on the basis of more than one column:
  (i) Click the **Sort & Filter** button on the **Home** tab.
  (ii) Choose which column you want to sort by first.

(iii) Click **Add Level**.
(iv) Choose the next column you want to sort.
(v) Click **OK**.

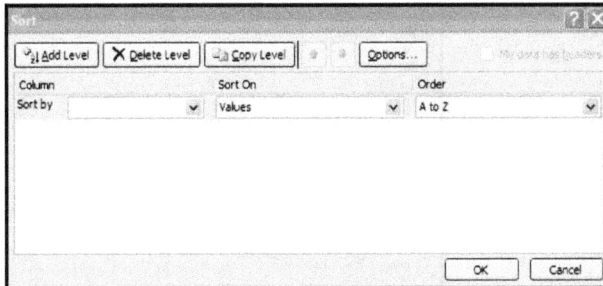

Fig. 6.61: Sort dialog box

Filtering:
- Filtering allows you to display only data that meets certain criteria.
- To filter follow the following steps:
    (i) Click the column or columns that contain the data you wish to filter.
    (ii) On the **Home** tab, click on **Sort & Filter**.
    (iii) Click **Filter** button.
    (iv) Click the **Arrow** at the bottom of the first cell.
    (v) Click the **Text Filter**.
    (vi) Click the **Words** you wish to Filter.

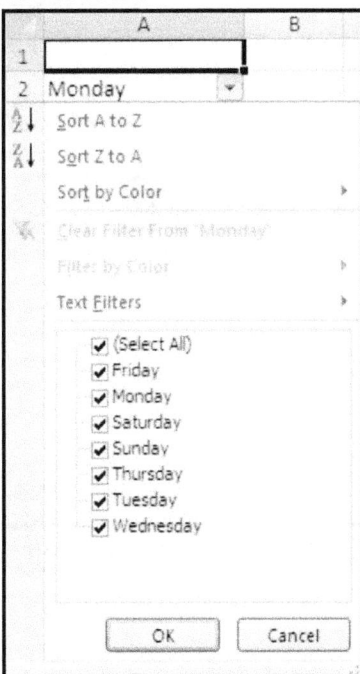

Fig. 6.62: Filtering options

(vii) To clear the filter click the **Sort & Filter** button.
(viii) Click **Clear**.

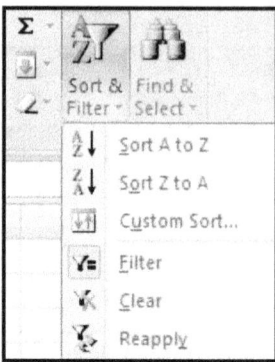

Fig. 6.63: Clear filter

Adding a Picture:
- To add a picture:
    (i) Click the **Insert** tab.
    (ii) Click the **Picture** button.
    (iii) Browse to the picture from your files.
    (iv) Click the **name** of the picture.
    (v) Click **Insert**.
    (vi) To move the graphic, click it and drag it to where you want it.

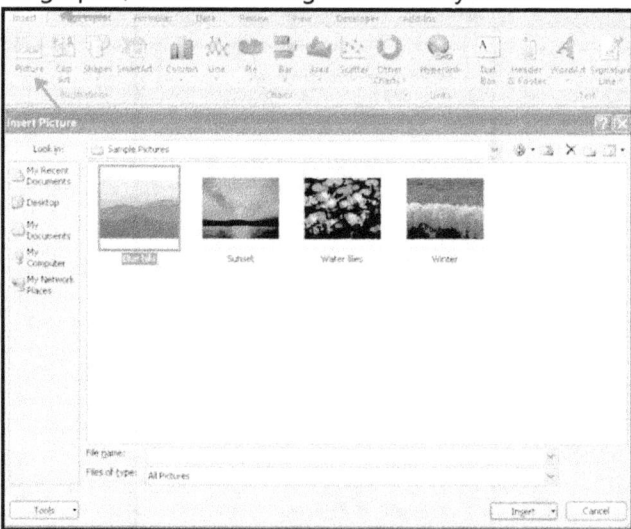

Fig. 6.64: Insert pictures dialog box

Adding Clip Art:
- To add Clip Art:
    (i) Click the **Insert** tab.
    (ii) Click the **Clip Art** button.

- (iii) Search for the clip art using the search **Clip Art** dialog box.
- (iv) Click the **Clip Art**.
- (v) To move the graphic, click it and drag it to where you want it.

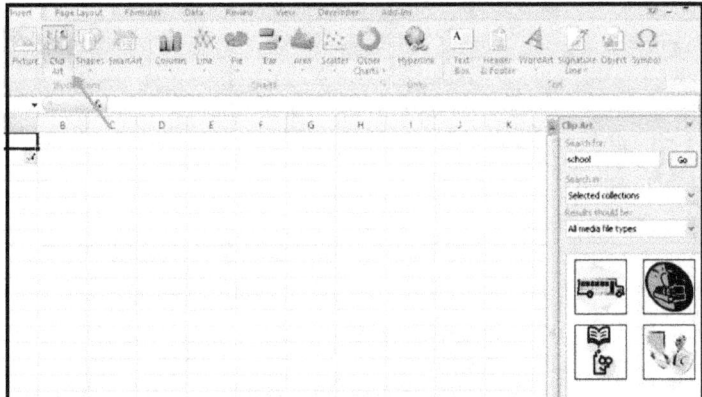

Fig. 6.65: Clip Art option

Adding Shapes:
- To add Shape:
    - (i) Click the **Insert** tab.
    - (ii) Click the **Shapes** button.
    - (iii) Click the shape you choose.

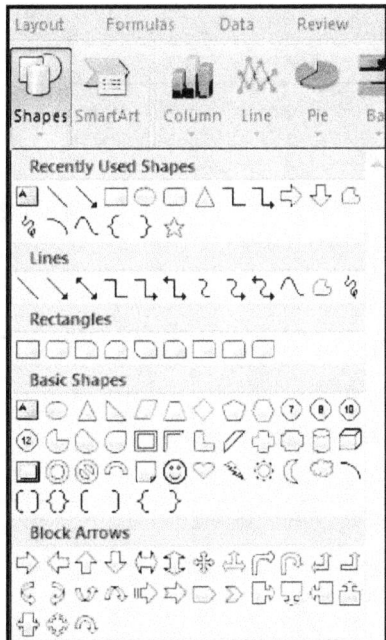

Fig. 6.66: Shapes options

- (iv) Click the **Worksheet**.
- (v) Drag the cursor to expand the Shape.

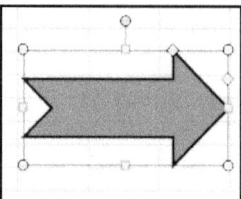

Fig. 6.67: A typical shape

- To format the shapes:
  (i) Click the **Shape**.
  (ii) Click the **Format** tab.

Fig. 6.68: Format options of a shape

Adding SmartArt:
- SmartArt is a feature in Office 2007 that allows you to choose from a variety of graphics, including flow charts, lists, cycles, and processes.
- To add SmartArt follow the following steps:
  (i) Click the **Insert** tab.
  (ii) Click the **SmartArt** button.
  (iii) Click the **SmartArt** you choose.

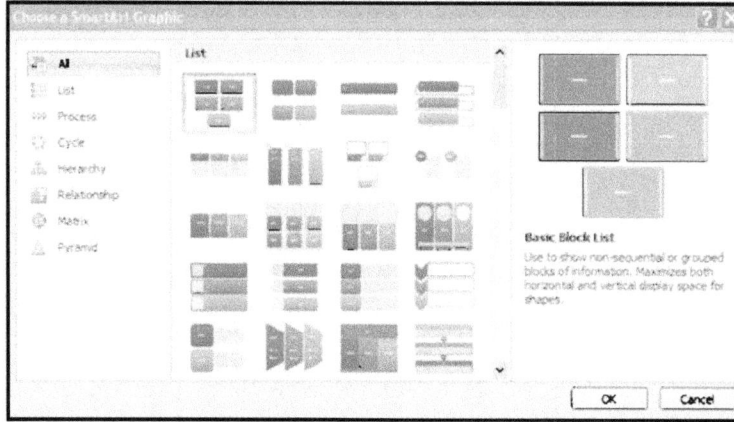

Fig. 6.69: Smart Art dialog box

  (iv) Select the Smart Art.
  (v) Drag it to the desired location in the worksheet.

Charts:
- Charts allow you to present information contained in the worksheet in a graphic format.
- Excel offers many types of charts including. Column, Line, Pie, Bar, Area, Scatter and more. To view the charts available click the Insert Tab on the Ribbon.

Creating a Chart:
- To create a chart:
    (i) Select the **cells** that contain the data you want to use in the chart.
    (ii) Click the **Insert** tab on the Ribbon.
    (iii) Click the type of **Chart** you want to create.

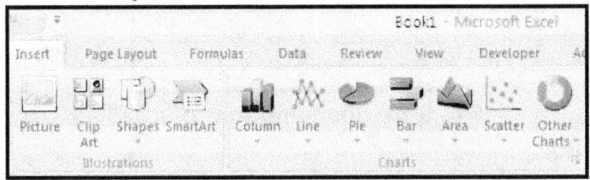

Fig. 6.70: Types of charts on Ribbon

Chart Tools:
- The Chart Tools appear on the Ribbon when you click on the chart. The tools are located on three tabs i.e. Design, Layout, and Format.
- Within the **Design** tab you can control the chart type, layout, styles, and location.

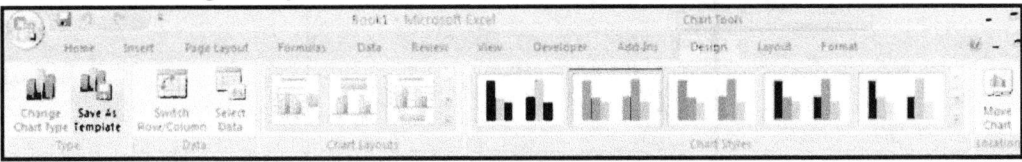

Fig. 6.71: Design tab of chart

- Within the **Layout** tab you can control inserting pictures, shapes and text boxes, labels, axes, background, and analysis.

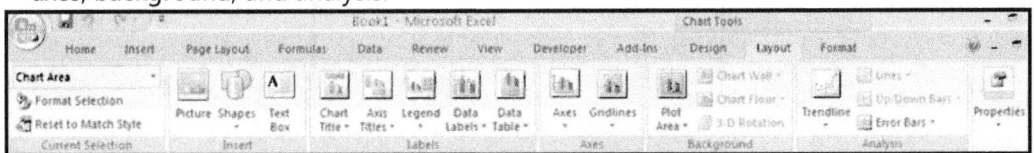

Fig. 6.72: Chart layout tab

- Within the **Format** tab you can modify shape styles, word styles and size of the chart.

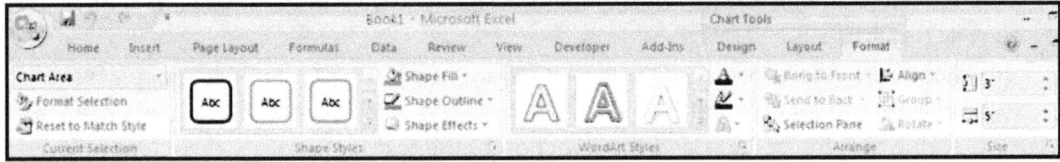

Fig. 6.73: Chart format tab

Modify Fonts:
- Modifying fonts in Excel will allow you to emphasize titles and headings. To modify a font:
    (i) Select the cell or cells that you would like the font applied.
    (ii) On the **Font** group on the **Home** tab, choose the font type, size, bold, italics, underline, or color.

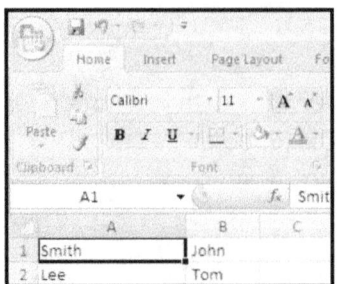

Fig. 6.74: Changing font of a cell

Format Cells Dialog Box:
- In Excel, you can also apply specific formatting to a cell.
- To apply formatting to a cell or group of cells:
    (i) Select the cell or cells that will have the formatting.
    (ii) Click the **Dialog Box** arrow on the **Alignment** group of the **Home** tab.

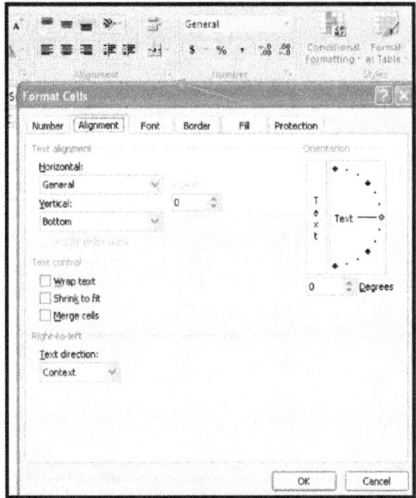

Fig. 6.75: Format cells dialog box

- There are several tabs on this dialog box that allow you to modify properties of the cell or cells.
    (i) Number: Allows for the display of different number types and decimal places.
    (ii) Alignment: Allows for the horizontal and vertical alignment of text, wrap text, shrink text, merge cells and the direction of the text.
    (iii) Font: Allows for control of font, font style, size, color, and additional features.
    (iv) Border: Border styles and colors.
    (v) Fill: Cell fill colors and styles.

Add Borders and Colors to Cells:
- Borders and colors can be added to cells manually or through the use of styles.
- To add borders manually:
    (i) Click the **Borders** drop down menu on the Font group of the Home tab.
    (ii) Choose the appropriate border.

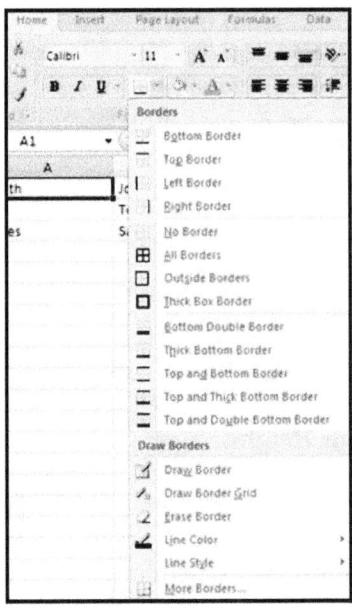

Fig. 6.76: Borders options

- To apply colors manually:
    (i) Click the **Fill** drop down menu on the **Font** group of the **Home** tab.
    (ii) Choose the appropriate color.

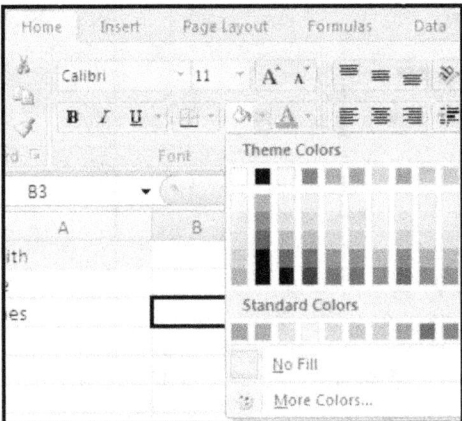

Fig. 6.77: Color options

- To apply borders and colors using styles:
    (i) Click **Cell** Styles on the **Home** tab.
    (ii) Choose a style or click **New Cell Style**.

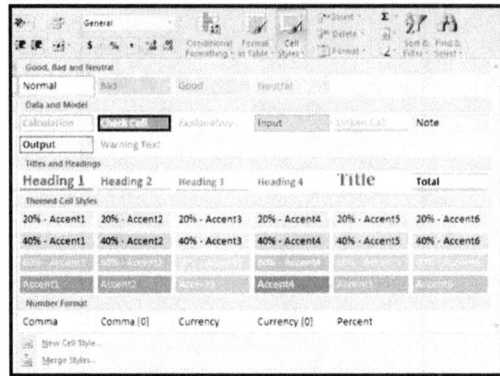

Fig. 6.78: Cell styles

Change Column Width and Row Height:
- To change the width of a column or the height of a row:
    (i) Click the **Format** button on the **Cells** group of the **Home** tab.
    (ii) Manually adjust the height and width by clicking **Row Height** or **Column Width**.
    (iii) To use **AutoFit** click **AutoFit Row Height** or **AutoFit Column Width**.

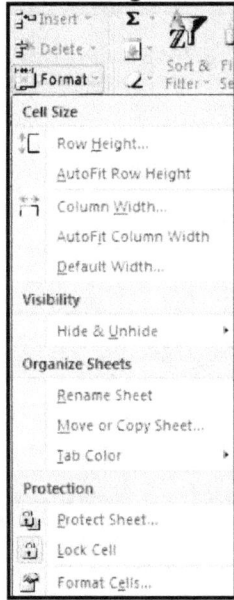

Fig. 6.79: Format cell options

Merge Cells:
- To merge cells select the cells you want to merge and click the Merge & Center button on the Alignment group of the Home tab.
- The four choices for merging cells are:
    (i) Merge & Center: Combines the cells and centers the contents in the new, larger cell.
    (ii) Merge Across: Combines the cells across columns without centering data.
    (iii) Merge Cells: Combines the cells in a range without centering.
    (iv) Unmerge Cells: Splits the cell that has been merged.

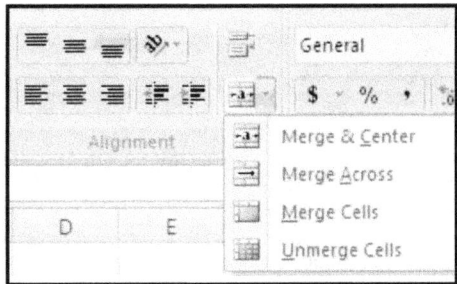

Fig. 6.80: Merge cells options

Align Cell Contents:

- To align cell contents, click the cell or cells you want to align and click on the options within the Alignment group on the Home tab.
- There are several options for alignment of cell contents:
    (i) **Top Align**: Aligns text to the top of the cell.
    (ii) **Middle Align**: Aligns text between the top and bottom of the cell.
    (iii) **Bottom Align**: Aligns text to the bottom of the cell.
    (iv) **Align Text Left**: Aligns text to the left of the cell.
    (v) **Center**: Centers the text from left to right in the cell.
    (vi) **Align Text Right**: Aligns text to the right of the cell.
    (vii) **Decrease Indent**: Decreases the indent between the left border and the text.
    (viii) **Increase Indent**: Increase the indent between the left border and the text.
    (ix) **Orientation**: Rotate the text diagonally or vertically.

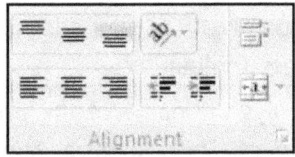

Fig. 6.81: Alignment options

6.4 MS-PowerPoint

- PowerPoint is a complete presentation graphics package. It gives you everything you need to produce a professional-looking presentation.
- PowerPoint offers word processing, outlining, drawing, graphing, and presentation management tools- all designed to be easy to use and learn.
- Fig. 6.82 shows various screen components of MS PowerPoint screen.

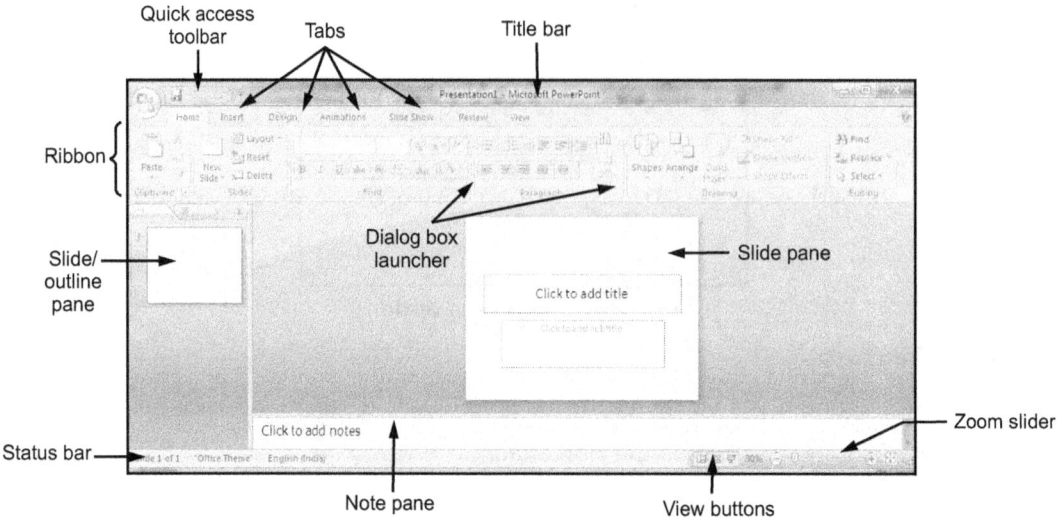

Fig. 6.82: PowerPoint program window

- Table 6.3 shows PowerPoint 2007 Screen Elements.

Table 6.3: PowerPoint 2007 program window element

Screen Element	Description
Ribbon	Organizes commands on tabs, and then groups the commands by topic for performing related presentation tasks.
File tab	Displays a list of commands related to things you can do with a presentation, such as opening, saving, printing, or sharing.
Quick Access Toolbar (QAT)	Displays buttons to perform frequently used commands with a single click. Frequently used commands in PowerPoint include Save, Undo, and Repeat. For commands that *you* use frequently, you can add additional buttons to the Quick Access Toolbar.
Title bar	Displays the name of the presentation and the name of the program. The Minimize, Maximize/Restore Down, and Close window control buttons are grouped on the right side of the title bar.
Ribbon tabs	Display across the top of the Ribbon, and each tab relates to a type of task-related activity within PowerPoint.
Program-level control buttons Groups	Minimizes, restores or closes the program window. Indicate the name of the groups of related commands on each displayed tab.
Slide pane	Displays a large image of the active slide in PowerPoint.

contd. ...

View buttons	A set of commands that control the look of the presentation window.
Notes pane	Displays below the Slide pane and allows you to type notes regarding the active side.
Status bar	A horizontal bar at the bottom of the presentation window that displays the current slide number, number of slides in a presentation, Theme Name, View buttons, and Zoom slider.
Slides/Outline pane	Displays either all of the slides in the presentation in the form of miniature images called thumbnails (Slides tab) or the presentation outline (Outline tab) .

Working with PowerPoint Document:

New Presentation or Creating New Document:

- You can start a new presentation from a blank slide, a template, existing presentations, or a Word outline.
- To create a new presentation from a blank slide:
    (i) Click the **Microsoft Office Button**.
    (ii) Click **New**.
    (iii) Click **Blank Presentation**.

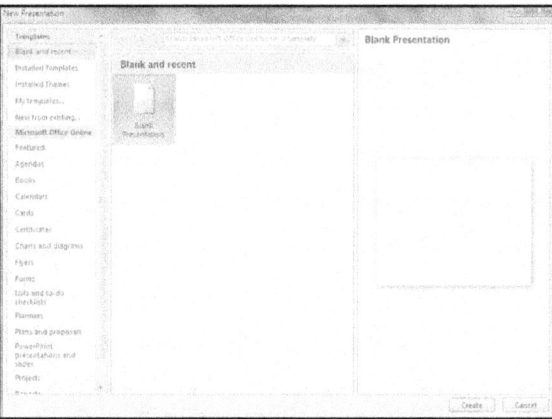

Fig. 6.83: Creating new presentation

Save a Presentation:

- When you save a presentation, you have two choices: **Save** or **Save As**.
- To save a document:
    (i) Click the **Microsoft Office Button**.
    (ii) Click **Save**.

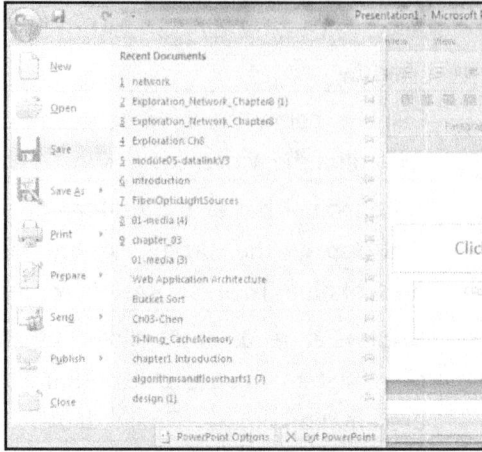

Fig. 6.84: Save options

Add Slides:
- There are several choices when you want to add a new slide to the presentation: Office Themes, Duplicate Selected Slide, or Reuse Slides.
- To create a new slide from Office Themes:
    (i) Select the slide immediately **BEFORE** where you want the new slide.
    (ii) Click the **New Slide** button on the **Home** tab.
    (iii) Click the slide choice that fits your material.

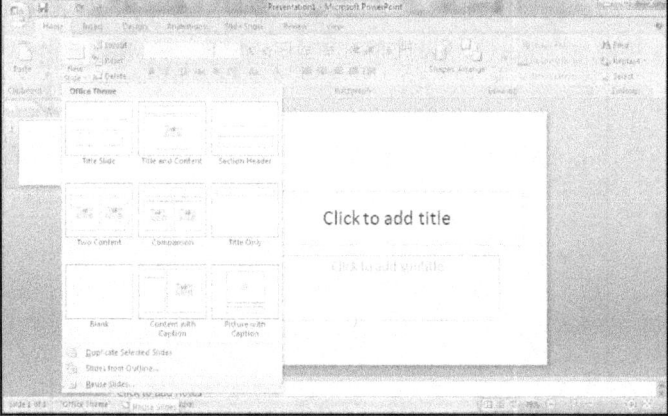

Fig. 6.85: Add slides in PowerPoint

Themes:
- Themes are design templates that can be applied to an entire presentation that allows for consistency throughout the presentation.
- To add a theme to a presentation:
    (i) Click the **Design** tab.
    (ii) Choose one of the displayed **Themes** or click the **Galleries** button.

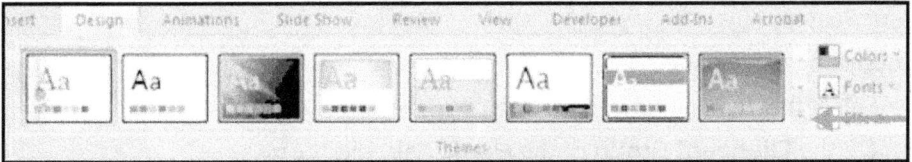

Fig. 6.86: Themes

Enter Text:
- To enter text:
    (i) Select the **slide** where you want the text.
    (ii) Click in a **Textbox** to add text.

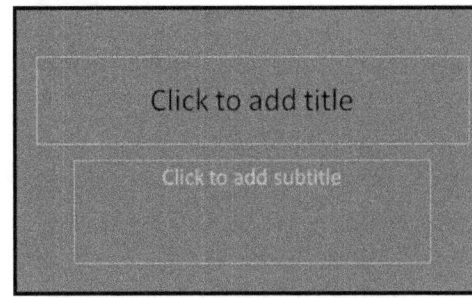

Fig. 6.87: Adding text in slide

- To add a text box:
    (i) Select the **slide** where you want to place the text box.
    (ii) On the **Insert** tab, click **Text Box**.
    (iii) Click on the slide and drag the cursor to expand the text box.
    (iv) Type in the text.

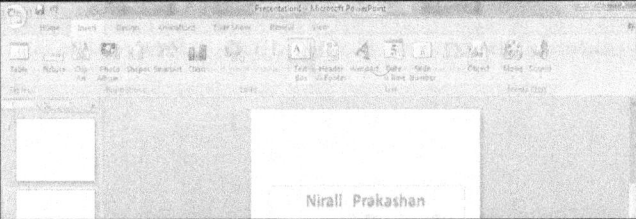

Fig. 6.88: Adding TextBox

Select Text:
- To select the text:
    (i) Highlight the text.

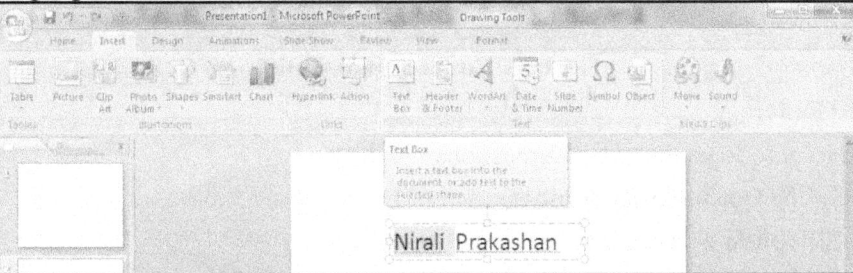

Fig. 6.89

Copy and Paste:
- To copy and paste data:
    (i) Select the item(s) that you wish to copy.
    (ii) On the **Clipboard Group** of the **Home Tab**, click **Copy**.
    (iii) Select the item(s) where you would like to copy the data.
    (iv) On the **Clipboard** Group of the **Home** Tab, click **Paste**.

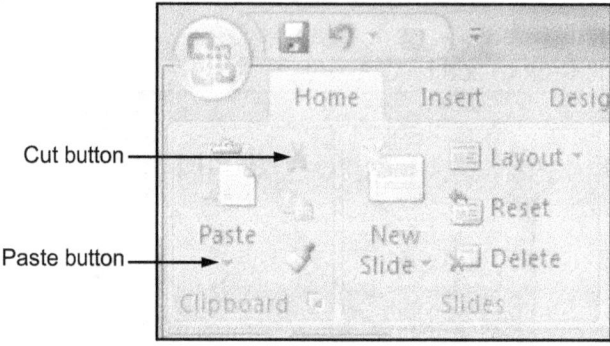

Fig. 6.90: Copy and Paste option

Cut and Paste:
- To cut and paste data:
    (i) Select the item(s) that you wish to copy.
    (ii) On the **Clipboard Group** of the **Home** Tab, click Cut.
    (iii) Select the items(s) where you would like to copy the data.
    (iv) On the **Clipboard Group** of the **Home** Tab, click **Paste**.

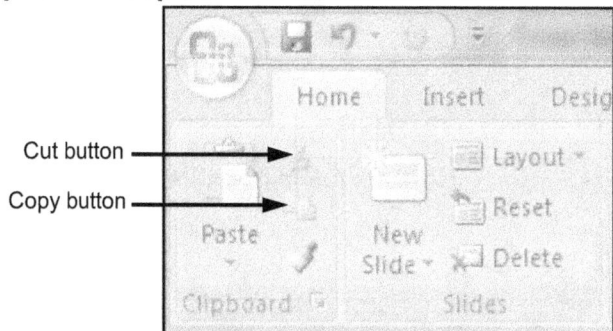

Fig. 6.91: Cut and Paste option

Undo and Redo:
- To undo or redo your most recent actions:
    (i) On the **Quick Access Toolbar**.
    (ii) Click **Undo** or **Redo**.

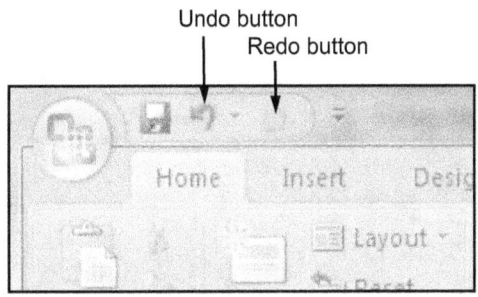

Fig. 6.92: Undo and Redo options

Spell Check:
- To check the spelling in a presentation:
    (i) Click the **Review tab**.
    (ii) Click the Spelling **button**.

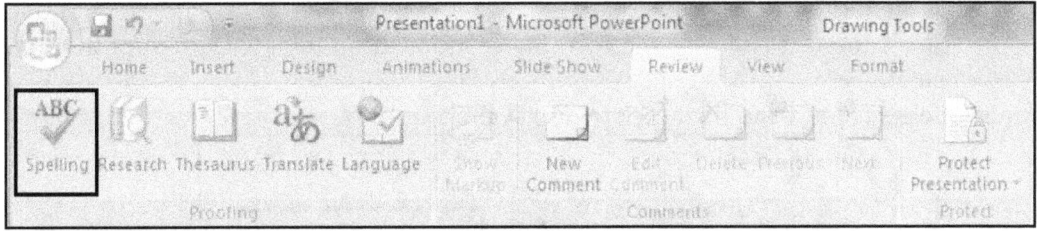

Fig. 6.93: Spell check options

Change Font Typeface and Size:
- To change the font typeface:
    (i) Click the **arrow** next to the font name and choose a font.
    (ii) Remember that you can preview how the new font will look by highlighting the text, and hovering over the new font typeface.

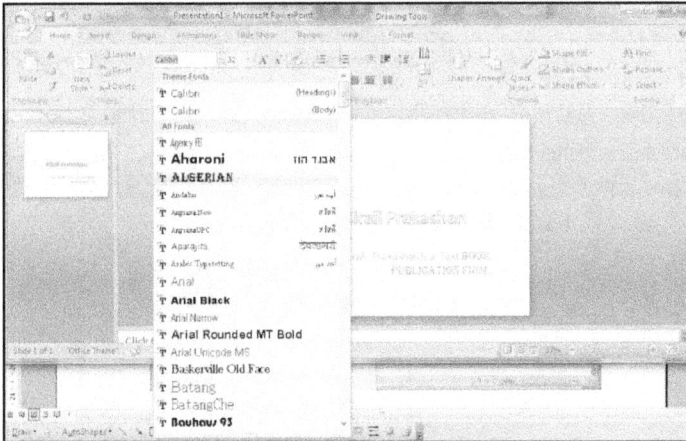

Fig. 6.94: Changing font

- To **change the font size**:
    (i) Click the **arrow** next to the font size and choose the appropriate size, or
    (ii) Click the **increase or decrease** font size buttons.

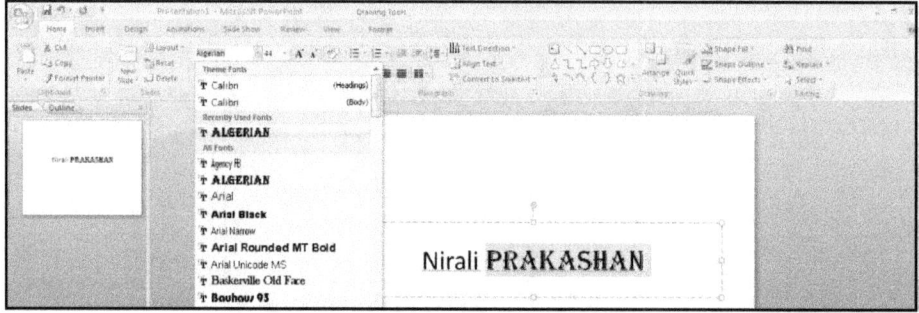

Fig. 6.95: Changing font size

Font Styles and Effects:
- Font styles are predefined formatting options that are used to emphasize text. They include: Bold, Italic, and Underline.
- To add these to text:
  (i) Select the text and click the **Font Styles** included on the Font group of the Home tab or
  (ii) Select the text and right click to display the font tools.

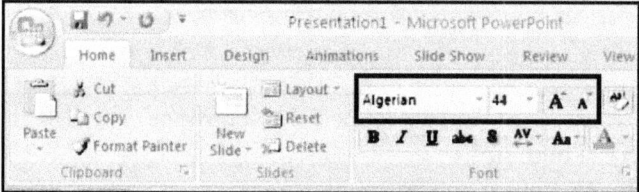

Fig. 6.96: Font styles

Change Text Color:
- To change the text color:
  (i) Select the text and click the **Colors** button included on the Font Group of the Ribbon, or
  (ii) Highlight the text and right click and choose the colors tool.
  (iii) Select the color by clicking the down arrow next to the font color button.

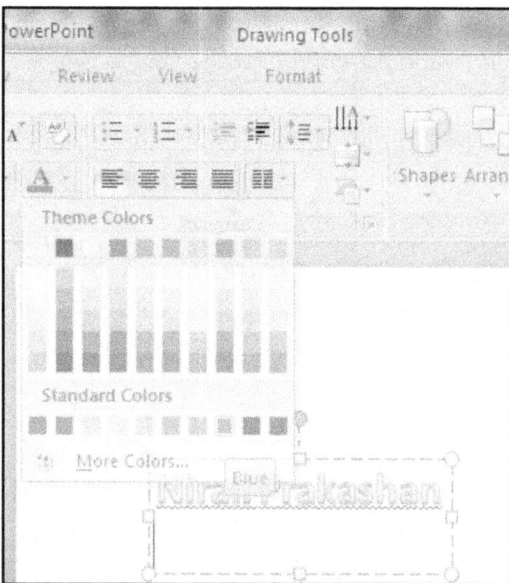

Fig. 6.97: Color options

WordArt:
- WordArt are styles that can be applied to text to create a visual effect.
- To apply Word Art follow the following steps:
    - (i) Select the text.
    - (ii) Click the **Insert** tab.
    - (iii) Click the **WordArt** button.
    - (iv) Choose the **WordArt**.

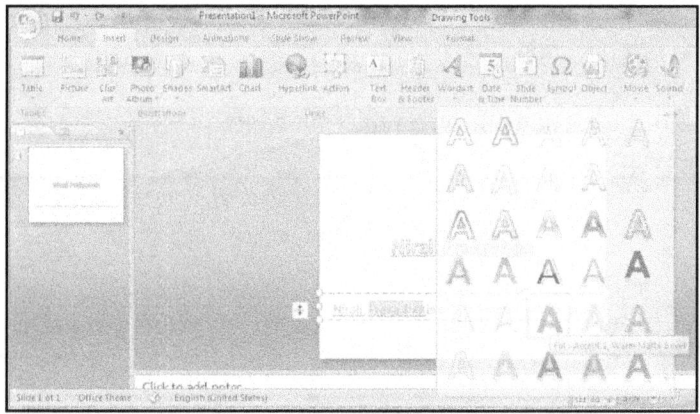

Fig. 6.98: Work Art options

Change Paragraph Alignment:
- The paragraph alignment allows you to set how you want text to appear.
- To change the alignment:
    - (i) Click the **Home Tab**
    - (ii) Choose the appropriate button for alignment on the Paragraph Group.
        - (a) **Align Left:** The text is aligned with your left margin.
        - (b) **Center:** The text is centered within your margins.
        - (c) **Align Right:** Aligns text with the right margin.
        - (d) **Justify:** Aligns text to both the left and right margins.

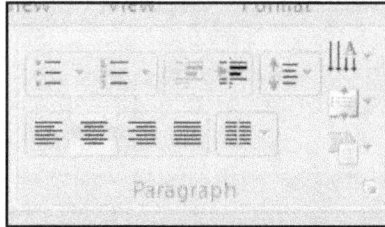

Fig. 6.99: Alignment options

Indent Paragraphs:
- To indent paragraphs, you can do the following:
    - (i) Click the **Indent** buttons to control the indent.
    - (ii) Click the **Indent** button repeated times to increase the size of the indent.

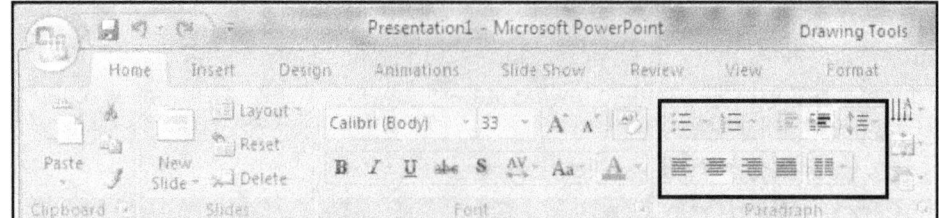

Fig. 6.100: Indent option

Text Direction:
- To change the text direction:
    (i) Select the text.
    (ii) Click the Text Direction button on the Home tab.
    (iii) Click the selection.

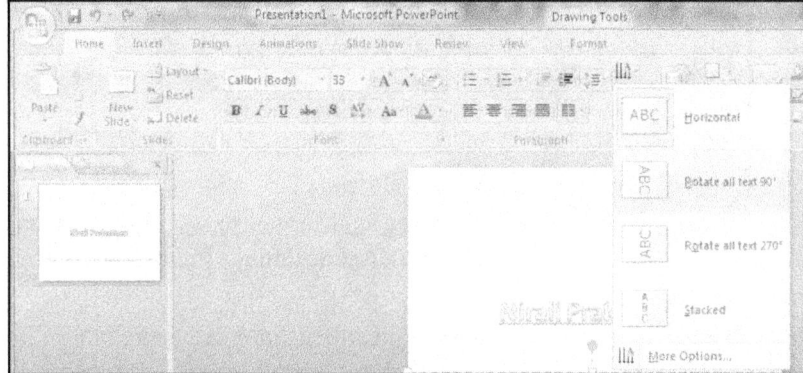

Fig. 6.101: Text direction option

Bulleted and Numbered Lists
- Bulleted lists have bullet points, numbered lists have numbers, and outline lists combine numbers and letters depending on the organization of the list.
- To add a list to existing text:
    (i) Select the text you wish to make a list.
    (ii) Click the **Bulleted or Numbered Lists** button.

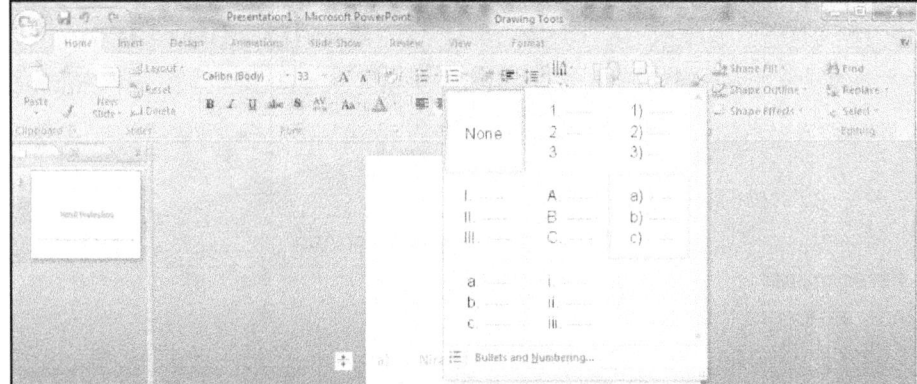

Fig. 6.102: Bulleted or Numbered lists

- To create a new list:
    (i) Place your cursor where you want the list in the document.
    (ii) Click the **Bulleted or Numbered Lists** button.
    (iii) Begin typing.

Nested Lists:

- A nested list is list with several levels of indented text.
- To create a nested list follow the following steps:
    (i) Create your list following the directions above.
    (ii) Click the **Increase or Decrease Indent** button.

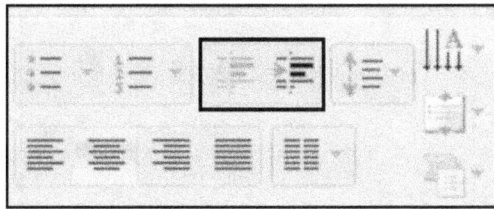

Fig. 6.103: Nested list option

Formatting Lists:

- The bullet image and numbering format can be changed by using the **Bullets or Numbering** dialog box.
    (i) Select the entire list to change all the bullets or numbers, or Place the cursor on one line within the list to change a single bullet.
    (ii) Click the arrow next to the bulleted or numbered list and choose a bullet or numbering style.

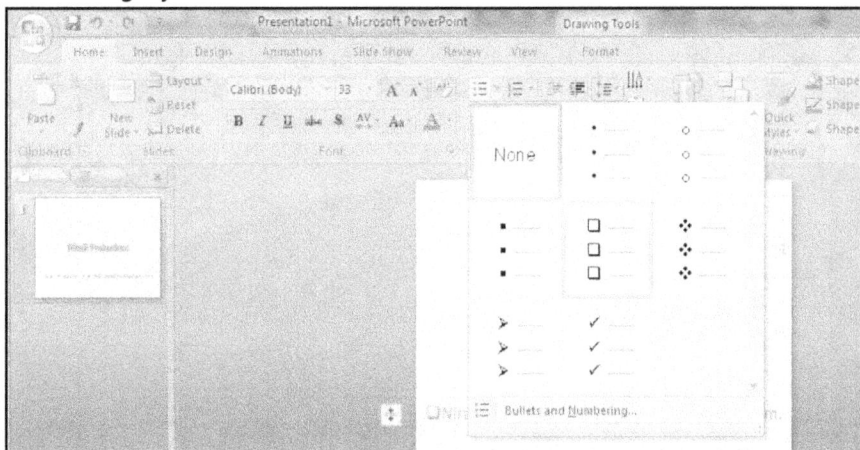

Fig. 6.104: Bullet or Numbering style

Adding Picture:
- To add a picture:
    (i) Click the **Insert** Tab.
    (ii) Click the **Picture** Button.
    (iii) Browse to the picture from your files.
    (iv) Click the **name** of the picture.
    (v) Click **insert**.
    (vi) To move the graphic, click it and drag it to where you want it.

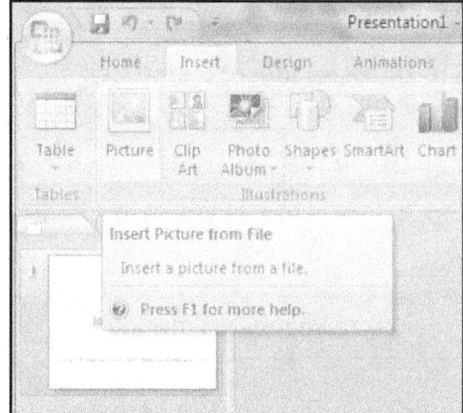

Fig. 6.105: Insert pictures dialog box

Adding Clip Art:
- To add Clip Art:
    (i) Click the **Insert** Tab.
    (ii) Click the **Clip Art** Button.
    (iii) Search for the clip art using the search Clip Art dialog box.
    (iv) Click the **Clip Art**.
    (v) To move the graphic, click it and drag it to where you want it.

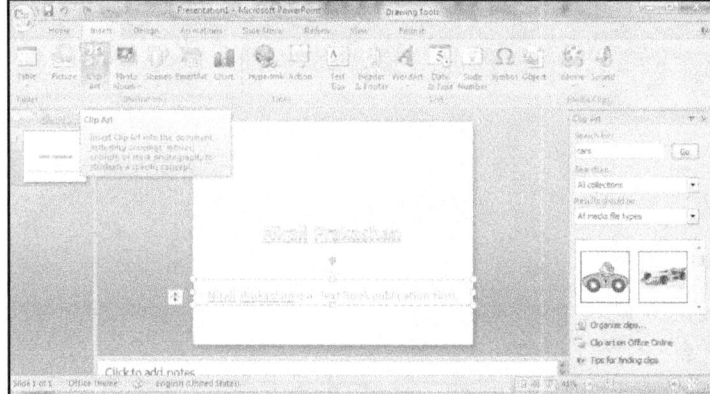

Fig. 6.106: Clip art option

Adding a Shape:
- To add Shapes:
    (i) Click the **Insert** Tab.
    (ii) Click the **Shapes** Button.
    (iii) Click the shape you choose.

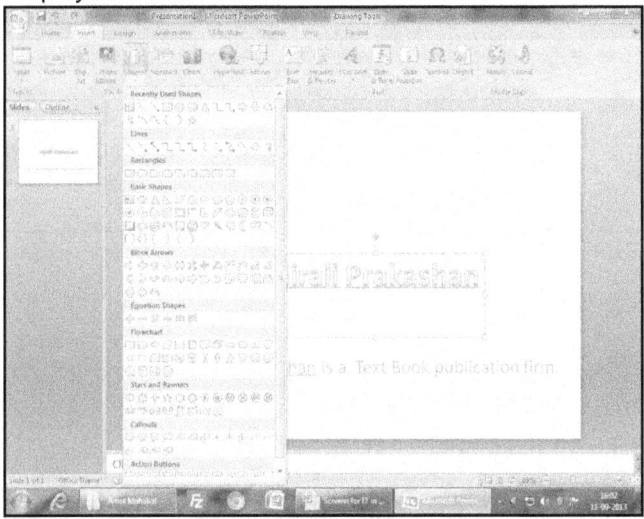

Fig. 6.107: Shapes option

  (iv) Click the **Slide**.
  (v) Drag the **cursor** to expand the Shape.

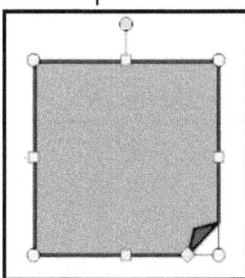

Fig. 6.108: A typical shape

Adding SmartArt:
- SmartArt is a feature in Office 2007 that allows you to choose from a variety of graphics, including flow charts, lists, cycles, and processes.
- To add SmartArt follow the following steps:
    (i) Click the **Insert** Tab.
    (ii) Click the **SmartArt** Button.
    (iii) Click the **SmartArt** you choose.
    (iv) Click the **SmartArt**.
    (v) Drag it to the desired location in the slide.

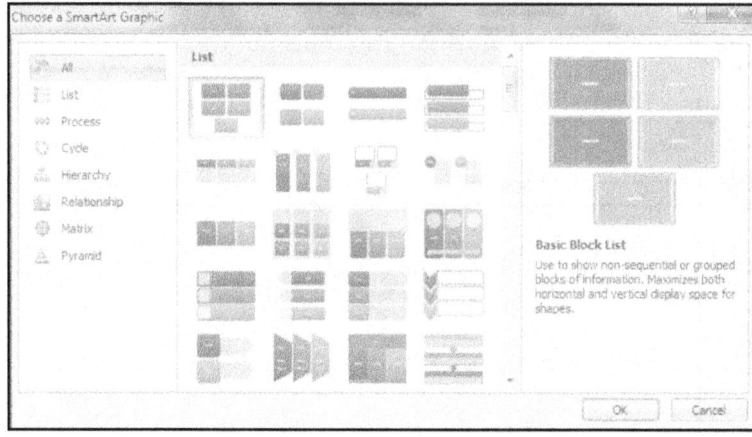

Fig. 6.109: SmartArt dialog box

Creating a Table:

- To create a table:
- Place the cursor on the page where you want the new table
- Click the **Insert** Tab of the Ribbon
- Click the **Tables** Button on the Tables Group. You can create a table one of four ways:
    (i) Highlight the number of row and columns.
    (ii) Click **Insert Table** and enter the number of rows and columns.
    (iii) Click the **Draw Table**, create your table by clicking and entering the rows and columns.
    (iv) Click Excel **Spreadsheet** and enter data.

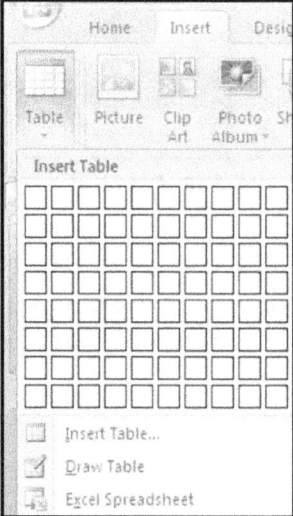

Fig. 6.110: Create table options

Charts:
- Charts allow you to present information contained in the worksheet in a graphic format.
- PowerPoint offers many types of charts including: Column, Line, Pie, Bar, Area, Scatter and more.
- To view the charts available click the Insert Tab on the Ribbon.

Fig. 6.111: Chart options

Creating a Chart:
- To create a chart:
    (i) Click the **Insert** tab on the ribbon.
    (ii) Click the type of **Chart** you want to create.
    (iii) Insert the **Data** and **Labels**.

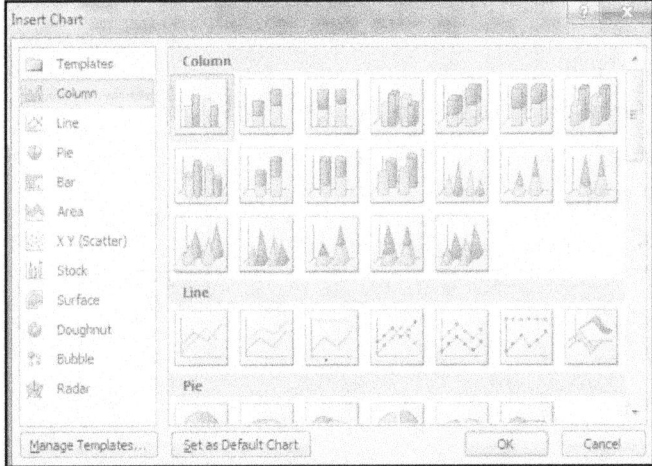

Fig. 6.112: Insert chart dialog box

Slide Transitions:
- Transitions are effects that are in place when you switch from one slide to the next.
- To add slide transitions:
    (i) Select the slide that you want to transition.
    (ii) Click the **Animations** tab.
    (iii) Choose the appropriate animation or click the **Transition** dialog box.

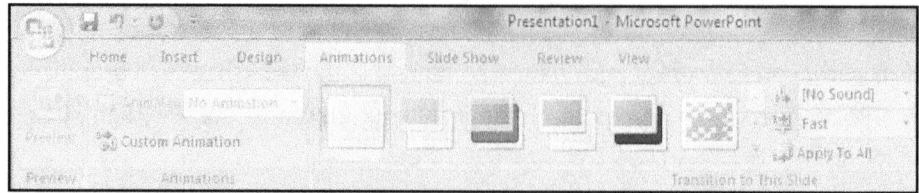

Fig. 6.113: Slide transitions

- To apply the transition to all slides:
    (i) Click the **Apply to All** button on the **Animations tab**.

Fig. 6.114: Apply to all option

Slide Animation:

- Slide animation effects are predefined special effects that you can add to objects on a slide.
- To apply an animation effect follow the following steps:
    (i) Select the object
    (ii) Click the **Animations** tab on the Ribbon.
    (iii) Click **Custom Animation**.
    (iv) Click **Add Effect**.
    (v) Choose the appropriate effect.

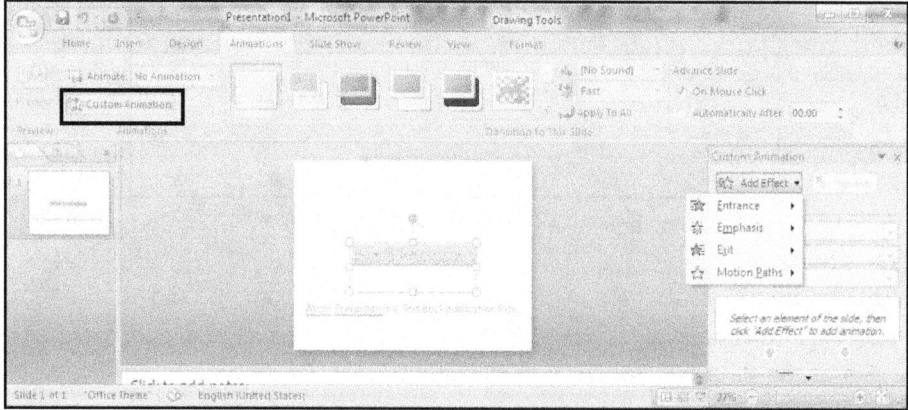

Fig. 6.115: Slide Animation

Animation Preview:

- To preview the animation on a slide:
    (i) Click the **Preview** button on the **Animations** tab.

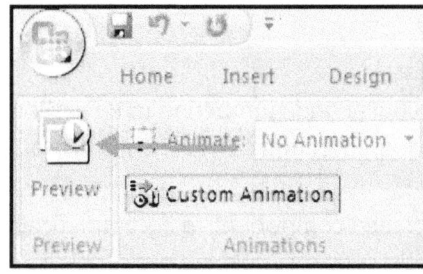

Fig. 6.116: Preview options

Slide Show Options:

- The Slide Show tab of the ribbon contains many options for the slide show. These options include:
    (i) Preview the slide show from the beginning.
    (ii) Preview the slide show from the current slide.
    (iii) Set up Slide Show.

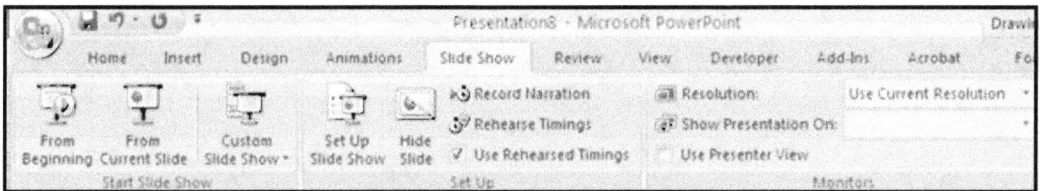

Fig. 6.117: Slide show options

Questions

1. What is meant by MS-Office 2007?
2. Enlist features of MS-Office 2007.
3. What are the components of MS-Office? Explain them in short.
4. What is MS-Word?
5. How to insert table in MS-Word?
6. What are the uses of MS-Word?
7. Explain the following word concepts:
    (i) WordArt
    (ii) ClipArt
    (iii) SmartArt
8. What is MS-Excel?
9. How to create formula in MS-Excel?

10. Explain the following MS-Excel concepts:
    (i) ClipArt
    (ii) Formula
    (iii) Cell alignment
11. What is PowerPoint?
12. Explain the uses of Excel.
13. Write short notes on Bullet and Numbering in PowerPoint.
14. With the help of diagram describe MS-Word screen components.
15. Describe Excel screen with its various components.
16. Explain PowerPoint screen components diagrammatically.

■■■

B.B.M. (IB) : SEMESTER II – IT IN BUSINESS OPERATIONS
QUESTION PAPER

Time : 3 Hours   October 2014   Max. Marks: 80

Q.1 Answer the following (Any Two): [20]
- (a) What is a Computer? Explain the block diagram of computer.
- Ans. Refer to Sections 1.1.1 and 1.3.
- (b) Explain the Normalization and its types?
- Ans. Refer to Section 4.3.
- (c) Write short notes on IT Act.
- Ans. Refer to Section 5.4.

Q.2 Answer the following (Any Two): [20]
- (a) Explain the difference between RAM and ROM?
- Ans. Refer to Sections 1.5.1.1 and 1.5.1.2.
- (b) What is DOS? Explain the difference between DOS and Window.
- Ans. Refer to Sections 3.2 and 3.1.8.
- (c) What is ER Diagram? Explain its tools.
- Ans. Refer to Section 4.4.

Q.3 Answer the following (Any Two): [20]
- (a) What is System? Explain the Types of systems?
- Ans. Refer to Sections 3.1.1 and 3.1.8.
- (b) What is MS-Excel? Explain the features of MS-Excel.
- Ans. Refer to Section 6.3.
- (c) Explain Digital Signature?
- Ans. Refer to Section 5.3.

Q.4 Answer the following (Any Two): [20]
- (a) Explain the feasibility study in detail.
- Ans. Refer to Section 2.4.
- (b) Describe the steps involved in creating any website.
- Ans. Refer to Section 3.5.
- (c) What is SQL? Explain the use of SQL.
- Ans. Refer to Section 4.5.3.

Q.5 Answer the following (Any Two): [20]
- (a) Explain Files and Directories.
- Ans. Refer to Section 3.3.
- (b) Explain the Failure of system.
- Ans. Refer to Section 5.5.4.
- (c) Explain any two Internal and External commands in DOS?
- Ans. Refer to Sections 3.4.1 and 3.4.2.

■■■

Information Technology in Business Operations · P.2 · University Question Paper

Time : 3 Hours **April 2015** **Max. Marks: 80**

Q.1 Answer the following (Any Two): [20]
(a) Explain the characteristics of digital computer.
Ans. Refer to Section 1.2.
(b) What is Operating System? Explain the services provided by an Operating System.
Ans. Refer to Section 3.1.
(c) Explain the concept of Prototyping.
Ans. Refer to Section 2.5.

Q.2 Answer the following (Any Two): [20]
(a) Explain the following SQL commands with its syntax and example:
(i) SELECT, (ii) DELETE
Ans. (i) Refer to Section 4.5.3.3.
(ii) Refer to Section 4.5.3.2.
(b) What is MS-PowerPoint? Explain its features.
Ans. Refer to Section 6.4.
(c) Explain the various security threats to information.
Ans. Refer to Section 5.5.

Q.3 Answer the following (Any Two): [20]
(a) What is System Development Life Cycle?
Ans. Refer to Section 2.4.
(b) Explain the various data recovery methods.
Ans. Refer to Section 5.6.3.
(c) What is secondary storage device? Explain any two secondary storage devices.
Ans. Refer to Section 1.5.3.

Q.4 Answer the following (Any Two): [20]
(a) What is MS-Word? Explain the features of MS-Word.
Ans. Refer to Section 6.2.
(b) Explain the concept of Cryptography.
Ans. Refer to Section 5.2.
(c) What is Normalization? Explain the goals of normalization.
Ans. Refer to Section 4.3.

Q.5 Answer the following (Any Two): [20]
(a) What is input device? Explain any two input devices.
Ans. Refer to Section 1.6.1.
(b) What is ER Diagram? Explain the types of Relationships.
Ans. Refer to Section 4.4.
(c) Explain the following DOS Commands: (i) Format, (ii) Copy, (iii) Attrib, (iv) Del.
Ans. (i) Format: Refer to Section 3.4.2, Point (28).
(ii) Copy: Refer to Section 3.4.1, Point (7).
(iii) Attrib: Refer to Section 3.4.2, Point (4).
(iv) Del.: Refer to Section 3.4.1, Point (12).

∎∎∎

Information Technology in Business Operations   P.3   University Question Paper

Time : 3 Hours   **October 2015**   **Max. Marks: 80**

Q.1 Answer the following (Any Two): [20]
- (a) What is Computer? Explain uses of Computer.
- Ans. Refer to Sections 1.1.1 and 1.1.6.
- (b) What is Operating System? Explain the types of Operating System.
- Ans. Refer to Sections 3.1.1 and 3.1.8.
- (c) Write a note on Cryptography.
- Ans. Refer to Section 5.2.

Q.2 Answer the following (Any Two): [20]
- (a) Explain the difference between RAM and ROM.
- Ans. Refer to Sections 1.5.1.1 and 1.5.1.2.
- (b) What is E-R diagram? Explain its tools.
- Ans. Refer to Section 4.4.
- (c) What is DOS? Explain the difference between DOS and Windows.
- Ans. Refer to Sections 3.2 and 3.6.

Q.3 Answer the following (Any Two): [20]
- (a) What is System? Explain the types of systems.
- Ans. Refer to Sections 2.1.1 and 2.2.
- (b) What is MS-Word. Explain its features.
- Ans. Refer to Sections 6.1 and 6.2.
- (c) Explain antivirus in detail.
- Ans. Refer to Section 5.6.1.

Q.4 Answer the following (Any Two): [20]
- (a) What is R.D.B.M.S.? Explain its advantages.
- Ans. Refer to Sections 4.2 and 4.2.7.
- (b) Explain feasibility study in detail.
- Ans. Refer to Section 2.4.
- (c) What is Batch File? Write the steps to create the batch file.
- Ans. Refer to Section 3.5.

Q.5 Answer the following (Any Two): [20]
- (a) What is System Development Life Cycle?
- Ans. Refer to Section 2.4.
- (b) Explain Micro-computers and Mini-computers.
- Ans. Refer to Sections 1.8.3 and 1.8.4.
- (c) Explain the following DOS Commands: (i) Del, (ii) Dir, (iii) Exit, (iv) Edit.
- Ans. (i) Del: Refer to Section 3.4.1, Point (12).
  - (ii) Dir: Refer to Section 3.4.1, Point (11).
  - (iii) Exit: Refer to Section 3.4.1, Point (18).
  - (iv) Edit: Refer to Section 3.4.2, Point (20).

■■■

www.ingramcontent.com/pod-product-compliance
Lightning Source LLC
Chambersburg PA
CBHW080726230426
43665CB00020B/2629